Texts AND Lessons

for Content-Area Reading

Harvey "Smokey" **Daniels**

Nancy **Steineke**

HEINEMANN
Portsmouth, NH

Heinemann
361 Hanover Street
Portsmouth, NH 03801–3912
www.heinemann.com

Offices and agents throughout the world

The authors and publisher wish to thank those who have generously given permission to reprint borrowed material:

Excerpt from *Wired Magazine*, August 2010, page 86. "Recommendation Engine //: Ask an Algorithm: Which TV for Me?" Copyright © 2010 Wired Magazine.

"School's lesson plan: No more homework; Students never did it; now it's no problem" by Jo Napolitano from *Chicago Tribune*, News Section, 5/8/2005 Issue, Page 1. Copyright © 2005 Chicago Tribune. All Rights Reserved. Used by permission and protected by the Copyright Laws

continues on page viii

Library of Congress Cataloging-in-Publication Data
Daniels, Harvey.

    Texts and lessons for content-area reading : with more than 75 articles from the New York times, Rolling stone, the Washington post, Car and driver, Chicago tribune, and many others / Harvey "Smokey" Daniels and Nancy Steineke.

      p. cm.

    Includes bibliographical references.

    ISBN-13: 978-0-325-03087-6 (pbk. : alk. paper)

    ISBN-10: 0-325-03087-1 (pbk. : alk. paper)

    1. Content area reading.   2. Periodicals in education.   I. Steineke, Nancy.   II. Title.
LB1050.455.D37 2011
372.47'6—dc22   2010051817

Editor: Margaret LaRaia
Editorial review and support: Zoë Ryder White
Production management: Sarah Weaver
Production coordination: Abigail M. Heim
Typesetter: Gina Poirier Graphic Design
Cover and interior designs: Lisa Anne Fowler
Strategy 19 poster artists: Gabrielle Einstein, Georgie Gardner, Gianna Riccardi
Manufacturing: Steve Bernier

Printed in the United States of America on acid-free paper

19 18 17 16 15   VP   6 7 8 9 10

Contents

PREPARING FOR TEXT SETS

TEXT SET LESSONS

Why Use This Book?

Greetings, colleagues.

Welcome, teachers of science, social studies, language arts, math, art, world languages, business, technology, shop, music, PE, and every other subject we teach in middle and high school.

These days, we are all expected to be "teachers of reading," no matter what our subject field, our college major, or our level of training in reading, right? There's pressure on us from our departments and principals, from our school districts, from the state and national standards, and especially from all those high-stakes tests. Everyone wants us "content-area" teachers to make sure that kids can read, understand, remember, and apply the subject matter in all of our disciplines.

And where is all that disciplinary knowledge stored? In *nonfiction texts*: reference books, textbooks, primary sources, charts, web pages, images, formulas, transcripts, and many other types of documents and data. So we are expected to give our kids tools for comprehending the whole range of informational, persuasive, procedural, and narrative documents that make up our disciplines. It's like we're supposed to issue every kid an "All-Access Pass" to the Body of Knowledge.

But our plates are already full. We have tons of content to teach if kids are going to pass those tests. We're already using every minute we have, every day. And weren't our students supposed learn how to read in elementary school anyway? You can't expect us to digress from our curricular duties to teach reading comprehension now. Can you?

But wait. This task doesn't have to be as hard or as time-consuming as it sounds. In this book, we'll show how to make your kids into much better readers in your subject field, using quick and engaging activities that add to, rather than steal from, subject-matter learning. We'll give you all the tools you need to work this magic: great short articles; explicit, step-by-step lessons; and real-life examples of kids and teachers at work. And in a minute, we'll show why we teachers also benefit big-time when we make this effort.

First, though, let's jump into some classrooms and see what these lessons look like with kids.

From Harvey (AKA "Smokey"), at Salazar School, Santa Fe, New Mexico

It's a crisp January day in New Mexico, and I am happily teaching sixth grade in Joyce Sanchez's classroom. Joyce's kids are a typical assortment of middle school readers—many are recent immigrants from Mexico, a smaller number are *Hispanos* (whose families came from Spain generations ago), and there's a sprinkling of Anglo kids. Some students are powerful readers, with homes full of books and relatives who love to read. Others struggle with text, or haven't spent much time in print-rich environments. Others are just learning English. The school, on the south side of town, is 100 percent free and reduced lunch.

Today, the kids and I are reading, writing, and talking about manure. *What?*

The middle school curriculum in New Mexico calls for kids to learn about nutrition, digestion, and food production and distribution. Now, a traditional way to launch this unit might be for the teacher to give a lecture about the food chain, or have kids read the appropriate textbook chapter. But I'm worried that those approaches won't hook the kids—won't get them engaged and eager to delve into the science, economics, and sociology of food production. In fact, good-hearted as they generally are, I can easily envision many kids "checking out" for this unit—faces down on their desks, hoods pulled over their heads, surreptitiously using their banned cell phones to text friends across town.

Nope, to have any hope of the kids investing fully in this subject matter, I have to first evoke their curiosity, activate their prior knowledge (including their misconceptions), and get them interested in the topic. Engaging the kids can't wait. By the time we move into the "meat" of the unit, students need to be pursuing their own inquiry questions. Not the kind that you answer at the end of the chapter, but the questions that skillful readers have in their heads *while they are reading*: "What's going on here? Does this make sense? What are the key points? Where's the evidence? Why does this matter? Who is this author, anyway? How does this all fit together? What does this mean to me?"

To get to that instructionally propitious place, I'm going to pander a little bit this morning. As Ivey and Broaddus showed in their 2007 study, the best way to get middle-level kids (especially ELLs) engaged in a subject is to reach into the required content, pull out whatever is most fascinating, puzzling, or provocative to students, and begin with that. Forget about the regular sequence; if we wait for the fun stuff that might pop up later, the kids will already have jumped ship. So instead, we begin with a stunning fact, a mystery, or some healthy disequilibrium.

Today, I toss the kids a question: "Does anybody know what a CAFO is?" I project the acronym on the screen. Kids gaze at each other and then back at me with looks that say, "Huh?"

"CAFOs are where a lot of our food comes from," I add, but puzzlement still prevails. Now I project and read aloud this definition, while also showing a picture of some milking cows in a feed lot.

> **Concentrated Animal Feeding Operations** (CAFOs) are agricultural operations where animals are kept and raised in confined situations. CAFOs congregate animals, feed, manure and urine, dead animals, and production operations on a small land area. Feed is brought to the animals rather than the animals grazing or otherwise seeking feed in pastures, fields, or on rangeland.
>
> —U.S. Environmental Protection Agency, 2010

We spend a few minutes clarifying the definition. The kids are shocked by the fact that dead animals can be part of a CAFO setting, not to mention the excretory by-products. Jose says his family keeps chickens at home, and we discuss whether this constitutes a CAFO. Since the hens peck freely around the yard, we decide not. Sky wonders aloud, "How many stomachs do cows really have?" so I google it on the spot. The answer is one stomach with four sections; then we talk about regurgitation for a few minutes. Now I have the kids' full, slightly perplexed attention. "Today," I declare, "we're going to learn about one way that our food is produced in America—in CAFOs, places that most of us have never even heard about."

To start the kids reading about this topic, I've brought along some "one-page wonders"—short, quirky nonfiction articles that engage kids while providing a platform for practice in reading and collaboration. Specifically, I'll offer a five-part article from *Rolling Stone* magazine about the dangerous and nonfragrant outcomes of large-scale pork production (see "Boss Hog" on pages 186–190). What I am going to do today is invest one class period in getting kids so fascinated with meat production that they'll be eager to learn more as the whole unit unfolds.

To structure kids' reading, writing, talking, and thinking, I will draw on some key comprehension and discussion strategies that Joyce taught earlier in the year. These students already know how to leave "tracks of their thinking" in an article, using *text annotation* (see page 41). They've also learned how to have four-member *jigsawed discussions* in which they discuss different articles about the same topic (see page 137). I've edited today's choices so there are both harder and easier selections; I want to make sure that every kid can find an article he or she *can* read and *wants to* read.

Now each student chooses one article and begins to read and annotate, while I circulate and observe. Most kids read silently. At one table, four kids take turns softly reading aloud to each other, one paragraph at a time, stopping to annotate in between. A pair—one English language learner and a bilingual classmate—have sat down together so the new arrival can hear the article read aloud and translated. Kids configure themselves to read however works best for them.

What is a one-page wonder?

Both of us are inveterate and passionate collectors of short nonfiction, in both its digital and tree-based forms, the more random the better. Nancy seems to have a direct feed into her brain from the nation's major newspapers, and among many other distinctions, has amassed the world's greatest collection of creepy animal stories. Smokey, who has subscribed to *Rolling Stone* since 1973, specializes in pop culture, politics, and stupid human behavior, a widely available genre of text. If you looked at our voluminous e-mail correspondence, you'd mainly see us trading short, current articles with subject lines like, "You're not gonna believe this one!"

We are also inveterate and passionate teachers of reading comprehension, thinking, and discussion strategies. This means we need a constant supply of text to use in short, lively, in-class lessons. So it's only natural that when we introduce our students to almost any strategy or topic, we bring out short nonfiction pieces from our collections—articles, essays, cartoons, charts, graphs, and images. We've come to call these texts "one-page wonders," because we hunt for (or trim down) kid-friendly reading selections that can be photocopied on a single page.

Now, when we do workshops around the country, teachers often come up to us all excited after the session. We expect them to compliment us on our stellar speaking skills, but instead they always ask the same question: "Where can I get those great articles?" Well, here they are, right in this book, seventy-five of our favorites, just for you. We secured permission from the publishers for each piece that we've asked you

Chicago Tribune

School's Lesson Plan: No More Homework
Students never did it; now it's no problem

May 8, 2005
By Jo Napolitano
Tribune staff reporter

Junior high students at the Marya Yates School in Matteson simply had too many crushes to attend to, Web sites to surf, and television shows to watch in order to sit diligently at their kitchen tables and crank ... School administrators saw ...

being able to study on one's own becomes crucial in high school and beyond.

Harris Cooper, director of Duke University's Program in Education, has studied homework for 20 years. Cooper said there is only a modest correlation between homework completion and academic success for middle school children, but the connection between the two becomes much stronger in high school. "Home-... teaches children study and time-... All kids should be ...

The Washington Post

Teens Are in No Rush to Drive
As modes of socializing change, digital generation delays rite of passage

By Donna St. George
Jan. 24, 2010

WASHINGTON – The quest to get a driver's license at 16—long an American rite of passage—is on the wane among the digital generation, which no longer sees the family car as the end-all of social life.

Federal data released Friday underscore a striking national shift: 30.7 percent of 16-year-olds got their licenses in 2008, compared with 44.7 percent in 1988.

"Driving i...

"Driving is real important to a lot of the kids in the culture, but it is not the central focus like it was 25 years ago."

Rob Foss, director of the Center for the Study of Young Drivers, and others suggest that these "graduated" state licensing systems— which have created new requir...

...n from every ...ents are more ... high school. ... Not surpris-... students on a ... one opposed to ...ydney Holt, 14, ...r teacher present ... Otherwise, she ...uld "be very con-...thing," Holt said,

DEADLY SPIDER REQUIRES LONG COURTSHIP—OR ELSE

Female Australian redback gets almost 100 minutes, or it will eat suitor

DISCOVERY CHANNEL   Jennifer Viegas, Oct. 21, 2009

Females of the Australian redback spider, one of the world's most poisonous spiders and a close relative to the black widow, demand 100 minutes of courting or else they usually cannibalize their male suitors.

Recent research shows that bigger isn't always better in the mating game. The tiniest of males sometimes approach female redbacks after offering the critical 100 minutes of wooing and successfully mate without being eaten.

The study shows that puny males of this species can win at love without exerting much effort and begins to explain the extreme size differences between males and females among some spider species. It appears as though females are not tuned to select male size, but rather the duration of courtship.

A male first performs a lengthy "courtship dance," where it vibrates the female's web and wraps it in his own silk to reduce the emission of pheromones that could attract other males. He then drums on her abdomen and may alternate between drumming and web dancing. If he does this for less than 100 minutes and then attempts mating, the female will begin her cannibalism.

But if he meets her desired courtship threshold, he may be able to mate and survive. If not, he's usually eaten and then other males enter her web, sometimes fighting with each other to get to her. Females appear to act as a referee and strike at males with their forelegs as males escalate aggression towards one another.

The bizarre process may help to explain why male spiders are often so much smaller than females. For this species, males carry 1 to 2 percent of the body weight of a typical female.

Smaller males likely mature faster and can therefore mate earlier in life. And tiny males may be better equipped to scramble faster towards females and their webs. Bigger females, on the other hand, may have greater reproductive success, so the species winds up with enormous females and minuscule males.

Researcher Mariella Herberstein concluded, "The question that remains is why females have not evolved a way of discriminating between two courting males in her web. It may be that distinguishing the sources of vibrations in a complex three-dimensional web is very difficult, an aspect that males clearly take advantage of."

to photocopy, so it is perfectly OK to slap these on the photocopier and run them off for your kids. In fact, that's the whole idea.

One-page wonders (OPW) allow us to do some good things for kids:

• Provide text that's packed with really interesting stuff

• Keep in-class reading time short, allowing all readers to keep up

• Allow for the efficient practice of comprehension and discussion strategies

• Minimize photocopying hassles at the school office

Now, these won't be our favorite seventy-five articles forever; we're always finding and adding new ones to the repertoire—and you should, too. As you work with these pieces, you'll start to internalize what makes a Wonder, and start collecting your own. As you search for more OPWs, keep an eye out for pieces that

• are interesting and relevant to kids

• are surprising, puzzling, funny, quirky, or weird

• invite the reader to visualize places, faces, and events

• feature people you can get interested in

• are complex enough to justify time and thought

• offer background knowledge in your content area

• contain open-ended or debatable issues that invite lively discussion

And when you are building bigger, multiarticle text sets, look for pieces that link directly to curricular units you need to teach. The goal is to create "launching lessons" that get kids interested in an upcoming topic. When you make those text collections, also be sure they are leveled: include selections at, above, and below grade level.

RollingStone

Boss Hog—Part 1

America's top pork producer churns out a sea of waste that has destroyed rivers, killed millions of fish and generated one of the largest fines in EPA history. Welcome to the dark side of the other white meat.

JEFF TIETZ

Dec. 14, 2006

Smithfield Foods, the largest and most profitable pork processor in the world, killed 27 million hogs last year. Hogs produce three times more excrement than human beings do. The 500,000 pigs at a single Smithfield farm generate more fecal matter each year than the 1.5 million inhabitants of...

Forty fully grown 250-pound male...

together, the immobility, poisonous air and terror of confinement badly damage the pigs' immune systems. They become susceptible to infection, and in such dense quarters microbes or parasites or fungi, once established in one pig, will rush spritelike through the whole population. Accordingly, factory pigs are infused with a huge range of antibiotics and vaccines, and are doused with insecticides. Without these compounds—...

HOUSTON CHRONICLE

If dress code doesn't suit teens, school district will

Parents say the inmate jumpsuit is too extreme for attire offense

By ELIZABETH WHITE
Associated Press, Aug. 1, 2008

GONZALES, Texas — Violating Gonzales High School's dress code is not a crime, but some of the offenders are about to start looking a lot like convicts. Soon after classes begin Aug. 25, violators of the district's beefed-up dress code must don navy blue coveralls unless they get another set of clothes from home—or serve in-school suspension. The outfits aren't just styled...

Mary Helen Douglas, who has a 17-year-old son starting his senior year. The 2,650-student district has ordered 82 coveralls, which are most often sold to county jails, state mental institutions and juvenile prisons. School districts have bought lunch trays and...

The 2,650-student district has ordered 82 coveralls, whic...

---

careerbuilder.com

My CareerBuilder | Find Jobs | Job Recommendations | Post Resume | Advice & Resources

10 Attitudes of Successful Workers

By Kate Lorenz, Copyright 2006 CareerBuilder.com

1. **I am in charge of my destiny.**
   If you spend your entire career waiting for something exciting to come to you, you will be waiting a long time. Successful professionals go out and make good things happen.

2. **Anything is possible.**
   If you think you can't, you probably won't. Adopt the attitude of The Little Engine That Could—"I think I can."

3. **No task is too small to do well.**
   You never know when you are going to be noticed. That is one reason to take pride in your work—all of it. Remember this the next time you feel like slacking because you are working on a menial task.

4. **Everyone is a potential key contact.**
   While you do need to be aggressive in the workplace, you can also go far by being courteous to those around you—you never know when your past contacts will play a role in your future.

5. **I was made to do this job . . . and the one above me.**
   If you spend your days feeling like you are not cut out to do the work you are responsible... Your job may not be the perfect fit, but successful workers ... no matter where they are.

National Geographic News

Scientists Successfully Clone Cat

David Braun, February 14, 2002

Scientists in Texas have successfully cloned a cat, opening the way to replicating pets and other valued animals once the technique is perfected. The work was funded in part by a company that hopes to use the technology to provide commercial cloning of companion animals for pet owners.

Cloned kitty, "CC"

The kitten, called CC (the old typist's abbreviation for carbon copy) and now almost two months old, appears healthy and energetic, although she is completely unlike her tabby surrogate mother, Mark Westhusin and colleagues at Texas A&M University, College Station, announce in the February 21 issue of Nature.

The cat was cloned by transplanting DNA from Rainbow, a female three-colored (tortoiseshell or calico) cat, into an egg cell whose nucleus had been removed, and then implanting this embryo into Allie, the surrogate mother.

"CC's coat color suggests that she is a clone, and a genetic match between CC and the donor mother confirms this," the researchers say.

She is not, however, identical to her DNA donor. The reason for this is that the pattern on cats' coats is only partly genetically determined—it also depends on other factors during development.

Out of 87 implanted cloned embryos, CC is the only one to survive—comparable to the success rate in sheep, mice, cows, goats, and pigs, the scientists say. "If these odds can be improved and CC remains in good health, pet cloning may one day be feasible," the scientists reported.

How They Did It

In their first attempt, researchers obtained the cells used to make the clone from the skin cells of a "donor" cat. But it didn't work. "We did...

188 nuclear-transfer procedures, which resulted in 82 cloned embryos that were transferred into seven recipient females," the scientists said. Only one became pregnant, with a single embryo. But this pregnancy miscarried.

In the next attempt, the scientists used cells from ovarian tissue to receive the DNA from the cat to be cloned. Five cloned embryos made in this way were implanted into a single surrogate mother. Pregnancy was confirmed by ultrasound after 22 days and a kitten was delivered by C-section on December 22, 2001, 66 days after the embryo was transferred.

Endangered Species Could Benefit

The Audubon Nature Institute welcomed the research. "Now we can take this technology and apply it for the preservation of endangered species," said their spokesman. "It proves that cloning can be applied not only to livestock but also to companion animals. Ultimately it will also be used for endangered species."

Humane Society Opposes Cloning

The Humane Society of the United States is opposed to the concept of cloning pets. "In the first place it is dangerous for the animals involved," said Brian Sodergren, who monitors the exploitation and abuse of companion animals for the society. "Take the cat that was cloned: The sheer amount of embryos it took is quite mind boggling."

"Secondly, cloning adds needlessly to the overpopulation of pets in the United States. There are millions of dogs and cats in shelters waiting to be adopted, looking for responsible owners and loving homes. About half of them will be euthanized because there are not enough homes for them."

Looking over students' shoulders, I see lots of codes and comments going down in the margins:

!   Disgusting

★   Wow! Surprised!

!★   OMG the manure lagoons are PINK

?   What does this [turbulence] mean?

?   This stuff has so much bacteria why would you jump in?

!★   Two guys drowned in that lagoon.

★   I didn't know lagoons had volatile gasses

★   These could be a contributor to global warming

★   Mmmm, not so good

?   Don't these companies have a heart?

★!?   It sounds like this company wants to pollute the planet because they don't really care.

★   They should clean up the lagoons so they are not so hazordes.

If some kids finish reading and annotating before others, they know to keep working silently, rereading their chosen article or starting on one of the other pieces in the set.

Now I form kids into discussion groups of five where each person has a different part of the article. They have five minutes to jigsaw. The kids begin by providing quick highlights from their chosen article, using their marginal notes and codes to remind themselves what's important to share. Then they shift into open-ended conversation for about three more minutes. I sit in and listen to the group meeting in the computer nook.

GREG: My article said this lagoon was as big as four Yankee Stadiums full of manure.

MARIA: And those guys drowned in there.

GREG: In my family, we would have saved them.

JOSE: Wouldn't it be horrible to live there, near one of these things?

MATT: I think I'd be really depressed. I think the smell would make me tense.

MARIA: I just feel sad for the animals. What about them? Ick! What a way to live.

GREG: I'd be angry. These companies just don't care about people.

Soon, we gather back together as a whole class. As I find so often with young people, the conversation quickly turns to questions of action: *what can we do about this*?

ADAN: The pollution stinks, but we can't just stop eating.

(pause)

NADIA: Well, you could switch from meat to vegetables.

ADAN: But I like meat! A lot. *(laughter)*

JUAN: Animals want to be hunted anyway.

NADIA: What? They want us to eat them?

JUAN: I mean they're made for us to eat. That's what they're for.

SKY: What can we do about all this pollution, though?

DEVIN: Just stop eating pork. Like bacon, ham sandwiches, and stuff . . .

NADIA: You can buy organic food instead.

DEVIN: Organic food is really expensive.

JUAN: Meat is cheap. You can get a hamburger for a buck at Mickey D's.

ILSE: That's not pork!

JUAN: Whatever.

SERENA: My mom always says steak is too expensive.

SKY: There's organic meat, you know, it's raised in a better way. Like Kobe beef. Without all the pollution and chemicals.

SERENA: But what if stores lie to you? Like maybe that meat is just the same, even though they say it isn't?

Our whole-class conversation goes on to touch on a dozen topics: pollution in the nearby Rio Grande River, climate change, animal cruelty, mad cow disease, the use of hormones and antibiotics in animal feed, the young adult book *Chew on This: Everything You Don't Want to Know About Fast Food* by Eric Schlosser, recent developments in the creation of artificial, "in-vitro meat," the wisdom of humans domesticating animals in the first place, and other engaging subjects. By the time the hour has passed, most of these sixth graders are actively thinking, wondering, debating, and posing questions about food production in the United States. Nobody is asleep, nobody is secretly texting in their pocket—and we are all late for gym.

From Nancy, at Victor Andrew High School, Tinley Park, Illinois

Last spring, the latest edition of the High School Survey of Student Engagement was released. Its most incendiary findings were shouted all over the media: "Kids spend seven hours a day on screen time, more than a full school day!" They might just as well have run headlines saying, "Eek! The Sky Is Falling!"

As I reviewed the report online, I knew that my juniors would be fascinated by this topic and ready to debate parts of it. I copied short key sections and brought them in. The survey focused on three dimensions of student engagement in school:

Cognitive/intellectual/academic

Social/behavioral/participatory

Emotional

It turns out that quite a few high school kids (66 percent to be exact) say they're bored at school almost every single day. As one respondent put it, "When I am not engaged, it is because the work is not intellectually engaging." Give that kid an A!

Later the report analyzes various instructional strategies as they enhance or detract from student engagement. Anyone want to take a guess at what the most boring strategy is according to students? Teacher lecture. On the other hand, a majority of students cited "discussion and debate" as the most engaging. Hey, isn't *that* good news, especially since *those* strategies are exactly what this book is about?

Moreover, those kinds of high-level discussions are just what the new Common Core State Standards (CCSS) call for in their Speaking and Listening sections. The language varies slightly from grade level to grade level, but here's what the CCSS say all kids should be able to do (2010):

Comprehension and Collaboration

- Initiate and participate effectively in a range of collaborative discussions (one-on-one, in groups, and teacher-led) with diverse partners on [grade-level appropriate] topics, texts, and issues, building on others' ideas and expressing their own clearly and persuasively.

- Come to discussions prepared, having read and researched material under study; explicitly draw on that preparation by referring to evidence from texts and other research on the topic or issue to stimulate a thoughtful, well-reasoned exchange of ideas.

- Work with peers to set rules for collegial discussions and decision-making (e.g., informal consensus, taking votes on key issues, presentation of alternate views), clear goals and deadlines, and individual roles as needed.

- Propel conversations by posing and responding to questions that relate the current discussion to broader themes or larger ideas; actively incorporate others into the discussion; and clarify, verify, or challenge ideas and conclusions.

- Respond thoughtfully to diverse perspectives, summarize points of agreement and disagreement, and, when warranted, qualify or justify their own views and understanding and make new connections in light of the evidence and reasoning presented.

Of course, the trick is to teach kids *how* to read deeply and then have those intellectually engaging discussions. It all starts with a combination of interesting text, instruction in smart-reader strategies, and an explicit understanding of what skills are needed for a good discussion. But boy, once those key ingredients are in place, watch out.

Here's part of what one group of my kids had to say after reading "Watch Your Driving, Kids—The Parents Are Watching" (see page 103), an article about installing cameras that monitor teen drivers and then send video snippets back to their insurance-paying parents.

> BRENDA: If my parents decided to install this in my car, I'd be highly upset. It's bad enough they can check my grades and my cell phone minutes online whenever they want. My privacy would be invaded because my parents could watch my every move.
>
> RANDI: I agree. Plus, it's creepy that an unknown person is watching you before your parents even do. I wonder what the company considers embarrassing footage. Like what do people do in their cars while driving?
>
> BRAD: What happens to the embarrassing footage that doesn't go to your parents? Do they delete it or toss it into a file somewhere? The fact that someone gets paid to sit at a computer and watch videos of some teenager in a car all day is kind of weird.
>
> BRENDA: A *lot* of things happen in a car, maybe not bad but just private. I hope my parents never put a camera in my car. I would feel like I was being watched 24/7 and that would probably make my driving even worse!
>
> BRAD: Having a camera in your car is *supposed* to make you paranoid; it's supposed to make you think more about your driving. I don't think it would make you drive any worse than you already do.

What do you notice about this discussion? First, it is pretty egocentric, focusing on one thing: how would this affect *me*? But hey, all humans, not just adolescents, are egocentric. Think about a revision of the teacher work rules at your school or a change in your contract. Sometime much later you may think about how this change will affect the bottom line of your district's budget, or how it will affect the long-term good of education in America—but I guarantee that your *first* thought will be: how does this affect me?

And, as you reread this conversation excerpt, notice that the kids are really thinking about the information in the article and responding thoughtfully to one another. As for me, it wasn't until I heard the kids' discussion that I started thinking about the "leftovers" angle myself. What *does* the company do with all that video? Do they save it for later sale to *The National Enquirer* once someone becomes a movie star—or a serial killer? What is the privacy language in the fine print of the contract—if there even is a contract?

Notice that the kids are engaged in conversation and staying focused on a discussion thread. They're asking questions, taking turns, responding respectfully, and talking about the article versus the latest video game. What just happened? Everyone read, everyone had interesting thoughts to share, and no one complained about having to read the article or participate in a discussion. The reason? Interesting text, an appreciation of various viewpoints, and an explicit understanding of good discussion skills.

Now, this sounds like a nice little activity, reading and reacting to an article about the surveillance of teen drivers. Maybe a bit of comprehension and collaboration practice, nothing wrong with that. But listen: at my school these kids are also studying the United States Constitution, and one of the biggest topics in that unit is the "right to privacy." This has been a highly controversial issue for generations: though privacy is not specifically guaranteed in our Constitution, many scholars and justices have argued that it is an implicit right, covered by the Second Amendment and the protections against unreasonable searches and seizures. There are also countless court cases and Supreme Court decisions that bear on (and often limit) the privacy rights of children, minors, and students in school. Our text set lesson on privacy (pages 226–233) covers exactly these issues.

So this engaging short surveillance article could be the bait that lures kids into a deeper study of American government, politics, and citizenship. That's one way we use our carefully selected "one-page wonders" and the lessons that go with them—not just to get kids hooked on topics, but also to get them *thinking and building knowledge through discussion and debate.*

OK. We just gave you two glimpses of what it might look like to teach "comprehension and collaboration" when you are mainly a teacher of science, French, social studies, economics, American government, math, or any other subject. Does this teaching look more fun and doable than when it was a mandate handed down? We hope so. Not only is such reading and discussion valuable for kids; it can really improve our teaching, enhance the staying power of our content, and even ramp up the enjoyment level of our work every day.

Why and How We Teach Reading

When many of us began working in the classroom, the job was to teach our subject matter, largely by assigning books that kids were supposed to be able to read on their own. Today, that's not working. (Did it ever?)

The distribution of students has changed, and their needs as readers seem far more complex. We see more kids with identified learning issues, more kids who are just acquiring English, kids who lack the background knowledge we took for granted back in the day, and still more kids who just seem to fight off reading with all their might. In any given class that walks though our door, the range of reading skills seems wider than ever. Fewer and fewer kids come to us ready to dig in and read our content on their own.

We also know that we are now competing for students' attention. Most of today's kids, even our academic stars, seek hours of screen time during their nonschool hours, where *they* are choosing the activities, running the mouse or joystick, being both in control and entertained. Maybe today's teenagers really are getting a little harder to reach, more alienated from the printed word.

If the kids in our classes can't read this year's material, we can't just blame the teachers in the grades below us. Reading is not a unitary skill that, once learned in elementary school, allows kids to understand any passage they encounter for the rest of their lives. Texts get harder, more specialized, more technical, more different from field to field as young people move up through the grades. So we accept that, whatever we teach, it really is part of our job to help kids crack open, connect to, and make sense of the tough texts in our field.

But we still wonder: Exactly, specifically, *how are we supposed to do this?* Show us the lessons, the materials. Oh, yeah, and while we're at it, all these new standards want us to make content literacy "interactive and collaborative"? With all the kids talking and working in groups? I mean, have you seen my sixth-period class? How can we train our students to read, work, talk, and think productively together?

Some Deeper Background: How Proficient Readers Think

Over the next few pages, we will dig deeper into the issues of teaching comprehension and collaboration as a content-area specialist. But you can bail out anytime and start trying the lessons. Then, you may want to come back here and read more about the issues and opportunities we face as we take up this role.

Still hanging in? Great.

Here's a question: how do skillful readers *think* when they are reading subject-matter text? If there are some effective patterns and strategies, we need to know what they are, so we can teach them to our students. Like today. But here's the weird thing: even though we adult teachers do have such strategies in our own brains, we might not even know what they are, since they probably were never explicitly taught to us. Instead, during our mostly fortunate lives as children, students, and teachers-to-be, we gradually cobbled together this repertoire of cognitive "moves" through our reading, storytelling, family literacy, school, and books, and then more books and more school. We may not be able to name our own strategies, but we do use them every time we read, and they work just fine. So well, in fact, that we might even deny their existence, scoffing: "Strategies, schmategies, I just read."

But the news is, we are not normal—we are teachers! And most of our students (rich or poor) are *not* growing up to be teachers, do not all come from fortunate and literate backgrounds, and will never cobble together a solid set of reading strategies—unless we name them, demonstrate them, and explicitly teach them. To do this, we need to become more aware of what's happening in our own minds so effortlessly that we don't even notice it.

Some reliable and well-replicated research done over the past few decades (Pearson and Gallagher 1983; Pearson, Roehler, Dole, and Duffy 1992; Pearson 2009) gave us a pretty clear picture of the cognitive strategies smart readers use. But we're not going to list them yet. Instead, we think you can discover them right in your own brain. Read the following passage and try to notice what's happening in your mind as you go. Do this with a colleague, spouse, or friend if one is handy. Really think about your thinking here.

// Recommendation Engine //

Ask an Algorithm

Which TV for Me?

I want that Panasonic 103-inch TV. My wife says that's too big. Is she right? Optimal viewing distance at 1080p = diagonal screen size ÷ 0.84, maximum OVD for 103-inch screen = 122.619 inches. **Recommendation:** If seat to screen distance >122.619 inches: Purchase TV; if <122.619 inches: Construct home theater space of necessary size; purchase TV.

OK, now we're going to guess what was just happening in your mind (except for you math teachers—this was too easy for you). From the start, you were **monitoring your comprehension** at an unconscious, unaware level. But soon, you ran into trouble. The meaning you were making didn't feel solid, and so you stopped and reread parts of the passage. Maybe you slowed down your reading rate. At this point, your thinking became more conscious and intentional. A lot of **questions** were popping into your head, like "what the heck is OVD?" or "what kind of publication did this come from?" You were trying to **make connections** to your background knowledge, perhaps about TVs you have known, certain mathematical operations, or classic spousal debates. You probably were **visualizing**, trying to make a mental image of the living room with that huge TV in it. "How big would a 103-inch TV actually be?" We'll bet you were doing a lot of **inferring**, putting together clues in the text with your own background knowledge in order to gain understanding. Along the way, you were constantly trying to **determine importance**, to figure out what were the most crucial facts and what were insignificant details. Does it really matter if the TV is a Panasonic or a Sony? And for sure, you were always trying to **synthesize**, to pull together all the information into one comprehensible summary, to get the gist of the piece.

As you worked, you may even have picked up a pencil or calculator to test out your thinking. Accessing any tool to make meaning—good for you! And, oh yeah, you showed stamina and persistence. If you were a student and this text were assigned for homework, you might very well have taken one look and tossed it aside, thinking, "This is too hard, I'm outta here."

Only when you synthesized all this thinking did you really "get it," and truly comprehend the passage. You realized that this "advice column" from *Wired* magazine (August 2010, p. 86) is completely tongue-in-cheek: the husband gets the giant TV either way. The guidance comes from "An Algorithm," a robotic voice answering questions with faux-scientific wisdom. Maybe not a gut-busting guffaw, but at least a chuckle. If you were superstrategic, you might have skipped right to the end, seen the joke, understood the genre that was being mimicked, and never even bothered to read the rest. Or if you were reading like one of your students, you might have just taken a gander at all that math in the middle and given up entirely.

Even after that experiment, you might still doubt the existence of your own internal cognitive repertoire. We surely don't notice ourselves using it very often. That's because when we adults are reading everyday text—from the newspaper to memos from the principal—we "just understand." The text clicks along, we get the meaning, no problem. As seasoned reading "pros," we have long since internalized that array of thinking patterns and we mostly use them unconsciously and automatically. But when the text is a little tougher (as this article was for us, and as our textbooks can be for kids), we can suddenly notice ourselves shifting to more conscious mental strategies.

So how did we do reading your mind? If we had any success, it is only because we expected you to make the same mental moves that any veteran reader would in this situation. Skilled readers:

Monitor their comprehension

Visualize and make sensory images

Connect to their background knowledge

Ask questions of the text

Draw inferences

Determine what's important

Synthesize and summarize

These seven core reading strategies are embedded in this book's thirty-three lessons, and kids will practice each one repeatedly as you lead them through the articles and activities. For the latest word on comprehension strategies research and practice, see *Comprehension Going Forward* (Daniels 2011).

How Skillful Collaborators Act

The new Common Core State Standards push pretty hard for us to get students working in groups a good part of the day. Among other things, the standards say that students should "assist in the formation and productive functioning of both formal and informal self-directed work groups" (2010). This embrace of student–student collaboration is also mandated by many individual state documents and by major subject-matter organizations.

How Proficient Collaborators Think and Act	
Strategy	**Examples/Actions**
1. Be responsible to the group	• Come prepared: work completed, materials and notes in hand • Bring along interesting questions/ideas/artifacts • Take initiative, help people get organized • Live by the group's calendar, work plan, and ground rules • Settle problems within the group • Fess up if unprepared and take on some other work
2. Listen actively	• Make eye contact • Nod, confirm, look interested • Lean in, sit close together • Summarize or paraphrase • Use names • Take notes when helpful
3. Speak up	• Join in, speak often, be active • Connect your ideas with what others have said • Ask lead and follow-up questions • Use appropriate tone and voice level • Draw upon the notes, materials, or drawings you've brought • Overcome your shyness
4. Share the air and encourage others	• Show friendliness and support • Take turns • Be aware of who's contributing; work to balance the airtime • Monitor yourself for dominating or shirking • Invite others to participate • Build upon and learn from others' ideas
5. Support your views and findings	• Explain and give examples • Refer to specific passages, evidence, or artifacts • Connect or contrast your ideas to others' • Dig deeper into the text or topic; revisit important ideas
6. Show tolerance and respect	• Receive others' ideas respectfully; no put-downs allowed • Try to restate opposing views • Use neutral language in disagreeing • Offer your different viewpoint; don't be steamrolled • Welcome and seek insight in divergent viewpoints
7. Reflect and correct	• Do frequent reflections or "think-backs" on group processes • Identify specific behaviors that helped or hurt the discussion • Talk openly about problems • Make plans to try out new strategies and review their effectiveness • Keep written record of group processing

From Stephanie Harvey and Harvey Daniels, *Comprehension and Collaboration: Inquiry Circles in Action* (2009).

What Social Strategy Use Looks and Sounds Like

Strategy	Looks/Sounds Like	Doesn't Look/Sound Like
1. Be responsible to the group	"Does everyone have their articles? Good, let's get going." "Let me show you this great website I found…" "I'm sorry, guys, I didn't get the reading done." "OK, then today I'll take notes on the meeting."	"What? There's a meeting today?" "I left my stuff at home." "Teacher, Bobby keeps messing around." Arriving late, unprepared, without materials
2. Listen actively	"Joe, pull your chair up closer." "I think I heard you say…" "So you think…" Asking follow-up questions	Not looking at others "Huh? I wasn't listening." Playing with pencils, shuffling materials
3. Speak up	"What you said just reminded me of…" "Can I piggyback on this?" "What made you feel that way?" "Let me show you my drawing."	Silence Whispering or shouting Not using/looking at notes Hiding from participation
4. Share the air and encourage others	"Can you say more about that, Chris?" "We haven't heard from you in a while, Joyce." "I better finish my point and let someone else talk." "That's a cool idea, Tom."	"Blah blah blah blah blah blah blah blah…" "I pass." "You guys are so boring." Declining to join in when invited
5. Support your views and findings	"I think Jim treats Huck as a son because…" "Right here on page 15, it says that…" "The person I interviewed said…" "My thinking was a lot like Jennifer's…"	"This book is dumb." "Well, that's my opinion anyway." "No, I didn't consider any other interpretations."
6. Show tolerance and respect	"Wow, I thought of something totally different." "I can see your point, but what about…" "I'm glad you brought that up; I never would have seen it that way."	"You are so wrong!" "What book are you reading?" "Where did you get that idea?" Rolling eyes, disconfirming body language
7. Reflect and correct	"What went well today and where did we run into problems?" "We are not sharing the talk time evenly." "OK, so what will we do differently during our next meeting?"	"We rocked." "We sucked." "It was OK." "Who cares?"

From Stephanie Harvey and Harvey Daniels, *Comprehension and Collaboration: Inquiry Circles in Action* (2009).

OK, so we need to get our students working together in groups. We want every single student to be willing—even eager—to work with any other classmate, at any time. We want to trust kids to stay on task when we put them in small groups. We do not want to hear chitchat about skateboards, video games, or the big dance when we stop by to listen in. We want peer collaboration, focused on the curriculum, right now, no grumbling, no hesitation, no arguments.

But, once again—have you seen my sixth-period class? Do you sometimes find yourself thinking: "Maybe *next year* I'll get some kids who can collaborate"? If so, stay tuned. Actually, collaborative, interdependent, high-morale groups are mostly made, not born. You don't have to wait for a just-right mix of kids to come along and be the exception to the rule. Every class—yes, of teenagers—can collaborate all year long *if we teach them how.* Kids are not born knowing how to work effectively in small groups; we have to show them explicitly. But that's exactly what the lessons in this book do.

So what are the component skills that good group workers have? Let's do a little thought experiment. You've been in a million small groups in your life, right? Just think for a minute—or chat with a colleague if one is handy—about some specific things that a group member can do that make the work speedier, more effective, efficient, or fun. Go ahead and jot down a couple of things. Now, ponder the reverse. What are some things that group members can do to obstruct, undermine, slow down group work—or make it less enjoyable?

Now take a look at the chart on pages 14–15, which is adapted from Smokey's book with Stephanie Harvey, *Comprehension and Collaboration* (2009). See if your own experiences aren't represented there, in the two right-hand columns. Of course, there are many ways to categorize the skills of effective collaborators. The field of study called *group dynamics* illuminates these skills in detail; we have never understood why this isn't part of our teacher training. Anyhow, this particular chart just shows how we label and group the collaboration strategies for our work with kids in school.

Here's the takeaway: just as with the comprehension strategies, we veteran collaborators have acquired a repertoire of social strategies that we draw upon, mostly unconsciously, to guide our participation in small-group work. And when the group work gets derailed, we can feel ourselves consciously deploying "fix-up" strategies to put things right ("Maybe we should get back to work now . . . ").

These seven strategies are embedded over and over again in his book's lessons. As you teach them, your kids will get plenty of practice and become better partners and group members.

How to Use This Book

This book offers thirty-three lessons: the first half of the book includes twenty-three strategy lessons, and the second half contains ten text set lessons. Every lesson focuses closely on at least one key comprehension strategy or collaboration skill that proficient learners use. You'll find that most of these lessons actually incorporate *several* such skills.

About the Reading and Thinking Strategy Lessons

Yes! It's OK to photocopy!

We secured permission from the publisher for each piece that we've asked you to photocopy, so it's perfectly OK to slap those on the photocopier and run them off for your kids. In fact that's the whole idea.

Each strategy lesson is accompanied by a "one-page wonder," a real-world article, text, or image that engages students in thinking and discussion. We selected and edited these pieces with engagement foremost in our minds; they cover a variety of current events topics, with a distinctly teenage spin. The lessons accompanying them are written as generally as possible, so you can use (and reuse) the steps and language with any compatible text you choose. The strategy lessons are quick: they are designed to be completed within ten to forty minutes.

The strategy lessons appear in what we'd call a "mild sequential order." You can't argue both sides unless you first know how to turn and talk with a classmate. As you can see from the table of contents, we present the strategies in families, beginning with the simplest and most basic ones, and moving toward more complex and challenging structures. But, that being said, use them however you like; no injuries are likely to result. You can also mix and match—any lesson with any article, ours or yours. But do read the articles first. There are a few spots where you need a fairly close genre fit, not just any random article. For example, in Lesson 23, you need two articles that use roughly the same internal structure.

Every lesson in the book has several sections or features. The following preview shows a typical strategy lesson. (When you get to the text set lessons, you'll find even more elements to get you organized: texts in order of use, lists of curriculum connections, and strategies used.)

Time: Tells the expected length of the lesson. Most strategy lessons range from ten to thirty minutes, averaging twenty. A handful run up to forty minutes. This estimate does not include extensions that may be offered in the Tips and Variations section, below.
For the text sets: Each lesson fills at least one fifty-minute class period—and we may give you steps and language to dig deeper over several additional periods.

Groupings: Tells what classroom configurations are used in this lesson, in the order they are used. You'll find that students are regularly shifting from working alone, to partners, to small groups, to the whole class. This sociability works toward student engagement, learning by doing, taking responsibility, and letting school be fun.

Materials Needed: We explain up front what article copies, projectable images, or other materials should be assembled in advance.

Steps and Teaching Language: This is the core of the lesson, where all the activities and teacher instructions are spelled out in sequence and in detail. Text that appears in regular type indicates our suggestions for the teacher. Text in italic is actual teaching language that you can try on and use. If you substitute your own article, check to see where the language might need to be adapted.

Title: Tells what reading, thinking, or collaboration skill is featured in each lesson. You'll probably notice that several other skills are introduced as well.

Introduction: The opening paragraphs give background on the strategies and structures being used, show when the lesson might be taught, and explain the value of the lesson for students.

Sc
Stua

May 8, 200
By Jo Napo
Tribune staff

Junior hi
School in
crushes to
television s

STRATEGY LESSONS / THINKING TOGETHER

THINKING TOGETHER

Strategy 1 ## Turn and Talk

Time:
10 minutes

Grouping Sequence:

Pairs, whole class

Here is the most basic collaborative learning strategy in the world: *turn and talk with somebody for a minute or two.*

Obviously, this is something that people in all walks of life do every day. We turn and talk to one another to connect, clarify, share, think things through, learn, and make decisions. If we want kids in our classrooms to shift from passive listening to actively engaging with the curriculum, this is a critical first step toward active thinking and energetic participation.

MATERIALS NEEDED

Copy of article for each student. If using an image instead of an article, have a projectable version ready.

Steps and Teaching Language

STEP 1 **Students read and talk** Have kids silently read the *Chicago Tribune* article "No More Homework" (or another engaging text of your choice). With this subject matter, students should have plenty of connections, reactions, and questions. Then just say:

Now turn and talk in pairs for two minutes. What are your reactions, feelings, or questions about this story?

STEP 2 **Share with the whole class** After kids have talked for two minutes, reconvene the whole class and invite pairs to share their thinking. Encourage kids to build on the ideas of other pairs. If you like, make a list of key phrases from the conversation as it unfolds.

TURN AND TALK is used in all the text sets.

STEP 3 **That's it** Your kids just turned and talked.

Tips and Variations

■ **PAIRS PREPARATION** Kids must know who their turn-and-talk partner is *before* you send them to chat. They should be sitting close to each other, so all they have to do when you call a meeting is put their heads together. Pairs are best; if numbers are uneven, it's OK to have one group of three, but airtime will be less per person in a larger group. Instead, you can partner with the leftover kid yourself—then everyone is in pairs.

34 Strategy Lessons / Thinking Together

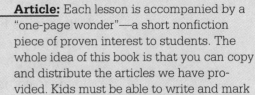

Chicago Tribune

Lesson Plan: No More Homework

r did it; now it's no problem

being able to study on one's own becomes crucial in high school and beyond.

Harris Cooper, director of Duke University's Program in Education...

at the Marya Yates ...nply had too many ...b sites to ...

Article: Each lesson is accompanied by a "one-page wonder"—a short nonfiction piece of proven interest to students. The whole idea of this book is that you can copy and distribute the articles we have provided. Kids must be able to write and mark directly on the page, so make copies for everyone (unless directed otherwise)—not just a class set that gets passed from one class to the next. Also keep in mind that you can substitute your own article and adapt our language to teach—or revisit—these skills.

■ **TOPICS** What do pairs talk about? Factual recall questions ("When was Gregor Mendel born?") give kids nothing to discuss. Instead, choose topics with a range of possible responses, interpretations, or points of view. You may use highly focused prompts ("To what extent do you think that deism affected our Constitution?") or more open ones ("What did you think about the story?"). Both can work well depending on the material.

■ **STAYING FOCUSED** How do you ensure kids stay on topic? Circulate and listen while they meet. Sit briefly with a few pairs and note their interactions. Back in the whole group, call on pairs to share their thinking. Require a short written outcome as well as an out-loud report. But you don't have to *grade* students' conversations to make them seem worthwhile; instead, listen to and use their ideas in class, honoring their thinking.

■ **DOUBLING PAIRS** Obviously, as kids get more adept at turning and talking in pairs, and if it adds value to do so, they can turn and talk in threes or fours. Often, we will have pairs discuss an initial point, and then have them quickly join up with another pair to make a group of four that can continue the conversation with a second prompt or question. Or kids can sit in a group of four, alternating between their "shoulder partners" (sitting beside them) and "face partners" (sitting across from them). See Strategy 17 on page 104 for an example of this variation, which also appears in several later text set lessons.

■ **TRY WRITTEN TURN-AND-TALKS** Instead of talking out loud, have pairs simultaneously write quick comments on index cards, exchange them at the teacher's signal, read the cards, and respond to them in writing. After a few swaps, have kids switch to talking. There are two complete lessons on such "write-arounds": Written Discussion on page 83 and Text-on-Text on page 89.

■ **READ AN IMAGE RATHER THAN TEXT** To be sure that talk-worthy information is available to everyone, teach Turn and Talk with a great projected photograph or painting instead of printed text.

Web Support: Anything you need to project or download as part of a lesson is ready for use on our website, www.heinemann.com/textsandlessons.

■ **DO THIS A LOT** In active learning classrooms, we often see turn and talk happening three, five, or ten times during a class period—along with other collaborative, small-group activities. With practice and reflection, kids get steadily better at these one-to-one conversations. A bonus: as you rotate students through different partners (daily early in the year, weekly later), they get to know many other class members, building a basis for more complex collaborative activities later on.

Tips and Variations: In this section you'll find two extra kinds of support: first, we offer advice on troubleshooting, solving predictable problems that may arise, and fine-tuning the lesson. Then, where appropriate, we offer ways you can vary, modify, or extend the lesson. Some of these variations extend the lesson into the following class period.

About the Text Set Lessons

The text set lessons are very similar in format and structure. The difference is that kids now choose from among multiple leveled texts on aspects of the same topic. (In each text set, we identify the easier choices. Also, be sure to read "What Makes Reading Easier," coming right up.) The text set lessons offer a deeper, longer engagement in the subjects and strategies being studied.

Unlike the opening strategy lessons, the text set lessons are directly aligned to commonly taught curricular topics (the U.S. Constitution, viruses and bacteria, the Civil War, force and motion, production and distribution, ecosystems, human geography, etc.) and so they require more classroom time for their exploration. Each text set lesson initially takes one fifty-minute class period to complete. Then, some have extensions—additional teaching ideas that can expand the lesson from one to three additional classes. We have arranged the text set lessons in a rough order of complexity; the first few are simple and straightforward, while the later ones add challenge and offer multiple extensions. As far as content is concerned, there is no teaching order to the ten lessons (as far as we can discern). Your own curriculum is probably the best source for timing clues.

About Text Difficulty

If you have already flipped through this book, you may have heard yourself thinking, "Whoa, some of these articles look way too hard for my kids." And you might be talking about your sixth graders, or your seniors! There is such a wide range of apparent reading levels in our classes these days that we have left-behind readers everywhere. We never see a class without a cohort of strivers, no matter what level we teach. And sometimes they're not even striving.

First, let us assure you that in the second section of the book—the text sets—we've provided a range of reading levels within each assortment. But what about the opening section—those twenty-three lessons where we use a single whole-class article? Normally, whenever we choose a whole-class text, something aimed for "the middle," it turns out to be too hard for some, not challenging enough for others, and "boring" to the rest.

Yes, we are saying that *your kids can read these articles*, from the sixth-grade strugglers to the English language learning seniors—but under the right circumstances, which you help to create. Aspects of the text itself are important, but we teachers choose to make any reading selection a lot easier—or a lot harder. So how did we identify and/or edit nonfiction pieces that *all* kids could find a way into?

As we were preparing this book, we looked for previously published, really easy nonfiction text—like fourth-grade level. But everything already in print that was aimed at below-level readers had the same chirpy, telegraphic, and patronizing voice: it was baby text, and our kids wouldn't go near it. Then we hired a professional writer to create new articles that would have the same

What Makes Reading
Easier?

☑ **THE TEXT** is shorter rather than longer.

☑ **THE READER** has chosen the text, versus it being assigned.

☑ **THE READER** has relevant background knowledge.

☑ **THE TOPIC** has personal interest or importance.

☑ **THE TEXT** embodies familiar settings and cultural values.

☑ **THE TEXT** evokes curiosity, surprise, or puzzlement.

☑ **THE TEXT** has high coherence, meaning that it explains itself
(e.g., "the plesiosaur, a Mesozoic period dinosaur . . . ").

☑ **THE TEXT** makes ample use of pictures, charts, and other visual
and text features that support and add meaning.

☑ **THE TEACHER** evokes and builds the reader's background knowledge.

☑ **THE TEACHER** teaches specific strategies for visualizing, inferring,
questioning, rereading, and other techniques.

☑ **READERS CAN** mark, write, or draw on text as they read.

☑ **READERS CAN** talk about the text during and after reading.

☑ **READERS CAN** hear text read aloud by the teacher,
by a classmate, or in a small group.

zest and interest as the "one-page wonders" we collected from adult sources, but still we got short, choppy sentences, an artificially controlled vocabulary, and the same chirpiness.

Meanwhile, we started trying out our own favorite "grown-up" articles with kids in Chicago and New Mexico, and, defying their grade levels, kids were reading them with delight. While doing this, we were reminded: not all reading tasks are alike. For any given kid, the exact same text can be easier or harder, depending on a lot of factors. In different situations, the very same marks on a page can either slam the door on most readers, or invite everyone in for a nice reading party. The list under "What Makes Reading Easier" summarizes the variable conditions we kept noticing.

Now let's use this list to think about how kids usually grapple with a traditional textbook assignment, like "Read Chapter 8 for Friday." They sit alone, overwhelmed by the length and text density, with little background knowledge available or activated, with no fellow reader to talk to, prohibited from marking on the pages, and probably with no interest in the topic.

Hmmm, maybe "text difficulty" is not so fixed after all. Indeed, we'd argue that the presence or absence of any of these conditions can determine how "hard" a given chunk of reading is, to any given student.

We've all had students who looked like they couldn't read a lick until they showed up with their biker, skater, gamer, music, gossip, or fashion magazines—or buried their face in a website covering similar topics. Just switching a few factors here—adding choice, interest, or background knowledge—can make a world of difference to what a student "can read." It almost makes us wonder, are some "struggling readers" struggling not so much from their own deficits, but from what schools fail to provide them?

That was a long answer to the original question: "Are these articles too hard for my kids?" We think not; we hope not. We have tried them with many students and they work—because so many of the factors that "make reading easier" are present in these pieces, and because the steps and teaching language support them.

All this being said, and having patted ourselves on the back for creating these accessible one-page wonders, if some pieces are too hard for your kids, don't use them! Substitute, grab another, use a picture with a caption, edit down to a single paragraph with a big font so everyone is reading "one whole article." It's gotta work for everybody. As Richard Allington (2000) keeps telling us: kids have to read text they can read. You cannot begin to become an Olympic pole vaulter by setting the bar at world record height. And you cannot get better as a reader by reading text you cannot read.

How We Edited the Articles

Many of the articles in the book are unedited, printed in their original form. Sometimes, if a tough word here or there impeded meaning, we swapped it out for an everyday synonym. Others began as two-, three- or even ten-page pieces, from which we extracted the most important, interesting, and kid-friendly elements, staying faithful to the thrust of the original piece. We got permission from all the copyright holders to edit this way; if they wouldn't allow such edits, we looked elsewhere.

About the Text Sets

In the second section of the book are ten more extensive lessons that use three to seven different texts on the same subject. For example, in the lesson on invasive species, kids choose among explanatory pieces about five different critters: Asian carp, Burmese pythons, killer bees, fire ants, and zebra mussels. Other text sets cover many forms of text, including six different maps of the same country and six images of children in forced labor as well as much more informational, persuasive, and even literary writings. Each of the text sets connects to one or more commonly taught school subjects, which we point out directly in the lesson.

Using these multiarticle sets allows us to differentiate for our young readers. Now, instead of using a whole-class text, kids get to choose an article they *can read* and *want to read*. The pieces are real-world, relevant, and current. Every set offers not just a range of topics, but also a range of reading levels.

Of course, not every article will be fascinating to every teenager. But there's a greater probability of grabbing kids with five options instead of one. In our selections, we've stressed the use of accessible, "hospitable" text wherever possible—and even incorporated nonprint choices in several sets. All these ingredients can, in effect, bring down the reading level, making one or more articles accessible to every student. And finally, when the teacher leads kids through the interactive and interesting steps of the lesson itself, students are even better supported to read, think, and build content knowledge.

Not all of these articles immediately look like "core material," do they? They don't necessarily cover the same topics as the textbook, or always focus on highly tested curriculum points. That's because these text sets are designed as "launching lessons," experiences that engage, puzzle, and involve kids at the start of a unit—much like the factory farming set we've already discussed.

For another example, consider American slavery and the Civil War. This material is routinely taught several times as kids move through the grades. Though we adults may find this period of history endlessly fascinating, the kids just find it endless. It's old, it's over, and that slavery stuff is so uncomfortable. So, to connect and engage students at the start of the unit, instead of beginning with, say, the triangular trade route, we plunge them into an inquiry about child slavery *today* (see pages 195–202).

How hard are textbooks?

While we were preparing this book, we dumped some five-hundred-word chunks of current middle school science and social studies textbooks into two different "lexile" scoring programs. Guess what? (And you *can* guess, because you know this in your DNA.) Every textbook sample scored two years above the grade level it is labeled for. Yeah, two years. No wonder so many middle and high school kids tell us their textbooks are "boring," which might just be teenspeak for "too damn hard." If you take this understanding back to the "What Makes Reading Easier" list (page 21), you can think further about how to better support students when using textbooks—and understand why it is so important to supplement these sometimes forbidding volumes with real-world text. We even advocate that you occasionally copy one really important page out of your textbook, so students can experience reading and marking it, just like a one-page wonder.

All in the family

This book stands on its own, offering immediately usable text and language for collaborative lessons in thinking across the curriculum. But it was also created to be used with several recent books by our "family" of coauthors. Over the past ten years, our own collaborative group has created a library of books focused on building students' content-area knowledge through the direct teaching of learning strategies in the context of challenging inquiry units, extensive peer collaboration, and practical, formative assessments.

Among these books are:

- *Best Practice: Today's Standards for Teaching and Learning in America's Schools* (Zemelman, Daniels, and Hyde 2003; 4th edition in press)

- *Subjects Matter: Every Teacher's Guide to Content-Area Reading* (Daniels and Zemelman 2004)

- *Content-Area Writing: Every Teacher's Guide* (Daniels, Zemelman, and Steineke 2005)

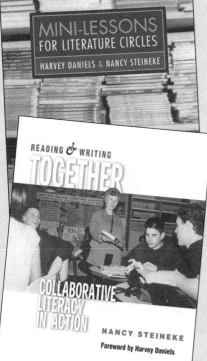

- *Comprehension and Collaboration: Inquiry Circles in Action* (Harvey and Daniels 2009)

- *Assessment Live! 10 Real-Time Ways for Kids to Show What They Know—and Meet the Standards* (Steineke 2009)

- *Mini-lessons for Literature Circles* (Daniels and Steineke 2006)

- *Reading and Writing Together: Collaborative Literacy in Action* (Steineke 2003)

Many of our readers have asked us to create a "practice book" to accompany these other titles. Though we are not in love with that term, we can see the need. If you are working with one of our other books, on your own or in a teacher study group, you can use the materials here to try out some of the ideas there. Indeed, these lessons are another way to provide your kids with lots and lots of *practice*.

Each of these books offers principles for teaching in different content areas—from the K–12 curriculum in *Comprehension and Collaboration* and *Best Practice*, to the secondary discipline areas in *Subjects Matter* and *Content-Area Writing*, to the book club strategies in *Mini-lessons* (though this is actually also a book about any kind of small-group work). Using the articles and lessons provided in this book, you can help kids practice and implement the ideas from any of these seven other titles.

Jigsawing Content

Who says that every student in America must learn the same things in the same order and at the same depth as every other kid? Why does everyone study every Civil War battle? Fort Sumter, Gettysburg, Antietam, Shiloh, Bull Run, Appomattox, oy! No wonder social studies teachers rarely finish the textbook—and the U.S. history course never gets past World War I! (OK, we have both taught American history and we never finished either.)

The important thing is not for students to know every detail of every battle, but to understand Civil War battles generally: What strategies were typically used, what weaponry, what injuries resulted? Who were the flesh-and-blood people who fought? The most important thing for kids to take away from the study of the American Civil War is not General McClellan's specific battle plans, but how the sudden advent of newly destructive weapons, just before the era of antibiotics and better battlefield medicine, yielded a catastrophic new level of casualties, dwarfing previous wars. (Our text set lesson on PTSD begins with a powerful Civil War battle scene on page 162.)

When we jigsaw curriculum, we have students pick one subtopic, aspect, or element (like one Civil War battle) to specialize in, working with a small group of kids who have chosen the same specialty. Using some class and homework time, each group is responsible for investigating its topic and then finding a powerful way to teach it to others. When these new "experts" share their learning, the audience—the rest of the students—is required to participate actively and keep notes, so that they will retain the highlights and synthesis provided. And the teacher is monitoring to be sure that the big, overarching ideas come across to everyone. We so often hear ourselves asking our jigsaw groups: "What do these things have in common? What are the overlapping features? What's different? How can you tell?"

When teachers hear about jigsawing, visions of the Big State Test sometimes loom in their heads, featuring material that all their students did *not* study in detail because they jigsawed that topic instead of lecturing. The six student "experts" knock it out of the park; the other twenty-four flunk. Those teachers are summarily fired, homeless the next day, and quickly forgotten.

Two quick answers to this fear: First, we have worked all around the country, and without exception, in schools where inquiry-based learning, along with curriculum jigsawing, is used, kids do just fine on state tests. That's because they have learned *how to think* (like a scientist, like a mathematician, etc.) and not just to memorize. Second, when kids become experts in one topic, that experience is, by definition, deep and valuable for them. It may even get them interested in a field of study. But we have to be equally sure that when these "expert" kids turn to teach others, their information has real staying power for the rest of the group. So we structure not just presenter, but also *audience responsibilities* into the DNA of our lessons.

Keep track of how we structure this as you work through the text sets. You'll see many different ways that we make sure kids benefit academically from jigsawing, learning even more from each other than from traditional lectures and textbook reading.

Assessment

So, you are using these lessons and articles to help kids learn and practice skills in comprehension, collaboration, and thinking. And you are also probably using the text sets to launch bigger units in your subject field. That means you're using maybe twenty minutes of class time for the solo strategy lessons and one or more class periods for the text sets. The question naturally arises: how do I grade these activities? After all, in today's schools, it seems like we have to assess, or at least assign a grade to, any activity kids spend time on.

Use Binary Grading

If you start *qualitatively* grading every piece of kids' work on activities like these, trying to defend the difference between a 78 and a 23, you're going to give up huge chunks of your own time marking, scoring, and justifying. Maybe this is some of our old Chicago "tough love" creeping in, but for smaller everyday assignments, we use binary grading: yes/no, on/off, all/nothing. We give 10 points for full participation and 0 points for less than full participation. No 3s, no 7.5s. Ten or 0, that's it.

Our colleague Jim Vopat has brought some poetry to this kind of grading in his book *Writing Circles* (2009). Jim calls this "good faith effort"—GFE. If a student shows up prepared to work, having all the necessary materials (reading done, notes ready), joins in the work with energy, and carries a fair share of the work—that's a good faith effort and that's 10 points. From a practical point of view, this means you only have to keep track of the few kids who don't put forth that GFE, and remember to enter that zero in your gradebook, even as you award everyone else their 10s.

The idea of good faith effort ties directly into sociability in the classroom. What kids might refuse to do individually, they are surprisingly willing to do when they can mix it up with others. Nancy adds a story: Just today I had a student who hates *everything*, like "Mikey" from the old cereal commercial. If he works alone, he does nothing. So today he comes in late. I've already given away his partner but I saved a seat so that he could join his old partner and a new person to form a trio. He sits right down, has them explain what they're working on, and in no time he's giving ideas and they're all working away making a poster about friendliness and support in the classroom.

Kids won't do much for just the teacher, but they'll do a heck of a lot when the task involves working with each other. So take note, resistant readers aren't so resistant when they start to enjoy working together. The likelihood of good faith effort rises exponentially.

Still, let's be honest. Giving points is not assessment, it's just grading. When we want to get serious and really monitor kids' thinking in these activities, we have to take further steps.

Collect and Save Student Work

As kids do the activities in these thirty-three lessons, they naturally create and leave behind artifacts, evidence, and tracks of their thinking: annotated articles, drawings, maps, diagrams, lists, notes, reports, and even podcasts or video clips. Who needs a quiz? As kids carry on with the work, you can collect, study, and save the naturally occurring by-products of their learning. This authentic residue of thinking is far more meaningful than a disembodied C+ in your gradebook. The kids' own creations are far more relevant in a parent conference or a principal evaluation than a string of recorded point totals. Instead, we maintain a firsthand record of a student's thinking all the way through a unit, quarter, or semester.

Observe Kids at Work

The form on page 29 is a tool we use when sitting with a group of kids, watching them work on a lesson together. As you can see, this form incorporates the good faith idea but goes much further. As we listen in on kids, we jot down one memorable quote from each student and reflect on what kind of thinking this comment or question represents; then we also jot notes about any conspicuous use (or neglect) of the collaboration skills called for in the lesson.

Orchestrate Authentic Teaching and Sharing Opportunities

When the time comes to assign grades for kids' work over long stretches of time and big chunks of content, we traditionally make up a big test and add that score to the points kids have earned along the way. Even as we do this, we quietly recognize that this assessment system invites cramming, superficiality, and the wholesale forgetting of content.

Instead, we like to devise authentic events at which kids share or perform their learning for an engaged audience—and then we use a rubric that carefully defines a successful performance to derive each kid's grade. Nancy has recently published a whole book with ideas on this kind of sociable, practical structure called *Assessment Live! 10 Real-Time Ways for Kids to Show What They Know—*and *Meet the Standards* (Heinemann 2009).

The Mechanics of Grouping

Every lesson in this book has kids working with other kids. That means there's always the question: how do you quickly and efficiently arrange students into partners or groups of various sizes? Some teachers are able to accomplish this "on the fly," without losing a moment of time or momentum for the lesson.

Observation Chart

Student Name	"Good Faith"	Quote	Thinking	Social Skills
1.				
2.				
3.				
4.				
5.				

Amazing. For the rest of us mortals, though, some advance planning is definitely required.

In the forthcoming lessons, we always tell you how groups should be formed right at the beginning, so you can get kids in the proper configuration. But it works even better if students have an ongoing understanding of how they can group and regroup during lessons. Before any class activity or reading, students should already be able to immediately identify their single turn-and-talk partner and know what larger group (usually four) they might join. We start with this at the very beginning of the year, so that within a week kids know what to do when we say "turn and talk" or "get in your groups."

While we highly value kids working with a variety of classmates over the year, we also prize regularity. Translation: kids keep the same partner and small group for several weeks before swapping around. There are some lively exceptions to this rule, spontaneous grouping activities like Where Do You Stand? or Jigsaw (you'll hear more about these shortly).

Finally, here's some more Chicago-bred tough love. Especially early in the year, we avoid allowing students to choose their own partners. Kids will inevitably choose their friends, which may increase off-task behavior and decrease divergent thinking. Self-choice can undermine our goal of keeping groups socially heterogeneous, as well as obstruct our attempts to differentiate instruction. And of course, there is always at least one "odd man out" circumstance, and we want to spare students from that painful moment. Nancy still remembers being picked second to last for PE teams (second to last because she was unskilled but had good hygiene—the last kid picked was the one who ate her boogers).

Materials and Equipment

These lessons are generally pretty low-tech. Mostly, you just photocopy the articles and help kids have meaningful, live conversations. But there are a few supplies we like to have around, especially for the text set lessons:

- Post-it notes of various sizes

- Index cards, 3x5-inch and 4x6-inch varieties

- Large chart paper or newsprint

- Markers, tape, scissors, glue sticks

- Clipboards: When kids are working with one-page articles, they may be moving around the room, sitting on the floor, meeting in various groups. They'll need to bring a hard writing surface; a textbook works, but clipboards were made to be portable desks.

- Projection tools: When we started teaching, there was one tool for showing documents to students: an overhead projector. Today we have a million ways of displaying material: document cameras, smart boards, whiteboards, you name it. Many of our lessons have either images or

On the Web

short chunks of text, which, though they are included in the book, work much better if projected for the class. So we have parked these on our website (www.heinemann.com/textsandlessons) or provided links that were active at the time of publication. Whenever projection would enhance a lesson, we'll remind you with this icon in the margin.

Have Fun

We're serious about putting this "F-word" back into school. In the education business these days, things too often seem monotonous and a little grim. The atmosphere feels increasingly mechanical and bureaucratic. We live under an onslaught of mandates, orders, directions, rulings, and marching orders; most come from afar and few have any immediate appeal. At the lowest moments, school feels more like a forced march than an adventure.

And now they want us to read real-world nonfiction with kids? And get them working together like human beings? Thinking, arguing, debating, interacting, actually doing stuff? Are you kidding? We'll take *that* job any time. Let us at 'em!

All the best,

Smokey and Nancy

Introduction to the Strategy Lessons

Just a few final tips before you launch into these twenty-three strategy lessons:

- **You go first.** The missing link in so much of our teaching (because it was probably lacking from our own school experience **and** from our professional training) is teacher modeling. In other words, if we want kids to read or think or interact in some way, we cannot just command them to do it. We have to *show them, ourselves, first.*

   If your kids have never turned and talked about the subject matter with a partner during class, pair yourself with one kid and demonstrate it, fishbowl style, before asking everyone to try it. If your kids might feel weird drawing their responses to a reading, project a text and "sketch it" in front of the class, so students see exactly what you mean and have their anxiety reduced when they see how simple and fun it can be.

- **Consider the source.** Flip through the twenty-four articles we have selected for this section of the book and you'll notice that they come from all over the place. Our sources range from the august and presumably reliable *New York Times* and the Associated Press to National Geographic News, the Discovery Channel, the Chicago Art Institute, CareerBuilder.com, and the Insurance Institute for Highway Safety. We chose these disparate sources on purpose. For young readers—hey, for all of us—evaluating the credibility of information always includes scrutinizing the source, the platform, the sponsor. For any of these twenty-three lessons, a worthy strand of the conversation can always be: How trustworthy is this information? How can you tell? What point of view does this entity represent?

- **Substitute your own articles.** After you've taught a few of these lessons, you'll quickly internalize their structure and want to plug in your own articles. Go for it! Not just for the variety, but also because these lessons need to be re-taught. We don't just teach these skills once, kids get it, and we're done. Instead, we return to the lessons over and over, using new text each time, to help students get better and better at, say, reading with a question in mind or jigsawing information. For most lessons, any high-interest article suited to the class reading level will work. Where some kind of structural match to our original selection is needed, we'll tell you.

| Strategy 1 | # Turn and Talk |

- Time:
  10 minutes

- Grouping Sequence:
  Pairs, whole class

Here is the most basic collaborative learning strategy in the world: *turn and talk with somebody for a minute or two.*

Obviously, this is something that people in all walks of life do every day. We turn and talk to one another to connect, clarify, share, think things through, learn, and make decisions. If we want kids in our classrooms to shift from passive listening to actively engaging with the curriculum, this is a critical first step toward active thinking and energetic participation.

MATERIALS NEEDED

Copy of article for each student. If using an image instead of an article, have a projectable version ready.

Steps and Teaching Language

STEP 1 **Students read and talk** Have kids silently read the *Chicago Tribune* article "No More Homework" (or another engaging text of your choice). With this subject matter, students should have plenty of connections, reactions, and questions. Then just say:

Now turn and talk in pairs for two minutes. What are your reactions, feelings, or questions about this story?

STEP 2 **Share with the whole class** After kids have talked for two minutes, reconvene the whole class and invite pairs to share their thinking. Encourage kids to build on the ideas of other pairs. If you like, make a list of key phrases from the conversation as it unfolds.

TURN AND TALK
is used throughout the text sets

STEP 3 **That's it** Your kids just turned and talked.

Tips and Variations

■ **PAIRS PREPARATION** Kids must know who their turn-and-talk partner is *before* you send them to chat. They should be sitting close to each other, so all they have to do when you call a meeting is put their heads together. Pairs are best; if numbers are uneven, it's OK to have one group of three, but airtime will be less per person in a larger group. Instead, you can partner with the leftover kid yourself—then everyone is in pairs.

■ **WHEN TO USE** When do you call for kids to turn and talk? Any natural stopping place will do—at the end of a read-aloud or a chapter, after watching a video, after a key idea has been introduced, or after a science experiment. Think of Turn and Talk as pausing so kids can think about and synthesize what you have just been teaching, and solidify their understanding.

■ **MODEL IT FIRST** While turning and talking is a fairly natural interaction, don't take any chances if your students haven't done it before. Kids need to understand that when they get together, they are supposed to have a lively back-and-forth conversation—not just each say a few words and then shut up. The key skill that students may be missing is asking the kind of follow-up questions that keep conversations going. So teach the activity explicitly. Grab one student (or another adult) and demonstrate in a fishbowl for the class to watch.

All right, everyone. Becky and I are going to do a turn-and-talk for you and we need a topic. Who can give us a subject that we two could discuss for a couple of minutes? It should be something that we both have some knowledge about. Who's got one? OK, what animal makes the best pet?

TEACHER: OK, Becky, let's turn and talk. What do you think—what's the best pet?

BECKY: Hmmm. My grandpa had this collie, she was the greatest dog.

TEACHER: What was so great about her?

BECKY: Queenie—she just loved people, she would snuggle up to you all the time, and kiss you and get dog spit all over you, but it didn't matter.

TEACHER: What did you do with her?

BECKY: My grandpa has a farm, so she could run around with the other animals, out in the orchard and stuff. She loved to run.

TEACHER: You keep saying Queenie "used to" do stuff—is she still alive?

BECKY: No, she got run over by the neighbor's tractor. It was really sad.

TEACHER: Aw, that's terrible. What happened? Were you there? Did your grandparents think about getting another dog?

Invite kids to notice how you listened to Becky and then asked her questions based on what she said, digging deeper into her story. That's how we do a turn-and-talk in class, using follow-up questions to find out more about what each other is thinking—whether it is about a poem or about photosynthesis. Now let Becky take a turn interviewing you, and then put the whole class into pairs to practice. Finally, come back and debrief, stressing the use of follow-up questions.

■ **TOPICS** What do pairs talk about? Factual recall questions ("When was Gregor Mendel born?") give kids nothing to discuss. Instead, choose topics with a range of possible responses, interpretations, or points of view. You may use highly focused prompts ("To what extent do you think that deism affected our Constitution?") or more open ones ("What did you think about the story?"). Both can work well depending on the material.

■ **STAYING FOCUSED** How do you ensure kids stay on topic? Circulate and listen while they meet. Sit briefly with a few pairs and note their interactions. Back in the whole group, call on pairs to share their thinking. Require a short written outcome as well as an out-loud report. But you don't have to *grade* students' conversations to make them seem worthwhile; instead, listen to and use their ideas in class, honoring their thinking.

■ **DOUBLING PAIRS** Obviously, as kids get more adept at turning and talking in pairs, and if it adds value to do so, they can turn and talk in threes or fours. Often, we will have pairs discuss an initial point, and then have them quickly join up with another pair to make a group of four that can continue the conversation with a second prompt or question. Or kids can sit in a group of four, alternating between their "shoulder partners" (sitting beside them) and "face partners" (sitting across from them). See Strategy 17 on page 104 for an example of this variation, which also appears in several later text set lessons.

■ **TRY WRITTEN TURN-AND-TALKS** Instead of talking out loud, have pairs simultaneously write quick comments on index cards, exchange them at the teacher's signal, read the cards, and respond to them in writing. After a few swaps, have kids switch to talking. There are two complete lessons on such "write-arounds": Written Discussion on page 83 and Text-on-Text on page 89.

■ **READ AN IMAGE RATHER THAN TEXT** To be sure that talk-worthy information is available to everyone, teach Turn and Talk with a great projected photograph or painting instead of printed text.

■ **DO THIS A LOT** In active learning classrooms, we often see turn and talk happening three, five, or ten times during a class period—along with other collaborative, small-group activities. With practice and reflection, kids get steadily better at these one-to-one conversations. A bonus: as you rotate students through different partners (daily early in the year, weekly later), they get to know many other class members, building a basis for more complex collaborative activities later on.

Chicago Tribune

School's Lesson Plan: No More Homework

Students never did it; now it's no problem

May 8, 2005
By Jo Napolitano
Tribune staff reporter

Junior high students at the Marya Yates School in Matteson simply had too many crushes to attend to, Web sites to surf, and television shows to watch in order to sit diligently at their kitchen tables and crank out homework. School administrators saw they were fighting a losing battle outside their walls. But they were confident most students were absorbing the lessons in class. So what did they do? They virtually eliminated homework.

Homework used to account for about 30 percent of students' grades. The shift in policy began after Principal Lucille Adams Johnson consulted with teachers a few years ago about why so many students were earning C's when tests and quizzes showed they had command of the material.

The answer was simple: homework. "Teachers were assigning it. Kids weren't doing it. Teachers found themselves entering dozens of zeros where better grades should have been," Adams Johnson said. As the policy has evolved, homework at Marya Yates now accounts for only 10 percent of grades, with some teachers making it as small a factor as possible.

But education experts are divided on the wisdom of adapting to the desires of junior high students, with some praising that flexibility and others noting that being able to study on one's own becomes crucial in high school and beyond.

Harris Cooper, director of Duke University's Program in Education, has studied homework for 20 years. Cooper said there is only a modest correlation between homework completion and academic success for middle school children, but the connection between the two becomes much stronger in high school. "Homework teaches children study and time-management skills. All kids should be doing homework," he said.

> *"...there is only a modest correlation between homework completion and academic success for middle school children, but the connection between the two becomes much stronger in high school."*

Adams Johnson said that from every indication she has, her students are more than adequately prepared for high school. And her students are happy. Not surprisingly, a small sampling of students on a recent afternoon found no one opposed to the school's approach. Sydney Holt, 14, said she likes having her teacher present when she has a question. Otherwise, she said, the assignments would "be very confusing. I'd forget everything," Holt said, speaking mainly of math.

STRATEGY LESSONS / THINKING TOGETHER

| Strategy 2 | # Read with a Question in Mind |

Our old friend and reading scholar Marilyn Bizar has always preached that students must "enter the text thinking," meaning that they should begin reading with a conscious purpose (Daniels and Bizar 2004). But too many times in school, kids are reading with mere compliance in mind, not comprehension. Reading strategies gurus Stephanie Harvey and Anne Goudvis turned this insight into a succinct lesson and process—"Reading with a Question in Mind"—in their wonderful *Comprehension Toolkit* (2008). Here's our version.

- Time:
  20 minutes
- Grouping Sequence:
  Pairs, whole class

MATERIALS NEEDED

Copy of article for each student, projector for sharing the list of ideas.

Steps and Teaching Language

STEP 1 **Introduce the topic**

Today we are going to read an article about teenagers and driver's licenses. That's a topic you guys have some ideas and opinions about, I bet. This article had quite a surprise in it—a set of facts that are way different from what I expected. Something has changed recently about teenagers getting their driver's licenses. What do you think that might be? Turn and talk in pairs (or small groups) for a couple of minutes. What do you think has changed? Jot down your ideas.

Then allow two to three minutes of talk time as you circulate and listen.

STEP 2 **Share ideas** Invite volunteers to offer hypotheses, guesses, or answers and list or project them.

STEP 3 **Read aloud** Now, read aloud the headline and second paragraph only. (If using a different article, select a similarly pivotal section.)

STEP 4 **Kids respond** Let kids react and comment. If it is appropriate, you can offer your own reaction. For Smokey it would be:

Are you kidding? On my sixteenth birthday, I made my mother drive me thirty miles through a Minnesota blizzard all the way to St. Paul to get my license. And she didn't even complain—we both knew this was a sacred rite of passage. Every kid in my class got their licenses as soon as they could—it was a coming-of-age ritual and ticket to freedom.

STEP 5 **Brainstorm** Now, invite students to brainstorm reasons *why* they think the rate of license-getting has declined among today's teens. They can work in pairs or small groups, with someone serving as recorder. After some work time, regather and create a whole-class list of possible explanations. It will likely include entries like these: state licenses for teens are more restrictive now; insurance, gas, and repairs are too expensive; parents are less trusting; I have other things to do; I can get a ride from someone else; and who needs a car? I can connect with my friends by cell, Twitter, text, and email.

If you teach in New York or Chicago, your kids can probably get anywhere on public transportation, faster and cheaper than with a car. So this may be another reason not to hurry and get a driver's license. But is it a *new* reason for the decline in license applications from sixteen-year-olds?

STEP 6 **Read with questions in mind** Now hand out the article and have the kids read with their questions and predictions (still projected) in mind. Tell them to mark in the text with an *A* (for Answered) when their question is answered or a prediction confirmed. They should also flag new, unpredicted reasons with an *N* (for New). Allow reading and writing time. (For more about the use of codes like these, look ahead to Strategies 3 and 4, pages 41–49.)

STEP 7 **Share and debrief** Either in small groups or back in the whole class, have kids share in two steps:

1. *Which of your questions got answered or guesses were confirmed?*

2. *What new reasons did you discover for why fewer kids seek their driver's licenses?*

READ WITH A QUESTION IN MIND is used in Text Sets 4, 7, 8

Tips and Variations

■ **SKIM FOR QUESTIONS** Another basic way to practice this strategy, no matter what the text, is to have kids very quickly skim the reading, paying close attention to text features like titles, bold type, boxes, charts, and sidebars. Sometimes we just say, *You have one minute to skim—go!* Then have each student develop one question they believe/hope this text will answer. Appropriate after-skimming queries might sound like these:

• What are negative ions, anyway?

• How did Custer end up losing at the Little Big Horn?

• So what does probability say about plane crashes and lottery winners? Don't your odds increase if you "get in the game" more often?

• How come some people think Shakespeare didn't exist or didn't actually write all those plays?

■ **PAIR READING** For a ramped-up alternative, where partners use repeated turn-and-talks to work their way through a text, see Strategy 9, Pair Reading.

The Washington Post

Teens Are in No Rush to Drive

As modes of socializing change, digital generation delays rite of passage

By **Donna St. George**
Jan. 24, 2010

WASHINGTON – The quest to get a driver's license at 16—long an American rite of passage—is on the wane among the digital generation, which no longer sees the family car as the end-all of social life.

Federal data released Friday underscore a striking national shift: 30.7 percent of 16-year-olds got their licenses in 2008, compared with 44.7 percent in 1988.

"Driving is real important to a lot of the kids in the culture, but it is not the central focus like it was 25 years ago," said Tom Pecoraro, owner of I Drive Smart, a Washington area drivers' education program, who added that plenty of his students are older teens. "They have so many other things to do now," he said, and, with years of being shuttled to sports, lessons and play dates, "kids are used to being driven."

A generation consumed by Facebook and text-messaging, by Xbox Live and smartphones, no longer needs to climb into a car to connect with friends. And although many teens are still eager to drive, new laws make getting a license far more time-consuming, requiring as many as 60 supervised driving practice hours with an adult.

> "Driving is real important to a lot of the kids in the culture, but it is not the central focus like it was 25 years ago."

Rob Foss, director of the Center for the Study of Young Drivers, and others suggest that these "graduated" state licensing systems—which have created new requirements for learner's permits, supervised practice hours, night driving and passengers in the car—are responsible for much of the decline in the number of licensed 16-year-olds. At the same time, drivers' education has been cut back in some public schools, so families must scrounge up money—often $300 to $600—for private driving schools.

Then there is car insurance and gas, expenses that make driving too costly for some families and a stretch for others.

But waiting too long also has its drawbacks. "Learning to drive is a fundamental part of adolescence," said psychologist Joseph Allen of the University of Virginia. "It gives teens a major responsibility they have to handle, and it also gives them the chance to move about on their own, to function independently of their families."

Strategy 3	# Text Annotation

- Time:
  40 minutes
- Grouping Sequence:
  Pairs, whole class

We'll bet that when you encounter a piece of "high-stakes text"—a document you really need to understand well—you drag out a pen or highlighter and "mark it up" with underlines, marginal notes, symbols, or even doodles. Are we right? Well, you're not that unusual—it turns out that annotating text is one of the most common comprehension-enhancing strategies used by proficient readers.

But our students often think that annotation simply means highlighting almost every sentence in a text, so that the whole thing becomes a wall of yellow. This misconception is so widespread that even the Harvard University library feels it must put incoming students on notice: "First of all, throw away the highlighter in favor of a pen or pencil. Highlighting can actually distract you from the business of learning and dilute your comprehension. In actual fact, it can lure you into a dangerous passivity" (2005).

For kids to annotate in a way that empowers later discussion, they must do two things: mark only the most important sections, and then stop to write down their thinking *in words*.

When students annotate as they read, it keeps them focused and engaged with the text. It makes comprehension a little more conscious and intentional. This heightened awareness becomes especially useful when the text gets more difficult, or when students need to remember information for later discussion and application. Since all content areas have their information stored mostly in print, this strategy is a winner across the curriculum. The next three lessons, Text Coding, Sketching Through the Text, and Two-Column Notes, show different ways for kids to stop, think, and react—to capture their responses while they read.

MATERIALS NEEDED

Copy of article for each student, text suitable for modeling via projector.

Steps and Teaching Language

STEP 1 **Prepare to demonstrate** Get a short piece of text that you can project and annotate "live" in front of the class. This text might be another article from this book or something short and provocative that you'd enjoy reading aloud. Aim for a text chunk less than a hundred words long, and then blow up the font so kids can easily read along when it is projected onto a whiteboard or from a transparency. This small sample also makes the demonstration appropriately brief.

STEP 2 **Model annotation** Now just read the article aloud, stopping to underline the really important parts. At each underline, jot quick notes describing your thinking—question, connection, image—and record that thinking right in the margin of the projected text. As you jot, share your thinking aloud: *This part reminds me of . . .* or *Wow, I never knew that . . .* or *I wonder where the author got these facts . . . .* (For a full-length lesson on this kind of reading, see Strategy 8, Think Aloud.)

STEP 3 **Give instructions for student reading and annotation**

As you read this article, I want you to do what I've just demonstrated: First, underline information that is important, surprising, interesting, or thought provoking.

Then, before continuing to read, stop and jot down a sentence or two that explains why you chose that bit to underline. The goal is to explain your thoughts, opinions, or questions. Try to imagine that you are having a conversation with the text inside your head. Your notes are your side of the conversation.

STEP 4 **Monitor reading** Circulate as kids work. Annotating can feel unnatural at first. Some students will simply read, others will only underline, and some will just underline and say they want to go back and record their thoughts after they finish. This may be a genuine learning style issue, but for now, encourage kids to follow the given instructions. *Stopping to think is a really key strategy of effective readers. Just play along with me, OK?*

If you notice some students finishing sooner than others, you can say: *If you are finished, go back to the article, reread your annotations, and try to add enough details so that you could just glance at your underlining and notes to easily remember the article without having to completely reread it.*

STEP 5 **Pairs discuss the article**

Get with your partner and have a quick discussion of this article. Compare what you've annotated and your thoughts connected to those underlines. Also, be sure to discuss and answer any questions you posed.

STEP 6 **Share with the whole class** Invite volunteer pairs to read aloud and discuss the annotations that produced particularly interesting conversation.

TEXT ANNOTATION is used in Text Sets 2, 4, 9, 10

Tips and Variations

■ **COLLECT KIDS' WORK** It may take practice with a few text pieces before students' annotations become more detailed. Though it is not always necessary to grade their work, collecting annotated articles can be helpful for assessing how students are mastering this skill and what kind of thinking they are doing. Kids' recorded thoughts might indicate a need for you to further model your own thinking, continuing to annotate in front of them. Or their misconceptions might lead you to a subsequent lesson for refining their thinking on the topic.

■ **BUT I'M USING A TEXTBOOK!** Don't bypass this powerful activity because your kids are reading a textbook or library book that they're not allowed to mark up. Xerox a key page from a textbook, just so kids can practice annotating it. How's that for strange? Then bring out the smallest size Post-it notes and have kids carry on annotating! Alternatively, have kids make two-column notes (Strategy 6).

Example of text annotation (shown on an earlier version of this article)

If dress code doesn't suit teens, school district will—Parents say the inmate jumpsuit is too extreme for attire offense

By ELIZABETH WHITE Associated Press

Aug. 1, 2008, 10:35PM (Appeared in Houston Chronicle)

GONZALES — Violating Gonzales High School's dress code is not a crime, but some of the offenders are about to start looking a lot like convicts.

Soon after classes begin Aug. 25, violators of the district's beefed-up dress code must don navy blue coveralls unless they get another set of clothes from home — or serve in-school suspension. The outfits aren't just styled like prison jumpsuits — they're actually made by Texas inmates.

[handwritten: Can we where stuff that they can't?]

[handwritten: School really WANTS TO MAKE Kids A joke]

"We're a conservative community, and we're just trying to make our students more reflective of that," said Larry Wehde, Gonzales Independent School District deputy superintendent.

The new policy in Gonzales, about 70 miles east of San Antonio, has drawn plenty of criticism — along with some speculation that all the district will accomplish is to set off a new fashion trend.

[handwritten: IT WOULD BE FUNNY IF 100's OF KiDS broke code and they rAn OUT OF JUMPSUiTs!]

Some parents and students are crying foul. "They're not little prisoners," said Mary Helen Douglas, who has a 17-year-old son starting his senior year.

The 2,650-student district has ordered 82 coveralls, which are most often sold to county jails, state mental institutions and juvenile prisons. School districts have bought lunch trays and similar items from inmate labor, but no other school district has ordered the jumpsuits in the last year, said Michelle Lyons, spokeswoman for the Texas Department of Criminal Justice.

[handwritten: THiS iDEA IS CReepy. Why doesn't school cAre About real problems?]

The jumpsuits aren't the only option for dress-code violators from fifth through 12th grade. School board President Glenn Menking said parents can still bring a change of clothes, or they may request that the student go to in-school suspension instead.

[handwritten: WOULD YOUR PARents make You wear A Jumpsuit?]

http://www.chron.com/disp/story.mpl/metropolitan/5920441.html

---

HOUSTON CHRONICLE

If dress code doesn't suit teens, school district will

Parents say the inmate jumpsuit is too extreme for attire offense

By ELIZABETH WHITE
The Associated Press, Aug. 1, 2008

GONZALES, Texas — Violating Gonzales High School's dress code is not a crime, but some of the offenders are about to start looking a lot like convicts.

Soon after classes begin Aug. 25, violators of the district's beefed-up dress code must don navy blue coveralls unless they get another set of clothes from home—or serve in-school suspension. The outfits aren't just styled like prison jumpsuits—they're actually made by Texas inmates.

"We're a conservative community, and we're just trying to make our students more reflective of that," said Larry Wehde, Gonzales Independent School District deputy superintendent.

The new policy in Gonzales, about 70 miles east of San Antonio, has drawn plenty of criticism—along with some speculation that all the district will accomplish is to set off a new fashion trend.

Some parents and students are crying foul. "They're not little prisoners," said Mary Helen Douglas, who has a 17-year-old son starting his senior year.

The 2,650-student district has ordered 82 coveralls, which are most often sold to county jails, state mental institutions and juvenile prisons. School districts have bought lunch trays and

> *The 2,650-student district has ordered 82 coveralls, which are most often sold to county jails, state mental institutions and juvenile prisons.*

similar items from inmate labor, but no other school district has ordered the jumpsuits in the last year, said Michelle Lyons, spokeswoman for the Texas Department of Criminal Justice.

The jumpsuits aren't the only option for dress-code violators from fifth through twelfth grade. School board president Glenn Menking said parents can still bring a change of clothes, or they may request that the student go to in-school suspension instead.

Strategy 4

Text Coding

- Time:
  25 minutes
- Grouping Sequence:
  Pairs, whole class

Did you ever put a question mark in the margin of a text when you felt puzzled? Did you ever put a star or exclamation point beside an important fact or idea? If so, you're already a practitioner of *text coding*. In this kissing cousin of text annotation, readers jot simple symbols in the margins of a text to represent their thinking. Most of us adult readers have developed our own coding system, though probably nobody ever taught us one. We just invented our own idiosyncratic symbols through a lifetime of school reading and literacy.

Harvard University's library (those guys again) thinks we text coders are doing a smart thing. In a letter sent to all freshmen, Harvard advises: "Develop your own symbol system: an asterisk for a key idea, for example, or use an exclamation point for the surprising, absurd, bizarre . . . Like your marginalia, your hieroglyphics help you reconstruct the important observations you made at an earlier time" (2005).

Often, we merge these codes with underlining, circling, and marginal notes to create a robust way of excavating meaning from a text, marking it up to open it up. If your students already know how to annotate text—identifying important sections and making marginal notes—adding coding can kick comprehension up another notch.

There are several ways you can introduce this to kids: by modeling it yourself (just as you may have modeled annotation on pages 41–44); by simply showing a set of codes and letting students practice using it; or by having the kids themselves think up useful codes, based on the range of responses they typically have when reading. For this lesson, we'll do it the quickest way—letting kids try out a system you provide. In the Tips and Variations section, we'll share a more inductive approach.

MATERIALS NEEDED

Copy of the text codes (available on the website) and the article for each student, projectable article on which to model coding.

STEP 1   **Introduce codes**   Present kids with the text coding symbols shown in the chart opposite. Explain each symbol.

STEP 2   **Demonstrate coding**   Project the chimp article and model by coding part of the text yourself. Read the first three paragraphs aloud, stopping periodically to show kids how you use codes to mark your reactions. Also show how you always write a word or two to help you remember what the code means. This should take four or five minutes.

STEP 3   **Kids try coding**   Now, have students text-code the rest of the article for themselves. Encourage them to find at least three places to put a code. Be honest and tell kids this may feel forced or mechanical at first. If it makes things easier, you can have kids put a code after each paragraph. This will be less "natural," but will give a defined stopping point.

STEP 4   **Monitor**   Circulate, confer, and assist individuals. Allow enough time for most kids to finish the article, but it is not vital that everyone finish every line.

STEP 5   **Pairs discuss**

Get with your partner and have a quick discussion of this article. Compare the codes you used as well as your reactions connected with them. Pay special attention to the parts you both noticed yet marked with different codes.

STEP 6   **Share with the whole class**   Reconvene the class and invite a few kids to share by asking: *Who used a check mark somewhere in the text? Where? What were you thinking? Who used a star? For what? Who used an eye? What were you seeing?* When you have reviewed the thinking that codes helped kids to flag, be sure to ask: *Did anyone have a reaction or some thinking that there was no code for? What new codes should we create?*

TEXT CODING is used in
Text Sets 1, 6, 7, 8, 9

Consider adding valuable new symbols to the classroom inventory, and post them in the room for kids to refer to when reading.

Tips and Variations   ■   **THE INDUCTIVE VERSION**   As we said earlier, you can let the kids invent their own inventory of text codes instead of simply presenting them with one. In this approach, begin by saying: *OK, guys, when you read, what are some of the reactions you have?* If your kids are halfway normal, you'll probably get "boring" or "stupid" right away. But persist. Kids will come up with "I don't understand" or "It reminds me of something." List all the suggestions, and for each one, ask: *What could be a code or symbol for that?* Keep probing: *Are you ever surprised?* Invite kids in small groups to design graphic symbols for each suggested reaction. Bring everyone together to decide on favorites and create the official class "code menu."

We think individual kids should be able to adopt the codes they value from the class inventory and add their own as appropriate. Now you can pick up the lesson at Step 3, letting kids practice using the class-created codes.

■ **OTHER SYMBOLS** There are many other codes that can help kids focus their thinking. In Strategy 2, Read with a Question in Mind, we already sneaked in one variation, where kids coded text with an *A* for Answered and *N* for New learning. In later sections of this book you'll see other kinds of coding that we have tailor-made for specific texts to help kids focus on particular kinds of thinking as they read.

■ **BUT THE KIDS CAN'T MARK IN THE TEXTBOOK!** As with annotation, don't bypass this powerful activity because kids are reading a textbook or library book that they're not allowed to mark up. Bring out the smallest size Post-it notes and carry on coding! Or try Strategy 6, Two-Column Notes.

Text Codes	
✓	When you read something that makes you say, "Yeah, I knew that" or "I predicted that" or "I saw that coming."
X	When you run across something that contradicts what you know or expect.
?	When you have a question, need clarification, or are unsure.
!	When you discover something new, surprising, exciting, or fun that makes you say cool, whoa, yuck, no way, awesome.
★	When you read something that seems important, vital, key, memorable, or powerful.
👁	When the reading really makes you see or visualize something.
⌒⌒	When you have a connection between the text and your life, the world, or other things you've read.
ZZZ	This is boring, I'm falling asleep.

Empathy for one's fellow chimp

Experts now think the apes may relate to each other in very human ways

By Jeremy Manier
Chicago Tribune staff reporter
Published March 23, 2007

If chimpanzees truly followed what humans call "the law of the jungle," a mentally disabled chimp named Knuckles would never stand a chance.

Yet Knuckles has found acceptance and perhaps even sympathy from his fellow chimps in Florida, making him an unlikely star of Lincoln Park Zoo's international Mind of the Chimpanzee conference.

The meeting, which runs Friday through Sunday with 300 researchers from around the world, is billed as the first major conference devoted to chimp cognition and the first academic chimp conference at the zoo since 1991.

Although much of the meeting will examine the impressive intelligence of humanity's closest living relatives, Knuckles offers unique insight as the only known captive chimp with cerebral palsy, which immobilized one arm and left him mentally unable to follow the intricate protocols of chimp society.

my cousin has CP

Normally, older chimps would put on intimidating displays with a juvenile male such as Knuckles, screaming, grabbing and biting the youngster to put him in his place, said Devyn Carter, who has studied Knuckles and is presenting his research at the Lincoln Park Zoo conference. But even the dominant alpha male tolerates and gently grooms Knuckles.

★ *a person might be bullied*

"To my knowledge he's never received a scratch," said Carter, a research assistant at Emory University's Yerkes National Primate Research Center. "They seem to sense somehow that he's different."

Such behavior touches on a central theme of many presentations at the conference: How well do chimps understand what other chimps know, feel and perceive?

Some experts believe chimps and other higher primates have genuine empathy, the ability to imagine themselves in another animal's place. And that may be the first step in the evolution of morality.

? Chimps have morals? I wonder...

Chimps may use their empathic skills for good, but also to manipulate others. Researchers have found that chimps have a talent for deception, which requires mental sophistication, said conference co-organizer Elizabeth Lonsdorf, director of the zoo's Lester E. Fisher Center for the Study and Conservation of Apes.

"Lying and deceiving means you have to know what another individual thinks is the truth and act in such a way to work around that truth," Lonsdorf said. "It takes complex information processing."

! But you have to be smart to lie (well)

Example of text coding (shown on an earlier version of this article)

Chicago Tribune

Empathy for one's fellow chimp

Experts now think the apes may relate to each other in very human ways

March 23, 2007
By Jeremy Manier, staff reporter

If chimpanzees truly followed what humans call "the law of the jungle," a mentally disabled chimp named Knuckles would never stand a chance.

Yet Knuckles has found acceptance and perhaps even sympathy from his fellow chimps in Florida, making him an unlikely star of Lincoln Park Zoo's international Mind of the Chimpanzee conference.

The meeting, which runs Friday through Sunday with 300 researchers from around the world, is billed as the first major conference devoted to chimp cognition and the first academic chimp conference at the zoo since 1991.

Although much of the meeting will examine the impressive intelligence of humanity's closest living relatives, Knuckles offers unique insight as the only known captive chimp with cerebral palsy, which immobilized one arm and left him mentally unable to follow the intricate protocols of chimp society.

Normally, older chimps would put on intimidating displays with a juvenile male such as Knuckles, screaming, grabbing and biting the youngster to put him in his place, said Devyn Carter, who has studied Knuckles and is presenting his research at the Lincoln Park Zoo conference. But even the dominant alpha male tolerates and gently grooms Knuckles. "To my knowledge he's never received a scratch," said Carter, a research assistant at Emory University's Yerkes National Primate Research Center. "They seem to sense somehow that he's different."

Such behavior touches on a central theme of many presentations at the conference: How well do chimps understand what other chimps know, feel and perceive?

Some experts believe chimps and other higher primates have genuine empathy, the ability to imagine themselves in another animal's place. And that may be the first step in the evolution of morality.

> *"Some experts believe chimps and other higher primates have genuine empathy, the ability to imagine themselves in another animal's place. And that may be the first step in the evolution of morality."*

Chimps may use their empathic skills for good, but also to manipulate others. Researchers have found that chimps have a talent for deception, which requires mental sophistication, said conference co-organizer Elizabeth Lonsdorf, director of the zoo's Lester E. Fisher Center for the Study and Conservation of Apes.

"Lying and deceiving means you have to know what another individual thinks is the truth and act in such a way to work around that truth," Lonsdorf said. "It takes complex information processing."

| Strategy 5 | # Sketching Through the Text |

- Time:
  25 minutes

- Grouping Sequence:
  Pairs, whole class

Here's another way for kids to focus carefully as they read, locating and thinking about the big ideas. But unlike the annotation or text coding strategies introduced earlier, sketching asks students to *draw their thinking* in the margin, rather than jotting ideas in words. The drawings are quick representations meant to jog the memory and spur discussion. We reassure kids that these are not meant to be museum-quality artworks ready for a gallery showing. The idea is to speedily sketch a visual representation of one's response, interpretation, or a key question. And we know that, when it comes time for sharing, students love to discuss and compare each other's drawings.

MATERIALS NEEDED

Copy of article for each student. A document camera is handy for showing drawings.

Steps and Teaching Language

STEP 1 **Give instructions for reading**

As you read this article, please do two things:

Stop when you notice something important, surprising, interesting, or thought provoking.

Then, before continuing to read, make a quick sketch of what you were thinking, right there in the margin. The goal is to create a quick picture that will help you remember your thoughts and the information. Don't worry if you don't feel like you are an artist. Stick figures are fine. Sketching is a different way for you to think about the material. It actually activates a different part of the brain than writing does, so if this feels odd at first, hang in there; it's OK.

STEP 2 **Monitor reading and sketching** As students are reading, circulate, confer, and look for great examples to use with the whole class later. Some students may want to just read the whole piece first, and go back later to sketch. But *stopping to think while reading* is the whole point, so encourage them to try it your way. If you notice some students finishing sooner than others, you can say:

If you are finished, go back to the article, reexamine your sketches, and try to add further details so that you could just glance at your drawings and easily remember the article without having to reread it.

STEP 3 **Partners discuss and compare**

Pair up with a partner and have a quick discussion of this article. Compare what you've sketched and your thoughts connected to those sketches. Be sure to discuss the differences in your sketches and why you chose to highlight different parts of the article.

STEP 4 **Share with the whole class** Give partners the opportunity to offer ideas about what they drew and any particularly interesting conversations that arose. If possible, use a document camera so students can come up front to project and comment on their sketches.

SKETCHING THROUGH THE TEXT is used in Text Sets 4, 7, 9

Tips and Variations

■ **WAIT OUT THE RESISTANCE** Many kids will initially respond to this activity with art phobia: "But I can't draw" (so I won't even try). But once they understand that fine art is not the goal, and that sketching stretches their thinking, their complaints and cries of "This isn't art class!" will diminish. In fact, we often see students putting more thought into their sketched responses than their written annotations.

■ **MODEL IT YOURSELF** Another way to handle resistance, of course, is to go first and put your own sketching in front of the kids. Follow the instructions for text annotation on page 46. Project the article and sketch your thinking for the first half of it; then let the kids sketch through the rest. Even if you have an MFA and could channel da Vinci, don't let your drawing be too good. The idea is to keep it sketchy and focused on the ideas. If your art is just so-so, so much the better; it will lower kids' anxiety.

■ **LIMIT OBSESSIVE ILLUSTRATION** We love how this activity legitimizes a different kind of thinking in the classroom. Have you noticed, as we have, that every time you open up a new domain like this, suddenly there is a whole different group of kids who are engaged and succeeding? Anyhow, the downside is that you may find a handful of students who get so into the drawings that they depart from the reading, start obsessing over their sketches, spend way too long on each one, and start asking for more art supplies. That's your cue to gently direct them back to the article and the purpose of the drawing.

■ **GOING VERBAL** It's OK if students want to use words with their drawings by adding captions, labels, or talk or thought balloons. Just emphasize that the words should enhance the drawing's meaning, not be the main focus.

10 Attitudes of Successful Workers
By Kate Lorenz, Copyright 2006 CareerBuilder.com

1. I am in charge of my destiny.
If you spend your entire career waiting for something exciting to come to you, you will be waiting a long time. Successful professionals go out and make good things happen.

2. Anything is possible.
If you think you can't, you probably won't. Adopt the attitude of The Little Engine That Could -- "I think I can."

3. No task is too small to do well.
You never know when you are going to be noticed. That is one reason to take pride in your work -- all of it. Remember this the next time you feel like slacking because you are working on a menial task.

4. Everyone is a potential key contact.
While you do need to be aggressive in the workplace, you can also go far by being courteous to those around you -- you never know when your past contacts will play a role in your future.

5. I was made to do this job... and the one above me.
If you spend your days feeling like you are not cut out to do the work you are responsible for, your performance will suffer. Your job may not be the perfect fit, but successful workers act like they are in their dream job, no matter where they are.

6. It's not just what I know, but who I know.
Successful workers understand the importance of networking, both in and out of the office. You need to proactively establish professional contacts. Invite a colleague out to lunch. Join your professional association. Do your part to establish a networking path for your future.

7. What else can I do?
Since you are in charge of your destiny, it's your job to look for ways to improve your professional self. Volunteer to take on an extra project. Learn a new skill that will make you more marketable. Stay late to help your co-workers. Successful workers don't just complete the job and sign out -- they look for additional ways to make their mark.

8. Failure will help pave the way to my success.
While it seems like some people never experience setbacks, the truth is everyone fails from time to time. Those who find success are the ones who learn from mistakes and move on.

9. I am my own biggest fan.
Have you been waiting for someone in the office to recognize your talents and efforts? Maybe it's time you start tooting your own horn. Step up and talk about your accomplishments and what you have done for the company. Successful workers know how to point out their achievements without sounding boastful.

10. My opportunity monitor is never turned off.
Yes, there will be days when you will want to just be happy with the status quo. But remember that successful workers are always on the lookout for opportunities to improve. Keep your eyes, ears and your mind open to new opportunities -- you never know when you will discover the one that will change the course of your career!

Example of sketching one's thinking (shown on an earlier version of this article)

career**builder**.com

My CareerBuilder | Find Jobs | Job Recommendations | Post Resume | Advice & Resources

10 Attitudes of Successful Workers

By Kate Lorenz, Copyright 2006 CareerBuilder.com

1. **I am in charge of my destiny.**

   If you spend your entire career waiting for something exciting to come to you, you will be waiting a long time. Successful professionals go out and make good things happen.

2. **Anything is possible.**

   If you think you can't, you probably won't. Adopt the attitude of The Little Engine That Could—"I think I can."

3. **No task is too small to do well.**

   You never know when you are going to be noticed. That is one reason to take pride in your work—all of it. Remember this the next time you feel like slacking because you are working on a menial task.

4. **Everyone is a potential key contact.**

   While you do need to be aggressive in the workplace, you can also go far by being courteous to those around you—you never know when your past contacts will play a role in your future.

5. **I was made to do this job . . . and the one above me.**

   If you spend your days feeling like you are not cut out to do the work you are responsible for, your performance will suffer. Your job may not be the perfect fit, but successful workers act like they are in their dream job, no matter where they are.

6. **It's not just what I know, but who I know.**

   Successful workers understand the importance of networking, both in and out of the office. You need to proactively establish professional contacts. Invite a colleague out to lunch. Join your professional association. Do your part to establish a networking path for your future.

7. **What else can I do?**

   Since you are in charge of your destiny, it's your job to look for ways to improve your professional self. Volunteer to take on an extra project. Learn a new skill that will make you more marketable. Stay late to help your co-workers. Successful workers don't just complete the job and sign out—they look for additional ways to make their mark.

8. **Failure will help pave the way to my success.**

   While it seems like some people never experience setbacks, the truth is everyone fails from time to time. Those who find success are the ones who learn from mistakes and move on.

9. **I am my own biggest fan.**

   Have you been waiting for someone in the office to recognize your talents and efforts? Maybe it's time you start tooting your own horn. Step up and talk about your accomplishments and what you have done for the company. Successful workers know how to point out their achievements without sounding boastful.

10. **My opportunity monitor is never turned off.**

    Yes, there will be days when you will want to just be happy with the status quo. But remember that successful workers are always on the lookout for opportunities to improve. Keep your eyes, ears and your mind open to new opportunities — you never know when you will discover the one that will change the course of your career!

| Strategy 6 | # Two-Column Notes |

- Time: 20 minutes
- Grouping Sequence: Pairs, trios, or groups of 4; whole class

Did you ever draw a line down the center of a piece of paper, and then list items on the left and the right? You've probably done this when trying to make a decision: Which smart phone should I buy? Should I continue to rent or buy a house? Would my life be better with him or without him? (Yeah, we stole that last one from Ann Landers!) If so, you were reinventing a thinking tool called two-column notes or a double-entry journal.

When students cannot mark in the text, two-column notes are an alternative way to capture their thinking and feed discussion later on. Unlike text annotation and coding (Strategies 3 and 4), where learners write directly on the text, here students jot their notes on a separate piece of paper. In the left-hand column, students list important quotes or information. In the right-hand column, they record their reactions to those entries: thoughts, questions, or connections that arise as they read.

MATERIALS NEEDED
Copy of article for each student.

Steps and Teaching Language

STEP 1 **Determine groups in advance** After creating their notes, students will move into a discussion with two to four other students. So decide beforehand how large you want the discussion groups to be and how the groups will be formed; then no time is lost in the transition.

STEP 2 **Help kids set up the page** Demonstrate as you say this:

Take out a sheet of loose-leaf paper and fold it in half lengthwise, "hot dog" style, and then unfold it so you have two columns. At the top center of the sheet write "Video-Game Addiction." Label the left-hand column "Quotes/Information" and the right-hand column "Reactions."

STEP 3 **Introduce the topic and give instructions for reading** After passing out the article, ask: *How many of you play video games?* See the show of hands. *How many of you think you can become addicted to playing?* Note the show of hands. *The university researcher described in this article thinks that you can literally get addicted. As you read the article, please be on the lookout for interesting/important quotes or information about gaming.*

When you run across an important fact or idea, write it down in the left-hand column. Then across from it, in the right-hand column, jot down your response to the information. Why did that stand out to you? What reactions, connections, opinions, or questions do you have? OK? Go!

STEP 4 **Monitor reading** Wander the room, looking over shoulders and offering help as needed. If you notice some students finishing sooner than others, you might say:

If you are finished, go back to the article and reread your notes. Try to add additional details to your thoughts in the right-hand column so that you could just glance at them and easily remember the article without having to completely reread it.

STEP 5 **Groups discuss the article and their notes**

Meet with your group [or partner, if you've decided kids will work in pairs] and have a discussion about this article. Take turns reading aloud a quote or information byte from the left-hand column and then explain your thoughts using your notes from the right-hand column. Before moving on to the next member's quote, get reactions and comments from the rest of your group. Once discussion on that quote has concluded, the next person shares a two-column note and asks for reaction. Continue this way around the group until everyone has shared all of their quotes or until I call time.

TWO-COLUMN NOTES is used in Text Set 8 (can be used wherever text annotation is required)

STEP 6 **Share with the whole class** Offer groups the opportunity to read aloud and discuss the quotes or information that produced particularly interesting conversations.

Tips and Variations

■ **VARY THE TASK** Two-column notes are especially versatile. Though the left-hand column remains the same (quotes/information from the text), the right-hand column can vary depending on the kind of thinking you want students to do. You can invite an unlimited range of reactions, as in the example above, or you can narrow the right-hand column response to a skill you want students to practice. For example, you might direct students to record just one of these responses:

- Importance of the information

- Connections (prior knowledge, text to text, personal experience)

- Questions

- Feelings

- Opposing argument

- Graphic representation

As we said earlier, two-column notes are very useful when students cannot write in their books. And because these notes can be folded in half and serve as a bookmark, students seem to enjoy this kind of note-taking more than other, more traditional formats. Go figure.

■ **MARK PAGE NUMBERS** If the reading is longer than a couple of pages, remember to tell students to jot down the page number next to the quote/information they record in the left-hand column so that the original information can be easily accessed later.

Quotes/ Information	Reactions (Thoughts, questions, connections)
Struggle when kids try to cut back on gaming	Why is it so hard to quit? Not like being addicted to cigarettes or drugs.
First nationally representative study	People have been playing video games for decades. Why did it take until now to do a big study on the effects of playing?
Addiction: skipping chores or homework	I don't think kids need video games as an excuse to skip this stuff!
"Game addicted" kids did worse in school	I wonder how the kids did in school before they were addicted. I bet they were never straight A students.
88% of kids 8–18 play video games	I wonder if there's any difference in the way gaming affects little kids versus teens. Does it make a difference how old you are when you start playing?

Example of two-column notes

The *Washington Post*

Video-game addiction a real problem, study finds

About 8.5 percent of youths affected, according to researcher

By Donna St. George
April 21, 2009

WASHINGTON — A new study concludes that children can become addicted to playing video games, with some youths skimping on homework, lying about how much they play and struggling, without success, when they try to cut back.

In what is described as the first nationally representative study in the U.S. on the subject, researcher Douglas Gentile of Iowa State University found that 8.5 percent of American youths ages 8 to 18 who play video games show multiple signs of behavioral addiction. "For some kids, they play in such a way that it becomes out of balance. And they're damaging other areas of their lives; it isn't just one area, it's many areas," said Gentile.

To get at gaming addiction, he adapted diagnostic criteria for pathological gambling into a series of questions about video game use. The questions became part of a 2007 Harris Poll survey of 1,178 children and teens. Gamers were deemed "pathological" if they reported at least six of the 11 symptoms.

Symptoms included spending increasing amounts of time and money on video games to feel the same level of excitement; irritability or restlessness when play is scaled back; skipping chores or homework to play; and lying about the length of playing time.

Gentile said he started his research with doubts about the possibility of addiction.

> "I thought this was parental histrionics—that kids are playing a lot and parents don't understand the motivation, so they label it an addiction. It turns out that I was wrong."

"I thought this was parental histrionics—that kids are playing a lot and parents don't understand the motivation, so they label it an addiction," he said. "It turns out that I was wrong." What he found, he said, was that pathological gamers did worse in school, had trouble paying attention in class and reported feeling "addicted." Four times as many boys as girls were considered pathological gamers.

The study found that 88 percent of the nation's children ages 8 to 18 play video games. With 45 million children of that age in the country, the study would suggest that more than 3 million are addicted "or at least have problems of the magnitude" that call for help, Gentile said.

Gentile's research findings leave many questions unresolved; for example, whether pathological game-playing causes poor school performance or whether "children who have trouble at school seek to play games to experience feelings of mastery."

| Strategy 7 | # Reading a Visual Image |

- Time:
  20 minutes
- Grouping Sequence:
  Pairs, whole class

We know from recent studies that the average American teenager now devotes almost seven hours a day to "screen time," marinating in visual images. But does immersion equal *understanding*? Staring is not necessarily thinking. Kids need to be able to actively read and interpret pictures or paintings just as well as prose text. So this strategy explicitly teaches *viewing comprehension*.

Our content-area books are chock full of photographs, portraits, and paintings that we sometimes bypass in our hurry to send students straight to the text. Plus, nowadays our textbooks often come with complementary CDs, which make these images much easier to project and discuss. All these visual resources contain tons of content, if kids know how to access and think about it.

MATERIALS NEEDED

Prepared images for projection. On our website you'll find a link to *The Rock*.

Steps and Teaching Language

STEP 1 **Prepare an image in advance** Choose an image (such as a painting or photograph) that has abundant detail throughout (versus one that has content centered in the foreground or one corner, with little detail in the rest of the space).

Create a projectable version of the image. If you are using a transparency or document camera, create a cutout that can frame one quadrant at a time, blocking the rest of the image from view.

If you're using PowerPoint slides, your first and last slides will be the entire image while the four middle slides will reveal only one of the four quadrants (see the examples on page 61). Use the Drawing and Fill tools to mask three of the quadrants on each middle slide. Also, see the tip "For Optimal Viewing" on page 60.

STEP 2 **Have students form pairs** Make sure students know who their partner will be for the later discussion, and have them sit near each other.

STEP 3 **Help students set up note-taking forms**

Fold a sheet of notebook paper in half and then in half again (hot dog plus hamburger), so that four sections are created. Now unfold it to use for your viewing notes.

During the lesson, they'll jot notes in the same quadrant as the one you are showing.

STEP 4 **Project the full image**

I'm going to give you one minute to study this image. Just look and see what you notice, but don't write anything down.

STEP 5 **View by quadrants** Now project the image one quadrant at a time. In a very quiet and slow voice, offer suggestions like these as kids view:

As you study each part of the image, jot down your notes in the corresponding square on your sheet.

What do you notice about setting: objects, landscape, weather, light, buildings, setting, what people are holding? What do you notice in the foreground? What do you see in the background? At the edges?

What do you notice about the people: clothes, facial expressions, feelings, personality, jobs, importance, relationships?

What do you notice about action or activities: What seems to be happening here? Who's doing what? Notice those who are active versus inactive. What goals, emotions, or motivations are suggested by the image?

And most important, what questions do you have as you look at this part of the image?

Use all the time I am giving you to list details. Keep writing down anything you see.

STEP 6 **Monitor note-taking** Leave each quadrant up for a good minute. This almost compels viewers to look more deeply and patiently. Observe students as they write, and quietly confer with any who are struggling. As the note-taking winds down, move on to the next quadrant, and the next.

STEP 7 **Display the full image a second time** After kids have viewed and taken notes on all four quadrants, display the full image again. This can be a magical moment. Many times, when we re-see the whole image, the picture seems to jump into high definition and take on new meanings. Let students take another few moments and add to their notes.

STEP 8 **Pairs discuss**

OK, now turn to your partner and discuss your thinking about the image, using your notes as a guide. Try to notice the similarities and differences in what you and your partner saw and recorded.

After three to five minutes of open partner discussion, have the pairs come to some conclusions by answering these three questions:

What are the three most important details you and your partner noticed?

What conclusions about the image can you draw from these details?

If you were to give this image a title, what would it be?

STEP 9 **Share with the whole class** First, ask students to discuss their important details and how those details impact the whole piece's message. Encourage them to get out of their seats and actually point to what they are referring to in the image. It's often surprising what details someone notices but no one else sees until they are pointed out.

Next, share some of the suggested titles. Afterwards, if the image has an official title, share it and compare with the kids' version. This one is called *The Rock*.

READING A VISUAL IMAGE is used in Text Sets 3, 5, 10

Finally, direct the discussion toward connecting the image with the content under study.

Tips and Variations

◼ **FOR OPTIMAL VIEWING** Instead of masking three-quarters of an image, enlarge each quadrant to fill the whole screen, rather than just a quarter of it. See page 199 for tips on how to do this. Be sure to explain what quadrant (e.g., "lower left") you are projecting as you go.

◼ **FINDING GREAT IMAGES** Google Images is of course the go-to spot for arresting images of almost any historical, sociological, literary, mathematical, scientific, artistic, or political topic you can imagine. But remember, most major art museums also have online collections that are searchable by artist, genre, period, or theme.

◼ **PROMPTS** The words you use to guide students' viewing can be very powerful, helping to open up deeper comprehension. For another set of during-viewing instructions, see page 198.

◼ **MASKING** If an image exists only in a textbook and you have no easy means to project it, have students cut out individual frames from a piece of notebook paper and manually cover the image so that one quadrant appears at a time.

Original visual image: *The Rock* by Peter Blume

Viewing the image by quadrants

| Strategy 8 | # Think Aloud |

- Time: 30 minutes
- Grouping Sequence: Whole class, pairs, whole class

In "Why Use This Book" we explained that proficient readers (which definitely includes all of us grown-up teachers) have an internal repertoire of cognitive strategies that we use to make sense of text. As veteran readers, we mostly use these tools unconsciously, but when the text gets tougher, we can notice ourselves opening up that mental toolbox very intentionally (rereading, visualizing, asking questions, etc.).

This lesson allows you to open up your head (don't worry, this is just a metaphor) and show kids how a skilled reader thinks while engaging with nonfiction text. The mechanism is simple: you read a passage aloud, but you stop and interrupt yourself at several prechosen spots to explain to students what is going on in your mind right then. You directly model the thinking process we call *comprehension*.

MATERIALS NEEDED

Copy of article for each student, annotated copy of the article for modeling the strategy, chart paper.

Steps and Teaching Language

STEP 1 **Prepare the lesson** Well before class, read the article yourself, using Strategy 3, Text Annotation, or Strategy 4, Text Coding, to help you track your thinking. You should find yourself marking various spots in the text where you are having thoughtful reactions like: "Whoa!" or "I never knew that" or "Who says so?" or "Where's the evidence?" Be especially sure to mark any part where the text gets tougher and you notice yourself adjusting somehow—slowing down your reading rate, wondering about a word definition, or going back and rereading. Finally, select a few of these places (at least two per paragraph, ideally about one for every thirty seconds of read-aloud time) where you will stop and share your thinking with kids.

STEP 2 **Kids preread** Hand out a copy of the article to each student and have them quickly preread it.

STEP 3 **Model**

Today, you guys, I am going to give you a look inside my head. Yuck, right? I know. I'm going to show you how I think when I am reading a piece of text. I am going to read this article aloud to you, and whenever I come to a place where I am having a reaction and doing some thinking, I'm going to look up and tell you what's going on in my mind at that moment. And when I do that—when I "think aloud"—I want you to jot some quick notes on what I say. You write only when I am sharing my thinking, not when I'm reading the article. OK?

Read the *first third* of the article aloud, following your plan to stop at certain spots and share your thinking. Make your statements in present time, as in *Wait, I have a question here,* rather than *When I read this during my planning period, I had a question.*

When you stop and think, look up from the text so kids will know that you are no longer reading. Make your statement directly—for example, "I am starting to wonder which side the author is really on" or "This reminds me of a story I heard on the radio this morning." Tell your response and then *write your thought down in the margin* beside the section of text that sparked your thinking. Boil it down to the key phrase, such as "Which side is author on?" There will be some silence as students watch you write. That's one thing that makes think-alouds so important—you are showing kids how effective learners think about their thinking.

STEP 4 **Kids respond** When you are done, ask volunteers to share what they noticed about your reading and thinking process. Record these insights on a chart titled "How Smart Readers Think." Hopefully, you'll get items like: "You stopped to think. You asked questions. You were skeptical. You reread. You had lots of reactions and opinions."

STEP 5 **Pairs practice** Now it's the kids' turn to think aloud. Place them in pairs and help them divide the remaining text in half, with each student assigned a different section. Follow the same procedure as the whole-class lesson: pairs silently read their chosen section first, marking some spots where they noticed themselves thinking or reacting. Then kids take turns thinking aloud. The one with the coolest shoes (latest birthday, longest ride to school) thinks aloud first. The partner takes notes on the think-aloud, just as in the whole-class version. Warn them:

This is not a reading conversation like we usually have. You are not supposed to get into a back-and-forth about the article. Think of your partner as your audience, and partners, just take your notes.

STEP 6 **Monitor** Circulate and coach as kids turn and talk for their partners. Look for great examples or quotes that can be used in the whole-class "roundup," coming next.

STEP 7 **Share with the whole class** Reconvene the whole class and debrief. *How did that work? How did it feel to be talking about your thinking?* Return to the "How Smart Readers Think" list, let volunteers confirm how they used certain reading strategies, and add any new ones kids report.

THINK ALOUD is used in
Text Set 1

Strategy 8: Think Aloud **63**

Tips and Variations

■ **STOP AFTER PARAGRAPHS** In our baseline version, you are stopping at spots in the text where you genuinely have had a strong reaction or thinking process. To make it simpler (though perhaps less authentic), you can instead stop after each paragraph and share one highlight of your thinking from that section. This adaptation can also help kids when they are thinking aloud for each other, because it ensures that there will be a certain number of stopping places, even for kids who didn't mark anything during the preread.

■ **USE UNKNOWN, UNREHEARSED TEXT** It is even more powerful to think aloud "cold"—to model reading articles you have *not* read beforehand. Challenge the kids to bring in any text for you to think aloud in front them. Now you're really teaching! You're putting yourself in the same spot that kids are in every day—negotiating text they have never seen before. If you hesitate, struggle, or make wrong predictions—that's great for kids to observe. We want students to understand that reading is not magic; if you work at it, you understand more.

■ **DO THIS OFTEN** Thinking aloud is not a lesson you do once. You need to show kids, over and over, across different genres of subject-area text, how you make meaning when you read.

The New York Times

Dementia Risk Seen in Players in N.F.L. Study

September 29, 2009
By Alan Schwarz

A study commissioned by the National Football League reports that Alzheimer's disease or similar memory-related diseases appear to have been diagnosed in the league's former players vastly more often than in the national population—including a rate of 19 times the normal rate for men ages 30 through 49.

The N.F.L. has long denied the existence of reliable data about cognitive decline among its players. These numbers would become the league's first public affirmation of any connection, though the league pointed to limitations of this study.

The findings could ring loud at the youth and college levels, which often take cues from the N.F.L. on safety policies and whose players emulate the pros. Hundreds of on-field concussions are sustained at every level each week, with many going undiagnosed and untreated.

Sean Morey, an Arizona Cardinals player who has been vocal in supporting research in this area, said: "This is about more than us—it's about the high school kid in 2011 who might die on the field because he ignored the risks of concussions."

Scrutiny of brain injuries in football players has escalated the past three years, with prominent professionals reporting cognitive problems and academic studies supporting a link more generally. The N.F.L. and its medical committee on concussions have steadfastly denied the existence of reliable data on the issue.

> *"This is about more than us—it's about the high school kid in 2011 who might die on the field because he ignored the risks of concussions."*

Dr. Ira Casson, a co-chairman of the concussions committee who has been the league's primary voice denying any evidence connecting N.F.L. football and dementia, said: "What I take from this report is there's a need for further studies to see whether or not this finding is going to pan out, if it's really there or not."

Dr. Daniel P. Perl, the director of neuropathology at the Mount Sinai School of Medicine in New York, said: "I think this complements what others have found — there appears to be a problem with cognition in a group of N.F.L. football players at a relatively young age."

| Strategy 9 | # Pair Reading |

- Time: **20 minutes**
- Grouping Sequence: **Pairs, whole class**

How many times have we heard kids say, "I read it, but I don't get it"? Our pal Cris Tovani even made that phrase the title of her excellent book about high school reading (2000). One reason why kids so often "don't get it" is that they usually read alone.

In pair reading, students work with a partner, reading the text in tandem. They take turns reading the text aloud. One paragraph at a time. Then readers stop, turn to their partners, and discuss what they've just read: What did the author say? What information was important to remember? What is your personal reaction to what you've read? This strategy is a cousin of the Think Aloud (page 62)—except here, instead of the teacher stopping to share her thinking with a class, kids stop, think, and react with a peer partner.

Pair reading is especially useful when the material is very difficult, tempting some students to "space out." This strategy reduces the tendency for kids to zone for two reasons. One, students must closely monitor their thinking as they read, since they must stop frequently and compare understanding. Two, even the driest material becomes more fun when a little socializing is added.

MATERIALS NEEDED
Copy of article for each pair.

Steps and Teaching Language

STEP 1 **Prepare the lesson** Review the article (or another text you have chosen) to determine where you want students to stop and think. Paragraph breaks usually work. If not, before copying the article, mark dots in the margin indicating where you want students to stop and discuss. When class begins, hand out just one copy to each pair.

STEP 2 **Give instructions for reading**

Today we are going to use a strategy called Pair Reading. Instead of reading silently, you and your partner are going to take turns reading aloud. However, you are not just going to read aloud to each other. At the end of each paragraph, I want you to stop for a moment and talk about what you've just read. This includes three steps:

1. Summarizing the paragraph

2. Deciding which information is most important

3. Sharing your feelings/ideas about the information

Be sure to switch readers after each paragraph. And here's the catch: after one partner reads a paragraph, it is the other partner's turn to begin the discussion by summarizing the paragraph, explaining what the author was saying. I purposely gave each pair only one copy of the article so that you must share and help each other as you work through your discussion.

STEP 3 **Monitor reading** As pairs read and discuss, circulate, observe, and help kids follow the directions. Out of habit, kids may initially try to read silently and discuss the whole article at the end. Acknowledge their attempt to personalize the task, but remind them that *stopping to think* while reading is something we need to practice. You might also mention that discussing at defined intervals replaces having to underline and annotate. Sometimes students welcome a break from note-taking.

If you notice some students finishing sooner than others, you might say: *If you and your partner are finished, look through the paragraphs and take note of your discussion highlights so that you can share them with the rest of the class in a couple of minutes. Also, jot down any questions you have about the information or about the author's stance on the topic.*

STEP 4 **Share with the whole class** Invite volunteers to tell how they responded to specific parts of the text, and to share highlights of their conversations.

PAIR READING is used in Text Set 9

Tips and Variations

■ **GO SILENT** Once students become familiar with this strategy, you can switch to pairs reading silently as long as they stop reading at the designated points to do their summarizing and sharing out loud.

■ **USE CHALLENGING MATERIALS** The best use of this strategy is when the text is difficult and students need to closely monitor their comprehension. Remember that "difficult" text is not limited to prose; the diagrams and graphs in many textbooks can be devilishly complicated. Stopping and discussing each element in a graphic ("Wait, what does the y axis represent?") can increase comprehension substantially.

The New York Times

Not Grass-Fed, but at Least Pain-Free

February 19, 2010
By Adam Shriver
Op-Ed Contributor

More animals than ever suffer from injuries and stress on factory farms. Veal calves and gestating sows are so confined as to suffer painful bone and joint problems. The high-grain diets provided in feedlots cause severe gastric distress in many animals. And faulty or improperly used stun guns cause the painful deaths of thousands of cows and pigs a year. Because the amount of red meat that Americans eat per capita has held steady at more than 100 pounds a year as the population has increased, we are most likely stuck with factory farms. But it is still possible to reduce the animals' discomfort—through neuroscience. Recent advances suggest it may soon be possible to genetically engineer livestock so that they suffer much less.

Scientists have learned to genetically engineer animals so that they lack certain proteins that are important to the operation of the anterior cingulate cortex, a part of the brain that senses pain. Prof. Min Zhuo and his colleagues at the University of Toronto, for example, have bred mice lacking enzymes that operate in affective pain pathways. When these mice encounter a painful stimulus, they withdraw their paws normally, but they do not become hypersensitive to a subsequent painful stimulus, as ordinary mice do.

Given the similarity among all mammals' neural systems, it is likely that scientists could genetically engineer pigs and cows in the same way. Because the sensory dimension of the animals' pain would be preserved, they would still be able to recognize and avoid, when possible, situations where they might be bruised or otherwise injured.

> *If we cannot avoid factory farms altogether, the least we can do is eliminate the unpleasantness of pain in the animals that must live and die on them.*

If we cannot avoid factory farms altogether, the least we can do is eliminate the unpleasantness of pain in the animals that must live and die on them. It would be far better than doing nothing at all.

Adam Shriver is a doctoral student in the philosophy-neuroscience-psychology program at Washington University.

Strategy 10

Save the Last Word for Me

- Time:
  40 minutes
- Grouping
  Sequence:
  Groups of 4,
  whole class

A core activity in many group discussions is for individual kids to pick out important passages while they are reading, then bring these selections to a face-to-face discussion later. And kids are often quite good at the choosing part. They often select the same passages of the text we would ourselves.

However, instead of making sure that lively discussion blossoms from their passage, students will read it aloud and immediately explain what they were thinking about when they picked it. Conversation killer! Once an official-sounding interpretation has been uttered, further discussion often shuts down. Other kids in the group just say "I agree. Who goes next?" And the discussion death march through the notes continues . . .

But, if the person who picks the passage speaks *last*, everyone else has a chance to get their ideas out on the table and, therefore, revisit and think about the passage more deeply. When the conversation returns to the "passage picker," she can piggyback on the others' thoughts as well as explain any ideas that did not get mentioned by the others. Or, maybe, she can reveal a take on the text that no one else thought of.

MATERIALS NEEDED

Copy of article for each student.

Steps and Teaching Language

STEP 1   **Give instructions for reading**   For this first step, students will use Strategy 3, Text Annotation (pages 41–44).

As you read this article, I want you to do two things:

Underline information that is important, surprising, interesting, or thought provoking.

Then, before continuing to read, stop and jot down a sentence or two that explains why you chose that bit to underline. The goal is to explain your thoughts, opinions, or questions. Try to imagine that you are having a conversation with the text inside your head. Your notes are your side of the conversation.

Mark at least three passages you think would be important or fun to discuss in your group.

STEP 2 **Monitor reading** Use the customary classroom M.B.W.A., which means Managing By Walking Around. Observe, coach, and guide. If you notice some students finishing sooner than others, you can say:

If you are finished, go back to the article, reread your annotations, and try to add enough details so that you can just glance at your underlining and notes and easily remember the article without having to reread it.

STEP 3 **Form groups**

Move into your groups and number off one through three or four, depending on the size of your group. Number ones, raise your hands. Number ones, I want you to turn to your group, and point out the first passage you have chosen in the article, so that the others can find it. Everyone ready? Now, number ones, read your passage aloud to your group and then stop and look back at me.

STEP 4 **Set up sharing** When students have returned their focus to you, continue.

Now, number ones, instead of explaining the passage you just read aloud to your group, I want you to turn to them and say, "Save the last word for me." (Yes, we really do have students say this out loud; the kids may giggle at it the first time, but it is an explicit reminder of how the activity is supposed to go.)

Then let everyone else in the group say something about why that passage was important or what it makes them think about. Only after everyone else in your group has spoken can you add your own explanation. Now go ahead and try it. When the group has finished discussing this first passage, stop talking and look back at me.

STEP 5 **Coach discussion** As students try out Save the Last Word on the first passage, monitor carefully and give help as needed. Once groups have finished and refocused on you, ask if there are any questions. Then say:

I want you to continue to use Save the Last Word. Be sure to move around the group, letting members take turns reading their passages aloud. That means the twos go next, then the threes, and so on. Once everyone has read a passage, the ones will start a new round.

STEP 6 **Adjust the sharing procedure**

Hey, I think we might have a problem. How many of you were the last ones to give an idea before it went back to the person who picked it? Raise your hands. I bet you noticed that it was a lot harder to think of something new to say when you were the last person. From now on, as you read the passages aloud, the first person who answers is the one on the reader's right and the last person who answers is on the reader's left. That way the same person won't always be the first or last to comment on a passage. Got it? Go ahead and continue your discussion.

STEP 7 **Monitor groups** This is a complicated activity, especially the first time out. Continue to monitor groups and take note of whether they are taking turns reading passages as well as commenting first or last. If you notice the same people reading passages or answering first, intervene and coach.

STEP 8 **Share with the whole class** Reconvene the class when you notice the group discussions winding down. Ask each group to share one interesting passage and the ideas it generated. This is also a good activity to debrief from a process point of view: How did this activity work for you? Did anything get confusing? How can we make it easier next time?

STEP 9 **Brainstorm a response topic list** Finally, once again acknowledge that it is much harder for the last person in the group to come up with a really good comment. Then have the groups brainstorm ways members can expand their comments when the most obvious ideas have already been taken. Make a master list (it might resemble the one below) and then refer to it the next time you use this strategy in class.

Ways to Respond to a Passage

- Why the passage was important

- What surprised you about that passage

- What you pictured when you read that part

- Connect the passage with something else in the article

- Add on to what someone else has said

- Ask a question: What does this passage make you wonder about?

- Connect the passage to a personal experience

- Connect the passage to another text, movie, television show, song, etc.

SAVE THE LAST WORD FOR ME is used in Text Sets 4, 7, 9, 10

Tips and Variations

■ **REINFORCE THE PATTERN** Students easily fall back into the habit of immediately explaining their passages after they've read them. Keep reminding them to use this skill in subsequent discussions and monitor closely, intervening with a quick reminder when necessary.

Los Angeles Times

Well-off nations' kids not the best-off

In UNICEF report, United States and Britain rank at the bottom among 21 wealthy nations

February 15, 2007
By Maggie Farley
Tribune Newspapers

NEW YORK—The United States and Britain ranked as the worst places to be a child among 21 wealthy nations, according to a report by UNICEF released Wednesday. The Netherlands was the best, it said, followed by Sweden and Denmark. UNICEF's Innocenti Research Center in Italy ranked the countries in six categories: material well-being, health, education, relationships, behaviors and risks, and young people's sense of happiness.

Some of the wealthier countries' lower rankings were a result of less spending on social programs and "dog eat dog" competition in jobs that led to adults spending less time with their children and heightened alienation among peers, Jonathan Bradshaw, one of the report's authors, said in London.

The highest ranking for the U.S. was for education, where it placed 12th of 21 countries. But the U.S. and Britain landed in the lowest third for five of the six categories measured.

The United States was at the bottom of the list in health and safety, due mostly to its high rates of child mortality and accidental deaths. It was next to last in family and peer relationships and risk-taking behavior.

The U.S. has the highest proportion of children living in single-parent homes, which the study defined as an indicator for increased risk of poverty and poor health, though it "may seem unfair and insensitive," the report said. "But at the statistical level there is evidence to associate growing up in single-parent families with greater risk to well-being—including a greater risk of dropping out of school, of leaving home early, poorer health, low skills and low pay," the report said.

The U.S. was close to the bottom of the scale for children who eat and talk frequently with their families.

Children in the Netherlands, Spain and Greece said they were the happiest, and those in Spain, Portugal and the Netherlands spent the most time with their families and friends.

Child welfare in the industrialized world

Overall rankings from the UNICEF report on 21 industrialized nations

1.	Netherlands	12.	Canada
2.	Sweden	13.	Greece
3.	Denmark	14.	Poland
4.	Finland	15.	Czech Republic
5.	Spain	16.	France
6.	Switzerland	17.	Portugal
7.	Norway	18.	Austria
8.	Italy	19.	Hungary
9.	Ireland	20.	United States
10.	Belgium	21.	Britain
11.	Germany		

Strategy 11 | **Conversation Questions**

- Time:
  20 minutes
- Grouping Sequence:
  Pairs, whole class

What color was General Douglas MacArthur's uniform when he accepted Japan's surrender on the deck of the USS *Missouri*? Was the day clear or cloudy? What was the rank of the soldier who carried in the treaty? How many pens did MacArthur and General Umezu use?

Who cares?!

Our students dutifully answer questions at the end of a textbook chapter, the kind that are narrow enough that the answers can be quickly located (often in bold type) and then regurgitated in five words or less. However, if we want students to think deeply about text and talk about their reading in ways that enrich their understanding, they need to engage with questions that reach far beyond factual recall and simple summarization, and that invite extended discussion. Great conversation questions require students to draw upon specific information in the text, yet also use their prior knowledge to make accurate inferences.

This strategy is applicable to any reading in any content. When students read and ask questions, they are actively engaged with the text—and with each other in the ensuing conversation.

MATERIALS NEEDED

Copy of article for each student, projectable version of the "fat questions" list.

Steps and Teaching Language

STEP 1 **Instructions for reading** After passing out the article, say:

As you read this article, I want you to do two things:

Underline information that is important, surprising, interesting, or thought provoking. Look for at least four or five good passages to underline.

Then, before continuing to read, stop and jot down a question related to that passage, a question that would be interesting to discuss with others.

Now, what makes a good discussion question? It needs to be fat, not skinny. A fat question makes room for people to say a lot, to have different opinions, to build a whole conversation around it. It can't be something that can be answered with just a fact or a date or a number. Like "What kind of teeth did George Washington have?" Wooden, right? (Actually, we now know they were ivory.) That's a skinny question. But suppose you asked, "What was life like before modern dentistry?" That's a fatter question that could lead to a much wider conversation—and even to some interesting research.

Project the sample prompts for "fat questions."

Fat Question Starters

- How could that . . .

- What is your opinion on . . .

- How did you react when . . .

- Why do you think . . .

- Why is this . . .

- How do you feel about . . .

- What reasons would you give for . . .

- How does _____ relate to your own experiences?

- Explain . . .

- Give me some examples of . . .

- Why do you think _____ did that?

- What does _____ make you think about?

Certain kinds of sentences or lead-ins often help us pose good conversation questions. Here's a list of some of these. Let's have a look. Read the stems aloud. *Can anyone think of other stems like this, that lead to big, rich, open-ended questions?* Add student suggestions to the list. *OK, let's read the article. Remember to jot down three or four fat questions you can use when you discuss this article with your partner.*

STEP 2 **Monitor reading** Work the room, looking over shoulders, checking in, coaching and guiding students to pose fat questions. If you notice some students finishing sooner than others, tell them: *If you are finished, go back to the article, reread your questions, and imagine what others might say in response. If you realize that the question would probably lead to just a short answer without any further discussion, revise it to create a fatter one.*

STEP 3 **Pairs discuss**

In a minute, you will turn to your partner and use your questions to have a lively conversation. As you discuss, please do four things:

1. Start a discussion by pointing out to your partner a passage you have chosen and then reading it aloud as your partner follows along.

2. After reading the passage aloud, ask your question and then let your partner answer. Listen carefully and then, rather than immediately jumping in with your own ideas, ask a follow-up question that will get your partner to explain something they mentioned in a bit more detail. Listen carefully as they answer.

3. *After your partner is finished, go ahead and add any ideas your partner didn't mention or that you thought of as you listened to your partner's answer.*

4. *Once discussion on that question is finished, it is your partner's turn to ask a question. Be sure to take turns asking questions.*

STEP 4 **Monitor discussion** As students conduct their discussions, monitor their interactions and coach them along. Watch for students who forget to read the passage aloud or to take turns, resulting in one person asking all their questions at once. Be looking for really great questions that you can highlight in the whole-group roundup later.

STEP 5 **Pairs determine conversation highlights** As discussion is winding down, say: *Look back at your questions and mark the one that created the best discussion.* Give students a minute to reflect.

STEP 6 **Share with the whole class** Now ask for a few members to report on their discussion highlights. Prompt students to point out the passage, read it aloud, state the question, and then describe what was discussed. As students report, revise and add to the conversation question list you introduced earlier. Remember to revisit this revised list each time students prepare conversation questions.

CONVERSATION QUESTIONS is used in Text Sets 7, 9

Tips and Variations

■ **PRACTICE OFTEN** The more students practice writing and discussing their questions, the better they will get at it. After each subsequent discussion, have students reflect on which of their questions best created rich, extended discussion. You'll know they've gotten to be good questioners when their discussions last longer and, afterward, they have a hard time picking their best question!

■ **USE IN TEXT SET LESSONS** Conversation questions are often embedded in text annotation and automatically become part of a discussion when students have the chance to share with each other. Though not always specifically denoted, this strategy can be found to some degree in every text set.

More people escaping to world less ordinary
Virtual alter egos called avatars are growing in popularity -- and creativity

By Rick Montgomery
MCCLATCHY-TRIBUNE NEWSPAPERS
March 11, 2008

Avatar, in Hindu philosophy, refers to the embodiment of a higher being in earthly form, usually as a human or animal. On the Internet, the meaning gets reversed as humans assume otherworldly forms. Worldwide, at least 9 million 3-D avatars exist in the Second Life site, buying islands, racing cars, raising pets and attending church (or strip clubs). The fantasy role-playing game World of Warcraft boasts more than 10 million subscribers.

Do you play? How did you pick your AVATAR?

Avatar Bryan Mnemonic can fly. His suit never wrinkles, and his chiseled body never bruises -- not even if he crashes into trees.

His human counterpart, Bryan Carter, wishes he could afford Mnemonic's diamond cuff links. But a mouse click makes it possible for Carter -- Mnemonic's maker -- to indulge a little in the virtual world.

Why do you think people make up AVATARS?

How does spending time on this prepare you for real life?

Pixel by pixel, Carter created an online alter ego, an avatar mostly in his own image. True, Mnemonic's goatee lacks the gray hairs in Carter's. The waist is tighter, the biceps beefier. Understand that where avatars dwell -- and there are millions of them -- vanity alterations are expected.

What would you do/look like if you got the chance to have an AVATAR? *

Some avatars dance. Some educate or perform concerts, perhaps in the form of an ogre or a large squirrel. Some annihilate armies of other avatars. They are whatever you wish to be in a cyber-land that doesn't exist, yet does.

If no one is who they really are, how can kids who go online keep from being exposed to online predators?

"An avatar is your embodiment in virtual worlds and virtual game spaces," Matthew Falk, an Indiana University researcher, said of what he and others call "synthetic worlds."

Between people and their avatars, gender reversal is nothing. Ethnicity, too, is a matter of choice. Children with physical disabilities can heave boulders.

How could a virtual life help disabled kids in real life?

Students at the University of Kansas School of Medicine learn how to prepare someone for surgery by logging onto a site called Second Life and transporting to the hospital's "island," where an avatar patient awaits on a gurney.

* *Most interesting to discuss*

Sample annotated article (shown on an earlier version of this article)

Chicago Tribune

More people escaping to world less ordinary

Virtual alter egos called avatars are growing in popularity—and creativity

March 11, 2008

BY RICK MONTGOMERY

MCCLATCHY-TRIBUNE NEWSPAPERS

Avatar, in Hindu philosophy, refers to the embodiment of a higher being in earthly form, usually as a human or animal. On the Internet, the meaning gets reversed as humans assume otherworldly forms. Worldwide, at least 9 million 3-D avatars exist in the Second Life site, a virtual world where users can customize an avatar in order to socialize and connect with others using voice and text chat as well as explore alternative life paths. In this virtual world, avatars buy islands, race cars, raise pets, attend church, and meet friends. The fantasy role-playing game World of Warcraft boasts more than 10 million subscribers.

Avatar Bryan Mnemonic can fly. His suit never wrinkles, and his chiseled body never bruises—not even if he crashes into trees.

His human counterpart, Bryan Carter, wishes he could afford Mnemonic's diamond cufflinks. But a mouse click makes it possible for Carter—Mnemonic's maker—to indulge a little in the virtual world.

> *Avatar Bryan Mnemonic can fly. His suit never wrinkles, and his chiseled body never bruises—not even if he crashes into trees.*

Pixel by pixel, Carter created an online alter ego, an avatar mostly in his own image. True, Mnemonic's goatee lacks the gray hairs in Carter's. The waist is tighter, the biceps beefier. Understand that where avatars dwell—and there are millions of them—vanity alterations are expected.

Some avatars dance. Some educate or perform concerts, perhaps in the form of an ogre or a large squirrel. Some annihilate armies of other avatars. They are whatever you wish to be in a cyber-land that doesn't exist, yet does.

"An avatar is your embodiment in virtual worlds and virtual game spaces," Matthew Falk, an Indiana University researcher, said of what he and others call "synthetic worlds."

Between people and their avatars, gender reversal is nothing. Ethnicity, too, is a matter of choice. Children with physical disabilities can heave boulders.

Students at the University of Kansas School of Medicine learn how to prepare someone for surgery by logging onto the Second Life site and transporting to the hospital's "island," where an avatar patient awaits on a gurney.

| Strategy 12 | # Support Your Position |

- Time:
  40 minutes
- Grouping Sequence:
  Pairs, whole class

Arguments are won and lost on the evidence presented for or against them. (Well, sometimes the arguer with the biggest stick wins.) This reality is recognized in many state curricula, as well as the Common Core State Standards (2010), which are very emphatic about students being able to *defend an argument or interpretation.* At all levels of middle and high school, students must be able to "cite textual evidence to support analysis of what the text says explicitly as well as inferences from the text." As the standards rise from sixth grade up, the required level of support rises from "evidence" to "several pieces of evidence" to "strong and thorough evidence" (CCSS, pp. 1–11).

MATERIALS NEEDED

Copy of article for each student.

Steps and Teaching Language

STEP 1 **Select and copy an appropriate article** This is a lesson where not just any article will do. You need a text that allows for multiple interpretations or arguments as well as an abundance of both "right there" information and deeper, more implicit ideas—as our vampire bat article does. It must require kids to think inferentially, combining their background knowledge with details in the text to make meaning, analyze the document, take a position, and defend it.

That doesn't mean the text has to be long and obscure. When attempting to be objective, newspaper articles typically offer readers multiple viewpoints. It is the reader's job to draw conclusions but also to recognize the details that support them.

In addition to making article copies, decide in advance how students will pair up for later steps in the lesson.

STEP 2 **Introduce the topic** *When you hear the word* vampire, *what comes to mind?* Students will most likely mention the *Twilight* series and, if they are older, perhaps the HBO program *True Blood. How are the vampires in these works of fiction depicted?* Answers will range from heroic to sly to bloodthirsty demonic killers. *Mythological vampires seem to possess a wide range of character traits—just like people in general. However, real vampire bats do exist. What do you know about them?* Take answers from a few volunteers—just a quick survey of kids' background knowledge.

STEP 3 **Give instructions for reading the text**

Today we are going to read an article about vampire bats in Panama, the Central American country that connects directly with South America. It is located very close to the equator and has a tropical climate. As you read, I want you to think about the main points or arguments the article is trying to make. After finishing the article, jot down three or four conclusions this text leads you to make.

Circulate as students read and jot down conclusions. In the next step, you'll model finding evidence—and then the pairs of kids will go through the article a second time, seeking evidence for their own conclusions.

STEP 4 **Explain the process of finding evidence**

In a minute, working in pairs, you're going to share the conclusions you reached based on the information in the article. Then, you're going to pick one you think is important and work together to find at least two pieces of evidence that support your conclusion.

STEP 5 **Model for kids**

Let me give you an example: From this article, I'm going to take the position that most bats are harmless. But for my conclusion to be valid, I've got to prove it. To convince you, I need to use evidence that I can point to, right in the article. And I'll also have to do some inferring—combining my own background knowledge about bats with details in the article—to make my argument. OK?

So, I believe that most bats are harmless. First of all, the article states that out of the 1,100 known bat species, only three are blood-sucking. Second, the zoologist in the article hand-feeds bats and describes them as peaceful and cuddly. Third, I've been to the cageless bat exhibit at the zoo. If they wanted to, the bats could fly right at visitors and attack them since there is no barrier separating bats from viewers, but they don't. As a matter of fact, those bats ignore the people watching them.

So did I convince you?

Let the class respond. Explicitly show them how you found your position and then gathered support for it.

STEP 6 **Pairs draw a conclusion**

Now, working in pairs, I want you to share the conclusions you jotted down and pick one you think is important.

After groups confer, you may move on to the next step or, if kids need more support, develop a list of possible arguments or positions, such as the following.

Sample Positions

Vampire bats are dangerous to cattle.

Farmers should have a right to catch and kill all the vampire bats they can.

Vampire bats are important to research.

Vampire bats contribute to the local ecology.

People don't know much about vampire bats.

The natural habitat of vampire bats is being destroyed.

The presence of naturally occurring species within Panama makes cattle herding inappropriate for the environment.

Killing vampire bats is cruel.

Vampire bats might turn out to be important to people.

Now I want you to get ready to defend your position with at least two pieces of evidence that we can all see or infer from the article. Be sure to jot down careful notes as you go: you'll get a chance to present your conclusion to one other pair first, and maybe the whole class later on.

STEP 7 **Pairs examine their positions and search for evidence** Circulate, confer, and assist as pairs collaborate to develop their positions and search for support. You will probably hear yourself saying over and over again: *Exactly what part of the article supports that opinion? OK, now what else backs up your idea? Show me.*

STEP 8 **Two pairs join and present to each other**

OK, quickly join up with another pair that's sitting nearby. Pull your chairs together so you can hear. Now the first pair, take a minute to share one of your positions and evidence. After that, the other pair should challenge them. Even if you actually agree, go ahead and ask them tough questions. Try to poke holes in their evidence. But no attitudes or insults—you've got to support your objections with the text, too. You'll have a total of two minutes for this.

STEP 9 **Pairs switch roles** Rinse and repeat. This will take another two or three minutes, depending on how fulsome the conversation gets.

STEP 10 **Share with the whole class** Ask a few volunteers to explain their positions and show their two pieces of evidence. Once someone shares, ask if other groups who took the same position found any additional evidence. Record or project these lists of supporting points.

SUPPORT YOUR POSITION is used in Text Sets 5, 6

Tips and Variations

■ **GO DEEPER** A valuable addition after Step 9 is to have pairs return to their notes and upgrade their argument and evidence, based on the challenges they've had from classmates. Then, in a second round, they can meet with a different pair to present their new and improved evidence supporting their position. A fuller version of this process appears in Strategy 17, Arguing Both Sides.

■ **USING FICTION** We have intentionally used nonfiction text here (remember what the title of this book is?). However, Support Your Position is a strategy that is absolutely essential when discussing character motivation in fiction. Rarely does an author directly explain why a character does something. The reader must infer this via the details, the clues. Plus, the reader must put those clues to work in a logical, defensible way.

At the conclusion of a story or novel, we often ask students: If the story continued, what do you think would happen next? Before we started teaching this strategy, kids often came up with outrageous answers (typically involving space aliens and high-powered weaponry) that had nothing to do with the story. Now that students know their interpretations must be backed up by text details as well as logic, they've become much more thoughtful in their reading and subsequent discussion. It will be music to your ears when you overhear a group member respond to another's outlandish supposition with the words: "Prove it!"

Los Angeles Times

Vampire bat debate: To kill or not to kill

May 18, 2005
By Chris Kraul

TONOSI, Panama — Cattleman Francisco Oliva was on a round-up—of vampire bats. After a swarm of the blood-slurping creatures dive-bombed his herd and drank their fill one recent night, he corralled several dozen of them in special contraptions that look like giant badminton nets. He put each bat in a cage and then applied a poison called vampirin to their backs with a brush before releasing them. Back in the bat roost, the animals would be groomed by about 20 other bats, causing their deaths.

Here in the remote and hilly southwest corner of Panama, Oliva and other cattlemen wage a continual battle against a variety of livestock pests such as coyotes, crocodiles, ticks, worms and a host of tropical diseases. But he has been driven to the edge of desperation by the increasing bat attacks.

Surveying his cattle, most of Oliva's 300-head herd bore fang markings and red stains from the nightly bloodletting. During the month of April, Oliva said, he lost 10 calves to anemia caused by successive bloodlettings. He and other cattlemen bemoan the scarcity of the bat-catching nets, which are strictly controlled by the Panamanian government to prevent their use to capture endangered birds.

Oliva said adult vampire bats, which have a wingspan of 8 inches, swoop down by the hundreds over his herd, land on the ground and then jump up on the animals' legs, underbellies or faces to bite them. A bat's saliva contains an anti-coagulant that makes blood flow freely, and the bat laps up the blood. Oliva said he would exterminate every bat if he could.

Stefan Klose, a research zoologist, begged to differ. He not only stuck up for vampire bats, but described the animals as boons to humanity. Bat-based research led to the development of sonar and anti-coagulant medicines that prevent heart attacks, and scientists are only beginning to understand the creatures. "Very little of what we have invented has been made from scratch. Nature usually provides the template. Vampires could hold the key to a problem we want to solve, like AIDS or cancer. But if you destroy them, they are lost for eternity."

> *"Vampires could hold the key to a problem we want to solve, like AIDS or cancer. But if you destroy them, they are lost for eternity."*

Klose also confessed a fondness for the creatures. The scientist said feeding time, when the bats accept bits of banana from his hand, is a "really sweet and peaceful sight. It always reminds me of how close these animals are to us and how incredibly intelligent they are—certainly more exotic and wilder than my neighbor's dog, but no less smart or cuddly." In addition, Panama's bat population plays an important role in pollination and insect control.

Panama has 120 bat species and bats are found globally except in Antarctica. Non-vampire bats make up the majority of the 1,100 known bat species. There are only three blood-sucking, or vampire, species of bats.

Vampire bats have always been present in Panama, and their attacks have ebbed and flowed. but now the attacks have become more frequent. Scientists theorize that the increased attacks on livestock are due to timber cutting that has flushed bats out of food-rich forests to the cattle herds, a ready-made and usually stationary food supply for the bats.

| Strategy 13 | # Written Discussion |

- Time:
  30 minutes
- Grouping
  Sequence:
  Groups of 3 or
  4, whole class

This is Smokey's Number One Most Important Teaching Strategy Ever. Is that emphatic enough? Among many other good things, "write-arounds" can replace those dreaded whole-class discussions, where the teacher pulls teeth to evoke participation, one or two kids obediently parrot answers, and the other twenty-seven sleep with their eyes open. We've always thought this was a passive, low-impact use of class time. Instead, with written discussion, you can fully expect to see *every kid in your room* reading, writing, and thinking about a topic steadily, for ten, twelve, fifteen minutes at a time. Believe us, you won't know what to do with yourself when the kids are actually doing the thinking, and you only have to call for paper passing every couple of minutes.

If you are having trouble visualizing this activity, take a look at the sample on page 87. This is one of four pages that got created as a group of four high school juniors responded to the teacher's prompt: "Explain Holden Caulfield's attitudes toward sex as they are revealed in Chapter 9 of *Catcher in the Rye*."

This strategy lends itself to digital, online variations, where kids post and respond to topics either you or they have selected. But in this baseline lesson, we are kicking it old school—students sitting knee to knee (well, maybe not quite), writing with real pens on paper, and soon enough, talking face to face. And finally, when everyone has rehearsed something to say, we come back together for a livelier whole-class discussion, where kids join in from engagement, not coercion.

MATERIALS NEEDED

Copy of article for each student.

Steps and Teaching Language

STEP 1 **Form groups** Place kids in groups of three or four. Have each student get a full-size blank piece of paper and put their first name in the upper *left-hand* margin.

STEP 2 **Students read the article** Have kids read the article "School Cancels Graduation for Cheaters" or a similarly controversial piece.

STEP 3 **Explain the written conversation**

Interesting article, right? Today we are going to have a conversation in small groups. We have done this plenty of times, haven't we? But this time we are going to have that conversation in writing instead of out loud. We are going to write notes about our thinking, pass them around, and write back to each other. OK?

There are three rules for this kind of conversation:

1. *Use your best handwriting, so people can read what you are saying.*

2. *Use all the time I give you for writing. No fair writing a couple of words and putting down your pen.*

3. *Don't talk, even when passing notes to each other. We want to keep all the energy in the writing.*

You will probably need to reiterate these rules as you go along, especially with students who are new to silent discussion.

STEP 4 **Begin the silent conversation**

Now we are going to start our written discussion. Remember, you are just writing an informal note to the kids in your group. What did you think about while reading this? What reactions, thoughts, questions, or feelings did you have about the article or this topic? Just tell what's on your mind—spelling and grammar don't count. I am going to give you about two minutes to write and then we will start exchanging papers.

STEP 5 **Monitor** Circulate through the class, looking over shoulders. Keep time, not by exact minutes and seconds, but by walking around and watching kids write. When most students have filled about a quarter of a page, warn them that it is almost time to stop writing and pass.

STEP 6 **Call for the first pass**

OK, in about fifteen seconds we are going to pass papers for the first time, so you might want to finish the sentence you are working on right now. Ready? 5-4-3-2-1-pass! Decide which way the papers are going to go and stick to it.

Now what are you going to do? Just read the note your classmate wrote, and right beneath it, write an answer, just like you were talking out loud. You can tell your reaction, make a comment, ask questions, share a connection you've made, agree or disagree, or raise a whole new idea about the article. Remember to use all the time I give you and keep writing. Just keep the conversation going!

STEP 7 **Monitor the writing** Walk the room, looking over shoulders to get the timing right.

STEP 8   **Call for additional passes**

Pass again, please. Now you have two notes to respond to, right? So I'm going to give you a little more time. You can respond to one note, or the other one, or both. Just keep that conversation going.

Reiterate instructions if needed, especially about "no talking" while passing or writing: *Remember, we are having a silent discussion here. You'll get to talk out loud in a few minutes.*

Repeat and continue. Again, don't pace this activity by actual minutes, but by watching how kids are coming along, and call "Pass" only when most people have written at least a few lines.

Have kids write and pass three or four times. Three is usually plenty, and hands unaccustomed to handwriting will be tired by then. And yet, four turns sometimes pushes the conversation to a deeper level, as in the Holden Caulfield example.

STEP 9   **Return to sender**   When you are ready to stop, have the kids pass back their papers so that everyone gets the one they started with, the paper with their entry at the top. *Now read the whole thing over and see the conversation that you started.*

As soon as kids are done reading and they start talking—and they will— say: *OK, go ahead and continue this conversation out loud in your group. Use your writings however they help you to keep talking. And thanks for playing along with the silent part of today's class.*

At this point, you can let the discussions be open, or you can offer a more focused prompt ("Is it fair to punish everyone for the sins of a few?"). Or you can shift directly to whole-class discussion.

STEP 10   **Share with the whole class**

Let's gather as a whole class and see where our written discussion took us. Will each group please share one highlight, one thread of your discussion? Something you spent time on, something that sparked lively discussion, maybe something you argued about or laughed about? Take a second to scan the writings in front of you. Now, who'd like to share?

And here's the beauty part: there will be plenty of volunteers. Once you have given the subject matter its due, be sure to review the process, too.

Let's discuss this write-around process. What worked for you and what made it hard? How could we make it better next time?

Tips and Variations

■ **PREVENT DIGRESSIONS** The first thing you should say when starting this activity is: *I will be collecting these papers when we are done.* This really helps kids stay away from topics like the big game, somebody's new phone, who's dating who, or how boring this class is.

■ **ENJOY BALANCED PARTICIPATION** Notice some of the things this discussion structure does. It equalizes airtime; each kid gets the same amount of time and space to "speak" to the group. Dominant kids can't hog the whole conversation, and the shy (or silenced) students are invited to speak right up. In fact, we often see much better participation from our quiet ones when silent discussion later goes live. That's because they've rehearsed their thinking and gained confidence in their ideas—which everyone has just read and responded to.

■ **GO DIGITAL** Of course, you can hold written conversations online, in the cloud, even on cell phones, depending on what facilities your school offers or legalizes. In these formats, it's possible for kids to post notes much like mailing letters, to be picked up whenever the addressee has a minute to read and answer. The written discussion becomes asynchronous; students can join in a discussion when they have time, even from home, at three in the morning if they want.

These are great options, but notice: this is a quite different experience from when the notes are written "live," side by side, with immediate responses, where everyone can switch to talking out loud in one second.

■ **SELECTING TEXT** When trying written conversations for the first time, we use a highly kid-relevant and controversial text, so that students won't have to struggle for something to write about. Once they have learned the structure, we bring on more subject-related text.

■ **LEGALIZE DRAWING** Some kids are faster text producers than others, some kids struggle with handwriting, some kids have identified learning needs that make fast writing hard, others are just learning English. If you have such students in class, the answer is not to give up on written conversations, but to make accommodations so these kids can join in—and so the discussions work better for everyone. As we noted in Strategy 5, Sketching Through the Text, you can pack a ton of meaning into a drawing. So let everyone know from the start that drawing is a perfectly valid way to join in a written conversation.

Chapter 9 letter C.

MM — Why did Holden call himself the biggest sex manic you ever saw. Holden has really good values toward sex. I wonder why Holden dosen't realize that he truly does understand sex. He does

AK — Holden does hold women in high regard, but he still sees them as sexual beings. Madonna/whore scenario. Not like boob's cone madonna, but as in the pshchological sense. He still is an adolescent male and becoms sexually aroused. [A classic.]

Jn — I don't really think he knows exactly what his thoughts are about sex. He seems really confused by it.

CB — He has values, but he is still confused. He 'can uphold those values and still wonder why he has them because they might be so different from other guys he knows.

Sample written discussion of Chapter 9 of *Catcher in the Rye*. In this example, the teacher allowed very short writing times, so responses are brief, and passing of papers was brisk.

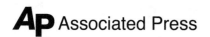
Associated Press

School Cancels Graduation for Cheaters

Ohio district says will still mail diplomas to 60 high school students

June 5, 2009

COLUMBUS, Ohio—An Ohio school district says it uncovered a cheating scheme so pervasive that it had to cancel graduation ceremonies for its 60 seniors—but will still mail their diplomas. A senior at Centerburg High School accessed teachers' computers, found tests, printed them and distributed them to classmates, administrators said.

Graduation was canceled because so many seniors either cheated or knew about the cheating but failed to report it, said officials of the Centerburg School District. Superintendent Dorothy Holden said the district had to take a stand and let students know that cheating can't be tolerated. "I am alarmed that our kids can think that in society it's OK to cheat, it's a big prank, it's OK to turn away and not be a whistle-blower, not come forth," Holden said.

> "We're not going to put that type of honor out there knowing that many of you are walking through there and you cheated, you lied, you denied."

The district says it has identified a student who apparently accessed shared file folders on teachers' computers. Officials believe the cheating involved at least five tests in a senior World Studies class dating to early January. One of the tests quizzed students on Aztec Indian history. Teachers had suspicions about some higher-than-expected grades during the semester, Holden said.

The cheating unraveled when a student discovered a congratulatory note to the perpetrator on a school computer Tuesday and gave it to Principal John Morgan. Administrators learned Friday that the cheating plot may have involved underclassmen, as well. Holden said so many students are involved that it was impossible "to separate the wheat from the chaff" in terms of deciding who could graduate. Instead, all students will be mailed their diplomas.

"We're not going to put that type of honor out there knowing that many of you are walking through there and you cheated, you lied, you denied," Holden said.

Some parents angry about the cancellation are organizing an unofficial graduation ceremony. Jeanette Lamb, whose son is a senior at the school, asked the Centerburg School Board to reconsider its decision to cancel graduation. The board declined. "At that point I did tell them that commencement would continue, it will be at the park, I will put it together and their presence wasn't welcome," Lamb told WTVN radio in Columbus. Lamb said parents and members of the community have offered help.

Centerburg High, with about 400 students, is one of the state's top schools, with an "excellent" academic rating last year, according to the state Department of Education. Last year, the school had a 99 percent graduation rate, compared to a statewide rate of 87 percent.

Some students admitted they cheated; others said they knew of the cheating but didn't participate; and others said they had the tests but didn't use them, Holden said. One student who used the test still failed.

Text-on-Text, or Collaborative Annotation

Strategy 14

- Time:
  20 minutes
- Grouping
  Sequence:
  whole class,
  groups of 3,
  whole class

We learned this rarely used strategy from teacher Sheila Newell in Houston, Texas. It is a powerful variant of the preceding strategy, Written Discussion. Here, groups of three kids gather around one large-print copy of a text, annotate it with individually colored markers, and write comments about each other's comments in the margin. Then, the groups join in a gallery walk (see Strategy 19), where they read and write about the ideas generated by other groups.

Like other forms of written conversation, text-on-text balances airtime, getting all group members involved in discussions. The shy kids cannot hide and the bloviators cannot dominate when the conversation is happening silently, in writing, and everyone gets the same amount of time to write. And later, once each student has built up a body of writing about a topic, all the kids usually have enough confidence to speak up when the discussion goes out-loud.

MATERIALS NEEDED

One article copy for every three students, enlarged as much as possible and pasted onto a large sheet of chart paper; several sets of different colored markers; Post-it notes or clipboards for gallery walk.

Steps and Teaching Language

STEP 1   **Prepare the lesson**   First you need to choose and prepare the text. Identify a very short selection (say a hundred words) that is relevant to kids *and* highly debatable, even inflammatory. The one we have provided, about teenage dishonesty, always evokes a range of comments from students—outrage, defensiveness, what-else-is-new, and even a little lying, just like on the survey itself.

Notice that our article appears in large type. Whatever text you use, blow up the font as big as you can get it on an 8½ × 11-inch sheet of paper. You are doing this because several kids will be reading from the same page. Make about ten copies of the article—one for every three students. Paste each article onto a big piece of chart or butcher paper (you may have to visit your local elementary school to retrieve this item). What you are doing is creating a huge margin around the text that kids can write in, using the colored markers.

STEP 2 **Get kids physically set up**

Today we are going to have a small-group discussion about a very short article. We've done that plenty of times before, right? But this time we are going to read the article silently on copies I have put on these posters. See? You'll get in groups of three, and push your desks together, and then put the poster on top. You'll want to sit or stand in a kind of U-shape around the poster. Let's try it.

Have one group of kids go through this process, moving their desks (or tables), placing the poster, and positioning themselves around it where they can easily read. Then let everyone else follow suit.

Students working on a text-on-text poster

STEP 3 **Show an example and assign colored markers** Show kids our example of a completed text-on-text poster on the next page, or display one from a previous group of your own students. Leave this up throughout the lesson so kids can get a feel for what these writings look like.

When we have a written discussion on the posters, we need to keep track of who said what, so you each need to pick a different colored marker. Got that? Now, at the bottom of your chart, make a key that shows who's using what color. Remember what a "key" is, from our study of maps? Reserve one color for yourself—we prefer purple—for joining in written conversations later on.

Ready?

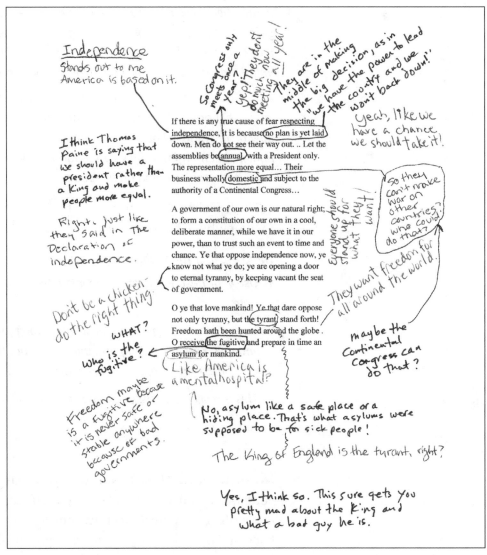

Text-on-text exercise using Tom Paine's *Common Sense*

STEP 4 **Read aloud** Now, introduce the article and read it aloud, slowly and dramatically, to really highlight the contents and issues.

STEP 5 **Offer instructions**

All right. You are now invited to reread the article and write your comments, reactions, feelings, questions, and connections in the margin. Feel free to underline or circle parts of the text, and use an arrow out into the margin to expand on what you are talking about. You can mark parts up with annotation codes, drawings or diagrams, anything that helps you put your thinking out there and get a conversation going.

Remember, three of you will be writing on the same page. So what are you going to do if two people are trying to circle the same word at the same time? Let kids offer suggestions. *Right, be polite, take turns, share space in the margins, don't shove anybody's hand around.*

As you guys finish annotating the text for yourself, you should start reading what other people have written, what parts they've marked, what comments they have made, what questions they have asked. And write back to them, right in that margin: share your thoughts, answer their questions if you can—just have a conversation on the page.

You will probably have to repeat this instruction later, as kids are trying to remember what to do next.

There are four rules when we do this:

1. *Use your best handwriting; people have to be able to read what you write.*

2. *Use all the time I give you for writing. Don't just write a word or two and quit. Keep rereading and thinking about the article and the other kids' posts—just keep that conversation going.*

3. *This is a silent discussion, so no talking until later on!*

4. *Have fun!*

STEP 6 **Monitor and coach** Now with your purple pen in hand, circulate, confer, and look for helpful examples. If kids are hovering over the text and writing, they are doing fine. Look for groups where kids have leaned back or stopped writing. Enter that group silently and read what kids have written so far. Using your teacher-color pen, write a good, meaty question in the margin to help them restart their discussion, and then move on. Come back a few minutes later to see if kids are on track. Allow plenty of time for this stage; if the activity is new to kids, you'll be doing a fair amount of coaching.

STEP 7 **Gallery walk** Next, have groups hang their posters up, spaced evenly around the room, and invite them to take a gallery walk (see Strategy 19). Be sure kids bring a clipboard or other writing surface so they can make notes on the similarities and differences among the charted conversations (three or four responses per poster is plenty). Or, supply them with Post-it notes, which they can use to leave comments on other groups' posters.

STEP 8 **Share** Now, reconvene the whole class and talk about what people noticed as they studied other kids' work, how ideas and interpretations developed, and what positions or themes emerged.

Tips and Variations

■ **IT'S WORTH THE TIME** This lesson is admittedly a bit of work to set up, but it can really spark thinking and conversation. With kids up and out of their seats, engaging with each other and with ideas, this activity opens some space for those students who crave the physical energy of movement, or who need a different way of representing their ideas in order to join in the thinking.

■ **MODELS HELP** The first time you try text-on-text with your kids, be sure to save copies of some well-done posters so you can use them as models for succeeding classes. It's always best to show kids what "the thing" is supposed to look like when it's done, whatever thing you are asking them to produce.

■ **INVITE DRAWING** When Smokey taught this lesson to English language learners in a rural New Mexico high school, many kids were initially reticent to write notes on the poster. But once he told them that drawing "counted," they loosened right up. For many kids, the chance to begin with a quick drawing or cartoon can open the door to writing. And, by the way, this is not "lowering standards." You can offer tons of meaning in a drawing, especially when you start adding labels, captions, and talk and thought balloons—exactly what we encourage kids to do.

crosswalk.com

American Teens Lie, Cheat, and Steal– And Think They're Okay

Chuck Colson, BreakPoint

December 9, 2008

The Josephson Institute of Los Angeles, which studies contemporary ethics and morals, recently released its "2008 Report Card on the Ethics of American Youth." According to the Institute, the "results paint a troubling picture of our future politicians and parents, cops and corporate executives, and journalists and generals."

The Report Card was based on a survey of 29,760 high school students across the country. They were asked 62 questions about their actions and their attitudes.

STEALING: Thirty percent of those surveyed "admitted stealing from a store within the past year." Contrary to what you might expect, girls were not significantly less likely to steal than boys—26 percent versus 35 percent.

Whatever drove kids to steal, it wasn't the impersonal nature of the offense—23 percent admitted to stealing from a parent or relative, and 20 percent acknowledged stealing from a friend.

CHEATING: Inside the classroom, 64 percent admitted to cheating on at least one test, and 38 percent said that they had cheated two or more times during the past year.

LYING: Forty-two percent said that they sometimes lie to save money, and 83 percent confessed that they had lied to their parents about "something significant." Twenty-six percent even admitted that they lied on some of their survey answers.

Yet despite all the admissions of lying, theft, and cheating, 93 percent described themselves as "satisfied with their personal ethics." Seventy-seven percent said that, when it comes to doing right, they are better than most people they know.

Alternative Perspective Writing

Strategy 15

- Time:
  40 minutes
- Grouping Sequence:
  Pairs

Early in the novel *To Kill a Mockingbird,* Atticus advises Scout that she'll get along better with others if she can take on alternative perspectives: "You never really understand a person until you consider things from his point of view."

Encouraging our students to examine a piece of content-area text from a variety of viewpoints strengthens them as readers—and as citizens. Writing from the perspective of a different role or character forces students to creatively reframe information from the text, using their background knowledge to make connections and draw inferences.

In a second phase of this strategy, we add the element of correspondence. After writing their initial piece, students trade with a partner and respond in the role of a new character. This offers kids an immediate audience for their work as well as a tangible response to their writing. In addition, assuming a different role forces writers to review the original text to incorporate factual information. This strategy is highly engaging and fun, plus students also get substantial writing practice along the way.

MATERIALS NEEDED

Copy of article for each student; projectable list of tips for writing an online dating profile, available on the book's website.

Steps and Teaching Language

STEP 1 **Prepare the lesson** Determine how pairs will be formed at Step 6. Before passing out the article, have students get out a sheet of loose-leaf paper.

STEP 2 **Introduce the article and explain annotation** After handing out the article, say: *I want you to read this article carefully, underlining important facts and details you discover about the Australian redback spider. Mark directly on the article; do not write on your loose sheet of paper.*

STEP 3 **Give coding instructions** As students are finishing up, give them the next instruction: *Return to the article and by each underline, mark whether the fact relates to male or female spiders. You can code this with* F *or* M.

STEP 4   **Define the genre and start kids writing**

After students have concluded their coding, continue:

Have you ever heard of websites such as match.com or eHarmony? These are sites that help people find dating partners. People post a description of themselves as well as a description of the kind of person they would like to date. Besides the actual dating sites, there are dozens of sites that offer tips on how to make your profile stand out. This is what they suggest: (Project the following list.)

- Write for the audience—the kind of person you want to date. That's your audience!

- Show, don't tell—rather than say you enjoy movies, name some of your favorites. Rather than say you like hiking, describe your favorite place to hike.

- Be positive. Don't talk about the losers you previously dated!

- Be unique, clever, witty, funny. Show your personality.

Now that you know something about the mating rituals of Australian red-back spiders, I want you to think about the information from a different perspective, that of a female spider. How would a female spider use this information to make herself more attractive to the opposite sex and find a suitable mate?

Using these dating profile tips, imagine what a dating profile for a female Australian redback spider might include. Be sure to use specific details from the text while also depicting your spider's vibrant personality.

Give students five to seven minutes to write their own female spider dating profiles.

STEP 5   **Monitor**   Help kids who need assistance. Warn students when they have a minute left.

STEP 6   **Pairs trade and write back in a new role**

Remember to sign off with an original spider name. Then pass your paper to your partner.

As you read the profile, you are all going to change roles. Now you are all male spiders who hope to find a mate but also live to tell about it. Read your partner's profile and then write back as an interested male.

Be sure to think about how your viewpoint will now be different as a male spider. What are his mating goals compared to the female's? What's in it for him? Once again, let your unique spidery personality show through while also including as many details from the article as possible.

Give students another five to seven minutes to read the female's profile and then write their responses. Warn students when they have a minute left and remind them to sign off with a closing and an original spider name.

ALTERNATIVE
PERSPECTIVE WRITING
is used in Text Set 10

STEP 7 **Read responses and share with the class** Partners trade papers again, read the responses, and then decide which of the two letters they like better. Depending on time, have several pairs volunteer to read their favorite letters and responses to the whole class.

Tips and Variations

- **USE VARIED GENRES** Students may write from an alternative viewpoint using a variety of genres: letter, email, text message, editorial, Internet site message board, diary, or blog. The genre you choose should lend itself to the text content. For this introductory lesson, to accompany the article "Deadly Spider Requires Long Courtship—or Else," we chose the genre of an online dating profile because female Australian redback spiders take their relationships very seriously—until they tire of their mates and eat them!

  That wasn't our only genre choice. Since this article does not show female redbacks in a very positive light (they are portrayed as cannibals), we also could have used the genre of letter to the editor and invited our students to speak as angry redbacks, trying to set readers straight as they refute the claims of this obviously biased article.

- **MATCH WRITING PROMPTS TO YOUR SUBJECT MATTER** Students enjoy the combination of information and creativity that alternative perspective writing calls for. As text varies within a unit or content area, feel free to shape the initial prompt in order to get students thinking about pertinent issues. Encourage students to use additional background information in creating the alternative perspective, as well as examine the characters' needs, motivations, goals, and reaction to the information presented in the article. When you see kids looking up additional information on the classroom computers, you'll know this activity is a hit.

- **USE MULTIPLE ROLES** Depending on the text, you can assign students to three or four different roles for the initial writing and responses rather than just one. In that case, have students number off by threes or fours (the same number of roles). All of a certain number then take on that assigned role and subsequent response.

Attractive Single Australian Redback Looking for STMR (Single Tiny Male Redback)

My name is Rachel Redback. I enjoy mating, the more love the better. The size of a male means absolutely nothing to me. I am looking for a spider with stamina, fighting skills, and no fear of death.

Just so you know, I am very selfish and picky. The loving must be at least 100 minutes—or else. My male must satisfy my needs. He must successfully complete the traditional courtship dance, and he better massage my abdomen; we Redbacks get very stressed out.

My spider must be a warrior, a great combatant to earn my love. I'm so tired of losers coming on to me when I'm just minding my own business. Losers are a dime a dozen. I eat losers for breakfast—literally! A spider that earns my love will have to battle his way through a gauntlet of fierce would-be mating partners.

The lucky hunk of a spider that wins my love must have no regard for his life. If you don't please me, I'll devour you like humans eat fast food. I can't stand it when males beg for mercy when I tell them they're not good enough for me. If you fear death, you had better stay away from this spider! Let me remind you, we female Redbacks are much larger than you males. And if it turns out you don't satisfy me, I hope you at least taste good.

Again, my name is Rachel Redback. I love a spider that can fight, has great stamina, and is fearless. If you think you are male enough for me, meet me in my web.

—Rachel Redback

Reply

I've read through your profile a million times and after careful consideration, I feel that I am the spider for you. I've got everything you're looking for and more. Stamina is my middle name. My small body allows me to court for hours. 100 minutes? That's nothing. I've got enough endurance to go longer than the rest of those losers that wind up in your web.

I'll do anything to prove my love for you. If it takes fighting off other spiders who want you, then so be it. I may be small, but I sure can fight for what I want. I have no fear and am willing to risk my life for a chance with you.

Death doesn't scare me. If you happen to eat me alive after we mate, that is fine by me. I'll die happily knowing that I fulfilled your needs; the more eggs I fertilize the better. I understand that you have neurotoxic venom that causes severe pain to larger animals and humans. Just knowing that you can kill me with one bite drives me crazy!

On top of all that power and control, you have the most beautiful long, black legs I have ever seen. The vibrant red stripe on your back makes you stand out from the rest of the females out there. I'm very excited to meet you. I've got everything you need, and I am sure you will pick me because your profile shows you have some pretty good taste! Give me a call.

—Rick Redback

Alternative perspectives—a "personal ad" and the response

DEADLY SPIDER REQUIRES LONG COURTSHIP—OR ELSE

Female Australian redback gets almost 100 minutes, or it will eat suitor

DISCOVERY CHANNEL | **Jennifer Viegas**, Oct. 21, 2009

Females of the Australian redback spider, one of the world's most poisonous spiders and a close relative to the black widow, demand 100 minutes of courting or else they usually cannibalize their male suitors.

Recent research shows that bigger isn't always better in the mating game. The tiniest of males sometimes approach female redbacks after offering the critical 100 minutes of wooing and successfully mate without being eaten.

The study shows that puny males of this species can win at love without exerting much effort and begins to explain the extreme size differences between males and females among some spider species. It appears as though females are not tuned to select male size, but rather the duration of courtship.

A male first performs a lengthy "courtship dance," where it vibrates the female's web and wraps it in his own silk to reduce the emission of pheromones that could attract other males. He then drums on her abdomen and may alternate between drumming and web dancing. If he does this for less than 100 minutes and then attempts mating, the female will begin her cannibalism.

But if he meets her desired courtship threshold, he may be able to mate and survive. If not, he's usually eaten and then other males enter her web, sometimes fighting with each other to get to her. Females appear to act as a referee and strike at males with their forelegs as males escalate aggression towards one another.

The bizarre process may help to explain why male spiders are often so much smaller than females. For this species, males carry 1 to 2 percent of the body weight of a typical female.

Smaller males likely mature faster and can therefore mate earlier in life. And tiny males may be better equipped to scramble faster towards females and their webs. Bigger females, on the other hand, may have greater reproductive success, so the species winds up with enormous females and minuscule males.

Researcher Mariella Herberstein concluded, "The question that remains is why females have not evolved a way of discriminating between two courting males in her web. It may be that distinguishing the sources of vibrations in a complex three-dimensional web is very difficult, an aspect that males clearly take advantage of."

Strategy 16

Point of View Annotation

- Time: 20 minutes
- Grouping Sequence: Groups of 3 or 4 (determined by the number of roles)

Once again, this strategy requires students to read, underline, and take notes. We are kind of big on that process.

But this time, rather than reading and reacting from their own perspectives, kids are required to *impersonate someone else* doing the reading. Yes, they take on a role outside themselves, and then annotate and respond in that role.

You can assign these roles, or the students can suggest ones of their own devising. In language arts, valuable roles might involve looking at a story from the viewpoint of particular characters. In science, perspectives might be based on the different components of a cell or an atom (e.g., How would the mitochondria react to this passage?). In history, different world leaders might interpret the same historical event in different ways.

This is an excellent way to keep students engaged as they read and create notes for a later conversation. Taking an alternative viewpoint dramatically reminds kids that everyone does not interpret information the same way—or even recognize the same details as important. Understanding multiple viewpoints becomes particularly important when students encounter content that has some controversy attached. And, when you think about it, how much content is really free of any controversy?

MATERIALS NEEDED

Copy of article for each student.

Steps and Teaching Language

STEP 1 **Form groups around roles** Before students read this article, decide which roles you want to use. For this piece, possibilities include teenager, parent, police officer, insurance executive, and president of DriveCam. Determine how roles will be assigned. Groups can negotiate who takes which role, or you can assign the roles randomly.

STEP 2 **Give instructions for reading**

As you read this article, you will be taking on a role other than yourself. You are going to pretend to be someone else reading the article, and annotate the text as you think that person would. Remember: you are not you! Respond to the information in your role, not as yourself.

Underline information that is important, surprising, puzzling, or thought provoking.

Then, before continuing to read, stop and jot down a sentence or two that explains why you chose that bit to underline. The goal is to explain your role's thoughts, opinions, or questions. Try to imagine that your role or character is having a conversation with the text inside their head. Your notes represent that conversation.

STEP 3 **Monitor reading** Circulate, confer, and coach. Gently enforce the process of stopping to think and write in your role—even though some kids may find it easier to read the whole thing at once and then backtrack to reconstruct. As our mantra goes: *stopping to think while you are reading* is a vital skill to practice.

If you notice some students finishing sooner than others, you can suggest: *If you are finished, go back to the article, reread your annotations, and try to add enough details that show you are really thinking in your role or character.*

STEP 4 **Give discussion directions**

Move into your groups and state what your assigned role was. Compare what you've underlined and your thoughts connected to those underlines. Be sure to find specific passages that everyone underlined and discuss how various roles reacted differently to the same information.

POINT OF VIEW ANNOTATION is used in Text Set 10

STEP 5 **Share with the whole class** Give group members the opportunity to read aloud and discuss the annotations they thought produced particularly interesting conversation threads or stark contrasts.

Tips and Variations

■ **MAKE SURE KIDS "GET" THEIR ROLES** Once students understand basic text annotation, they should have little difficulty making the leap to pretending they are someone else. However, to help students successfully pretend, make sure they have the background knowledge for understanding their roles. Usually a quick discussion of "What would be important to this person/character/object?" is sufficient. If a student still has difficulty imagining her role, the most expedient solution may be to reassign her to a different role. Though this might result in a group's doubling up on some of the roles, there is little likelihood that the annotations for the same role will be identical, and comparing the differences will still be interesting.

■ **BRING IN ROLES FROM OTHER TEXTS** Many times nonfiction is used to supplement the study of fiction. Rather than taking on nonfiction roles, students can become characters from a novel or play. For example, if students were reading about the Civil Rights Act of 1964 in conjunction with *To Kill a Mockingbird*, kids could read and annotate from the perspectives of Atticus, Jem, Scout, Tom Robinson, Bob Ewell, Miss Maudie, or Aunt Alexandra.

Watch your driving, kids. The parents are watching.

By Matt Zapotosky, *The Washington Post*, October 26, 2008

ASHINGTON — Ken Richardson does not have to ride in his 17-year-old daughter's Ford Escort to know when she takes a turn too fast. The camera system installed in her car will e-mail him about it.

The cameras are among the latest tools in the struggle to reduce teen car crashes, a problem that has been particularly vexing in Maryland. Last year, crashes involving drivers ages 16 to 20 killed 112 people in the state. Such accidents are often caused not by alcohol or overt recklessness but by simple driver inexperience. The problem has persisted despite efforts by lawmakers to restrict teen driving privileges.

The camera, mounted on the front windshield, captures footage of what is happening outside as well as in the vehicle. It saves about 20 seconds of that footage only when its sensors are triggered by excessive G-forces. Those forces tend to accompany unusual driving maneuvers such as sudden braking or swerving. Saved footage is transmitted back to DriveCam via a cellular network. DriveCam experts review the videos, add tips for the young drivers and post them to a Web site where parents can see them a day or so later. Parents receive an e-mail alert when the videos are posted.

The camera can capture anything going on in the car, but the company uploads only footage that involves unsafe driving. "If an event is captured that is embarrassing to the teen ... then we're not going to return it to the family," Carpenter said.

In the month or so since the camera was installed, Stacie has not been caught on camera doing anything too bad. But the camera has been a sore point since Ken Richardson told his daughter it would be installed, whether she liked it or not. "I feel like I'm being baby-sat, like I'm being watched constantly," said Stacie Richardson, Ken's daughter. "It drives me nuts."

Richardson has tried every possible angle to convince his daughter that the camera is a good idea. He has tried telling her she could earn new driving privileges by avoiding major incidents. He has appealed to her sense of benevolence, telling her that being a part of the study could save others' lives. And he has tried telling her that when she gets older, she'll want the same kind of device for her kids.

The limited research conducted on DriveCam elsewhere in the country seems to support her dad. McGehee, the researcher, tracked 25 new drivers using the camera and a feedback system for more than a year starting in 2006. The six people that McGehee classified as "high-frequency drivers," meaning they triggered the camera frequently early on, did so 86 percent less after using the DriveCam and McGehee's version of the feedback system. The study was funded by American Family Insurance, which uses the cameras as a marketing tool, offering them free for the young drivers it insures.

Handwritten annotations:

Parent's Perspective

I think this would be a great idea! As a parent, I should know how fast or slow my child is driving.

When I place this in my son's car, I will know everywhere they're going and everything they are doing inside the car.

My daughter would say the exact same thing. In fact, my son would too. They would think that I don't trust them, but the truth is I just want them to be safe.

Since my kids would complain about it, I wouldn't tell them about installing the camera in their car. Then I could keep an eye on their driving while I am doing work on my laptop.

Example of point of view annotation (shown on an earlier version of this article)

The *Washington Post*

Watch your driving, kids. The parents are watching.

By **Matt Zapotosky**
Oct. 26, 2008

WASHINGTON — Ken Richardson does not have to ride in his 17-year-old daughter's Ford Escort to know when she takes a turn too fast. The camera system installed in her car will e-mail him about it.

The cameras are among the latest tools in the struggle to reduce teen car crashes, a problem that has been particularly vexing in Maryland. Last year, crashes involving drivers ages 16 to 20 killed 112 people in the state. Such accidents are often caused not by alcohol or overt recklessness but by simple driver inexperience. The problem has persisted despite efforts by lawmakers to restrict teen driving privileges.

The camera, mounted on the front windshield, captures footage of what is happening outside as well as in the vehicle. It saves about 20 seconds of that footage only when its sensors are triggered by unusual driving maneuvers such as sudden braking or swerving. Saved footage is transmitted back to DriveCam via a cellular network. DriveCam experts review the videos, add tips for the young drivers and post them to a Web site. Parents receive an e-mail alert when the videos are posted.

The camera can capture anything going on in the car, but the company uploads only footage that involves unsafe driving. If an event is captured that is embarrassing to the

> "I feel like I'm being baby-sat, like I'm being watched constantly. It drives me nuts."

teen . . . then we're not going to return it to the family," Carpenter said.

In the month or so since the camera was installed, Richardson's daughter has not been caught on camera doing anything too bad, but the camera has been a sore point. "I feel like I'm being baby-sat, like I'm being watched constantly. It drives me nuts," said Stacie.

Richardson has tried every possible angle to convince his daughter that the camera is a good idea. He has tried telling her she could earn new driving privileges by avoiding major incidents. He has appealed to her sense of benevolence, telling her that being a part of the study could save others' lives. And he has tried telling her that when she gets older, she'll want the same kind of device for her kids.

The limited research conducted on Drive-Cam elsewhere in the country seems to support her dad. DriveCam tracked 25 new drivers using the camera and feedback system for more than a year starting in 2006. The six people who triggered the camera most frequently in the beginning, did so 86 percent less later on.

Strategy 17

Arguing Both Sides

- Time:
  45–50 minutes
- Grouping
  Sequence:
  Groups of 4
  working in 2 pairs

Where do our kids learn how to argue and debate? From TV attack ads in which politicians bombard each other with invective?

> "Dick Johnson hates our troops, pushes senior citizens down stairwells, and spits on the flag every day at 6:00 a.m.! Call Dick Johnson and tell him he is a traitor to our country!"

If we aim to nurture literate, thinking citizens, our students need to recognize the one-sidedness of many arguments presented in today's media. When students are presented with controversial—and sometimes sensational—statements, they need to automatically ask: what contradictory information or other viewpoints are missing from this debate?

The ability to articulate a well-constructed argument, one that acknowledges both sides and uses factual evidence to support its position, is very useful when you are sitting for a state graduation exam, writing essays for the ACT or SAT tests, or, later in life, convincing your employer that a raise/promotion is in order.

In this lesson, students learn how to argue both sides of an issue, as well as draw from both to create a deeper understanding. This strategy has more steps than most and will definitely take a full period when you first introduce it. However, once kids are familiar with the steps, this versatile strategy can be used with text, lecture, or films. And topics need not be the sensational, emotionally hypercharged controversies that splash across the news channels and Internet pages. Almost any scientific discovery or historical event results in complex and debatable issues.

MATERIALS NEEDED
Copy of article for each student.

Steps and Teaching Language

STEP 1 **Determine pairings** Students will be working with two different partners for this strategy: they will need a "shoulder partner" (a student sitting to the side) and a "face partner" (one across a table or possibly right behind them, so they can face the person by turning around). Decide ahead of time how you will arrange students so that they can easily move between their shoulder partners and their face partners. Students will be working with their face partner to prepare their arguments and their shoulder partner to argue their opposing positions.

STEP 2 **Students brainstorm arguments with their preparation (face) partner** Have students move into their groups and say:

Take out a sheet of loose-leaf paper and fold it in half lengthwise (hot dog style) in order to create two columns. Unfold and at the top center write "Why Cell Phones Should Be Banned in School." Label the left-hand column "Reasons" and the right-hand column "Examples." Now turn to your face partner and work together to come up with four good reasons why students should not use their cell phones during the school day. Then, across from each reason on the right-hand side, list specific examples that show why your reason is legitimate. (See the example on page 107.)

STEP 3 **Monitor the work of face partners** Probably about five to ten minutes will be needed. Observe progress, answer questions as they arise, and end the discussion as talk and note-taking wind down.

STEP 4 **Pass out the article and give reading directions**

It looks like everyone was able to come up with lots of good reasons why students are prohibited from using cell phones during the school day. Now I'd like you to read an article about a school that has the exact opposite policy. This school encourages students to bring their cell phones to class so they can use them during instruction. Allow a few minutes for students to read the article.

STEP 5 **Students brainstorm pro-phone arguments with their preparation (face) partner**

Turn your papers over and at the top center write "Why Cell Phones Should Be Used in School." Label the left-hand column "Reasons" and the right-hand column "Examples." Once again, I want you to work with your face partner to brainstorm four good reasons along with examples for using cell phones in school. Think about the information presented in the article but do not limit yourselves to it since you and your partner may think of other legitimate uses the article did not mention. (See the example on page 108.)

STEP 6 **Monitor work of face partners** Circulate and confer, clarifying instructions as needed. Track the energy and production in the room, allowing between five and ten minutes for this step.

STEP 7 **Introduce argument using shoulder partners**

Turn to your face partner and thank them for all their help so far. Now turn to your shoulder partner and listen for your assignment. The partner on the right [the student's right] *is a one and the partner on the left is a two.* Take a minute to walk the room and make sure partners understand who is the "one" and who is the "two."

Now all you ones, raise your hands. (If students have followed the directions correctly, all of the ones should line up behind one another.) *Twos raise your hand. Good. Ones, you are going to argue in favor of banning cell phones. Twos, you are going to argue in favor of using cell phones in school. Everybody clear on which side you are going to argue? Good. Get ready to start when I tell you.*

STEP 8 **Shoulder partners argue positions one at a time**

Ones, you will have one minute to argue in favor of banning cell phones. Twos, you may not interrupt. You can only listen. Go!

When a minute or so is up, call a halt to the presentations. Then give the twos a minute to present their side. Once again, remind the opponents that they can only listen.

STEP 9 **Students brainstorm solutions with their argument (shoulder) partner** At the end of the second presentations, say: *Now I want all of you to drop your advocacy for a specific side and work with your shoulder partner to come up with a solution that both teachers and students could live with.* Give partners a few minutes to discuss and then quickly have each pair state their solution to the whole class.

ARGUING BOTH SIDES is used in Text Set 8

Tips and Variations

■ **PLAY THE GAME WITH NEW RULES** This is a streamlined version (believe it or not) of a strategy David and Roger Johnson have named "academic controversy" (1995). Once students understand the basics demonstrated in this lesson, you can make the model more elaborate by incorporating some or all of the following additional steps. (Nancy's book *Assessment Live* [2009] treats this strategy at length.)

• Assign shoulder partners opposing viewpoints at the very beginning so that when they meet with their face partners to prepare, their desire to beat their adversaries is heightened.

• Once the initial presentations conclude, shoulder partners engage in an "open discussion" in which they try to break down their opponents' weakest arguments by pointing out those weaknesses or asking questions.

• Have shoulder partners switch roles, so that instead of arguing just one side, students must argue both sides. Encourage them to try to argue their new positions better than their partners did. Also, it is often helpful for students to return to their face (preparation) partners so that they can work together to devise their new positions.

On the Web

Reason for Banning Cell Phones	Examples
Cheating	• Students could text answers to their friends. • They could copy down test questions. • They could photograph test pages. • They could put their notes/answers on their phones.
Texting will distract from learning	• Kids in class text back and forth making smart alec comments about students and teacher. No one feels comfortable—like they're being talked about behind their backs. • Always checking for messages. Constantly engaged in silent off-task conversations.
Social networking will distract from learning	• Updating pages rather than paying attention. • Posting class photos without subjects' permission. • Updating Twitter without censoring content/thoughts.
Surfing the Internet will distract from learning	• Find ways to get around school's filtering systems. • Play games. • Watch YouTube.

Why cell phones should be banned in school—student brainstorming example

Reason for Using Cell Phones	Examples
Quick research	• Teacher can pose a question and students can look it up and share information. • Visual information—if students are reading about a setting or time period they are unfamiliar with they can find out what people wore, what places looked like, etc. • Students get more practice at best ways to research a topic and they can easily share tips/strategies with each other.
Saves time for students and teacher	• Teacher doesn't have to look everything up ahead of time or try to anticipate all the questions about a topic students might have. • No need to reserve the computer lab for a period when only 5 or 10 minutes of research is needed.
Cell phones eliminate need for students to carry calculators, cameras, and maybe even textbooks if they are available online	• Save money—family won't have to buy a cell phone, a calculator, and a camera. • Might save districts money if they don't have to buy as many textbooks. • Online textbooks would lighten backpack load and prevent injuries.
Students learn cell phone self-control	• Use cell phones for nonschool business during lunch and passing. • Since teachers are not hassling students, they have to make the choice to pay attention. Puts responsibility on students. • Schools could actively teach cell phone manners—important in real world.

Why cell phones should be used in school—student brainstorming example

St. Petersburg Times

Florida School Allows Cell Phones in Class

By **Jeffrey S. Solochek**
The Associated Press, October 4, 2009

WESLEY CHAPEL, Fla. (AP)—Jennifer Gould ended her class announcements and told her students to take out their cell phones. "I need at least three people who can get a signal in here," Gould said to her advanced placement literature class. "We're going to be studying the works of D. H. Lawrence, and I want you to find some things about him that you don't already know." Nearly everyone whipped out a phone and began tapping away.

"He lived during World War I."

"He had relationships with men and women."

"He lived the second half of his life in exile, considered a pornographer who had wasted his talents."

When the talk had run its course, the students set their phones down and turned their attention to another author.

The new cell phone rules have opened up a new world. Teachers no longer have to wait for a school computer lab to get a quick research project done. The few students who don't have phones share in small groups, or use alternative school equipment. Allowing students to use their cell

> Allowing students to use their cell phones in class means things get done immediately, which translates into more efficient use of learning time.

phones in class means things get done immediately, which translates into more efficient use of learning time, Gould said: "It puts the education in their hands."

In a world where most high schools have adopted a "we see them, we take them" policy on cell phones, Pasco County's Wiregrass Ranch High School swims upstream. It encourages teachers to allow students to use their phones in classes for educational purposes. Teens routinely use their phones to shoot pictures for projects, calculate math problems, check their teachers' blogs and even take lecture notes.

Senior Eric LaGattuta, who attended Freedom High in Hillsborough before moving to Wiregrass Ranch, called his new school "ahead of the game." "They're just following the rest of the world. It's going digital," he said, checking his phone for messages repeatedly during a short interview. "Once you're 16 or 17, there's things you need to know throughout the day. It was so inconvenient when I had to hide it all the time."

Chemistry teacher Peter Skoglund said he barely pays attention to texting teens anymore. He expects students having cell phones out in his class to be using them for learning. If not, that's their problem.

| Strategy 18 |

Where Do You Stand?

- Time:
  25 minutes

- Grouping
  Sequence:
  Solo, standing
  groups, whole class

We should never forget that school means mostly *sitting*, which is not conducive to active engagement—especially to adolescent humans. This lesson is the first in a series of "up and about" activities, designed to get students out of their seats into thoughtful written and out-loud discussions. Kids especially enjoy this activity because it gets them talking with classmates, deliberately making choices, and responding to text physically.

All the equipment you need is the four corners of your classroom. Got those? You're good to go. For text, you need articles, readings, or images that can invite a wide range of responses. The idea is that the teacher poses questions about the topic, and kids literally stand up and take a position. They walk to a spot on the spectrum of opinion and chat with the people nearby who agree with them—or reposition themselves to talk with classmates in other corners, who hold opposing views.

Often we literally label the corners of the room with signs. For example, you can arrange a classic agree-disagree continuum: strongly agree, agree somewhat, disagree somewhat, disagree. You can also label the corners for multiple-choice answers (A, B, C, D), or you can create your own customized corner labels.

For example, in a study of climate change we labeled four corners by four attitudes people commonly have about the topic.

1. It's a hoax; the climate will be fine.
2. It's a hopeless situation; it's too late to stop it.
3. It's real and dangerous, but can be solved.
4. I need more information.

You get the idea—let's go to class.

MATERIALS NEEDED

Copy of article for each student; signs to label the four corners (see Step 1); projectable image of "artificial meat"; clipboards, if using.

Steps and Teaching Language

STEP 1 **Prepare the lesson** Put up legible signs that label the four corners of your room (or four workable spaces where kids can gather): "For sure," "probably," "probably not," and "no way." Also, go to www.images.google.com and get an image of "artificial meat." If you can find it, use our favorite—a full-color petri dish of in vitro "chicken breast." Yeah, we know. If you have a class set of clipboards (see page 30) this is the perfect time to use them as a portable writing surface for roving students.

STEP 2 **Introduce the article**

Today we are going to read a short article about artificial meat, also known as in vitro meat. Has anybody heard of this? Who knows what in vitro *means? Look at this title: "PETA's Latest Tactic: $1m for Artificial Meat." Do you know what People for the Ethical Treatment of Animals is? What they stand for?* Clarify as needed. *OK, let's dive in and read the article, using your trusty tool of text annotation.* Let kids read individually, allowing them about five minutes to annotate the text as they choose. (See pages 41–49 for text annotation options.)

STEP 3 **Add more information** Now call the class back.

All right, so what did you think? While you were reading, I found this picture for you. This is a hunk of meat grown in a laboratory. Right now it is not in the grocery store, because it would be way too expensive. But when they ramp up production, it will probably become part of our lives. Let kids study and comment on the photo.

STEP 4 **Explain the activity**

So now we're going to use the four corners of our room to have some discussion. In a minute, I'm going to ask you to go and stand in the corner where you agree with the label that's hanging there. So the question is, when artificial meat becomes available, would you eat it? If you say "for sure," go to the corner by my desk. If you say "probably," go stand in the corner by the bookshelf. If you say "probably not," stand by the closet. And if you say "no way, I would never eat that stuff," stand in the corner by the door.

Before you get up, a couple of things: First of all, bring your article, a writing surface, and a pen, so you can compare notes with the people you'll meet. When you arrive and take your position, your job is to talk to some other people who are standing there, and take turns explaining your reasons. If someone says something new or smart, write it down. Find out why you agree.

Now, let's think: how many people can you really talk to at once? Right, one or two at the most. So form into pairs or threes right away when you arrive in the corner. Talk with a couple of people for one or two minutes and then move on. Keep mingling, meeting more and more people, and talking with them about artificial meat. OK? Go!

STRATEGY LESSONS / MOVING CONVERSATIONS

STEP 5 **Monitor and coach** The first time you do this activity, it may feel like the proverbial herding of cats. You'll need to be pretty active, nudging people to pick their corners and keeping them mingling.

STEP 6 **Kids report out** When kids have had a chance to talk with several pairs or threes, call the whole class to attention where they stand. Ask one or two students from each corner to explain why they have taken that position. Probe the thinking. Let kids from the other three corners ask them questions, too. When all corners are heard from, ask: *What could change your mind about this in the future?* Allow time for the same groups to talk over that question, taking notes, and then report out again.

WHERE DO YOU STAND?
is used in Text Set 4

Tips and Variations

■ **EXTENDING THE ACTIVITY** Where Do You Stand? can be a one-issue deal, or it can go on as long as students remain engaged. With this particular article, you could continue as follows:

Let's talk more about eating meat. To start, go and stand where you belong in terms of how often you eat meat.

Corner 1: Every day

Corner 2: Pretty often

Corner 3: Rarely

Corner 4: Never

Why have you chosen to consume meat at this frequency? Talk to the classmates around you. After a few minutes, invite volunteers to share.

You can add related topics as kids are standing. *Now, in your corners, discuss this: Who knows a vegetarian? Who knows a vegan, someone who eats no animal products of any kind? What are their eating rules and restrictions? Talk to several people, and we'll ask a few volunteers to share what they know.*

Now offer another choice: *Here are four reasons people say eating lots of meat is a bad thing. Let's relabel our corners like this:*

1. Negative health effects

2. Pollution from meat production

3. The waste and inefficiency of eating so "high on the food chain"

4. Cruelty to animals

Which one of these reasons do you feel the most concern about or find most interesting to discuss? Choose your corners!

And onward.

■ **THE HUMAN SPECTRUM** Our friend Sara Ahmed, a Chicago middle school teacher, has a version of Four Corners that she calls the Human Spectrum, which is especially good for displaying *predictions* students make about text. Instead of dividing themselves up by their views, kids place themselves on a living continuum based on their confidence in a prediction. Sara uses the spectrum with Jesus Colon's wonderful one-page memoir, "The Choice." In the story, the main character has to decide whether to help a white woman with two kids who is struggling through a subway station late at night. As a black Puerto Rican, Colon is worried about how he will be perceived if he offers to help. It's an elemental choice in his own life—is he going to observe the customary racial barriers and stay away from this woman's problems, or step across those boundaries and choose to be a different kind of person?

Sara copies just the first section of the story, right up to the point where Colon makes his decision. She reads it aloud as kids follow along in their own copies. Then she has them line up in a Human Spectrum, based on their prediction of the ending. "If you are really sure that he's going to help her," Sara says, "stand over on this side of the line. If you are uncertain, stand in the middle, and if you are sure that he will not help the woman, stand at the other end of the line."

When kids take their positions, she has them talk for a minute with students standing next to them, and then asks several to go public, to share their thinking: "Why are you standing where you are? What makes you think this way? What in the story makes you predict this outcome?" After hearing from seven or eight kids, Sara reads the rest of the story aloud. You've never seen students so eager to hear a story! As the ending is revealed, some kids gasp with amazement, others high-five each other, and still others stand there, stunned and pondering. Now, everyone sits down, and a lively whole-class discussion ensues about Colon's choice and why he made it.

The New York Times

PETA's Latest Tactic: $1 Million for Fake Meat

By **JOHN SCHWARTZ**

April 21, 2008

*P*eople for the Ethical Treatment of Animals wants to pay a million dollars for fake meat — even if it has caused a "near civil war" within the organization.

The organization said it would announce plans on Monday for a $1 million prize to the "first person to come up with a method to produce commercially viable quantities of in vitro meat at competitive prices by 2012."

The idea of getting the next Chicken McNugget out of a test tube is not new. For several years, scientists have worked to develop technologies to grow tissue cultures that could be consumed like meat without the expense of land or feed and the disease potential of real meat. An international symposium on the topic was held this month in Norway. The tissue, once grown, could be shaped and given texture with the kinds of additives and structural agents that are now used to give products like soy burgers a more meaty texture.

> The idea of getting the next Chicken McNugget out of a test tube is not new.

New Harvest, a nonprofit organization formed to promote the field, says on its Web site, "Because meat substitutes are produced under controlled conditions impossible to maintain in traditional animal farms, they can be safer, more nutritious, less polluting and more humane than conventional meat."

Jason Matheny, a doctoral student at Johns Hopkins University who formed New Harvest, said the idea of a prize for researchers was promising. Citing the example of the Ansari X Prize, a competition that produced the first privately financed human spacecraft, Mr. Matheny said, "They inspire more dollars spent on a research problem than the prize represents." A founder of PETA, Ingrid Newkirk, said she had been hoping to get the organization involved in advancing in vitro meat technology for at least a decade.

| Strategy 19 | # Gallery Walk |

- Time:
  40 minutes
- Grouping
  Sequence:
  Mobile groups
  of 3, whole class

Smokey lives in Santa Fe, New Mexico, a town that boasts 245 art galleries. On any given Friday evening, a dozen of those galleries will be having an "opening." This means that you can wander in for free snacks, a glass of Chardonnay, and ganders at brand-new artworks. What's not to like?

But what exactly do you *do* in an art gallery or museum? Well, usually you walk around from picture to picture, talking quietly with your companions. When you stop in front of a painting, maybe you try to understand what the artist was aiming for, compare it to other pictures or other artists, or make judgments about the quality of the work…and then, you move on.

That's exactly what happens in our school version of the gallery walk: the teacher or students post some kind of work, thinking, or art; then clusters of kids quietly circulate through the room, studying and responding to other people's thinking.

There are countless variations of gallery walks, as you will see through the rest of this book. The fundamental process involves hanging up various graphic and/or textual displays, and then having kids interact around them in a purposeful way, often leaving behind written comments as they go. A gallery walk can stand on its own, as we describe here, or it can be the culminating activity for many other lessons.

MATERIALS NEEDED

Copy of article for each student, large chart paper, different colored markers, tape, large (4x6 if possible) Post-it notes. (If you don't have any large sticky notes, you can instead hang a couple sheets of plain paper beside each poster when you get to Step 7.) You may want to use a projector to highlight discussion topics (see Tips).

Steps and Teaching Language

STEP 1   **Plan the lesson**   Decide how you will form kids into groups of three. Assemble the materials noted above.

STEP 2   **Explain the process**

Today we are going to read an article and have a discussion about it. Nothing new there, right? But with this text we are going to respond mainly with drawing, and we are going to have our discussion while walking around. Sound good?

STEP 3   **Kids read**   Invite students to read the article, "Motorcycle Helmet Use Laws," using Sketching Through the Text (Strategy 5). The idea is to get kids to respond visually to the article, making drawings in the margins, which they can draw upon to create a quick poster.

STEP 4   **Kids discuss their sketches**

Now, in your groups of three, take about one minute each to share some of your sketches with each other. Each person, hold up a sketch you think is worthwhile, and explain the thinking behind it. Partners, listen carefully, and when it's your turn, share a sketch you made about a different part of the article or that has a different point of view.

STEP 5   **Make a common poster**

Now, drawing on all your sketches and any other images that have popped up in your discussion, you are going to make a poster—another, bigger drawing—that represents your group's responses to the helmet law article. This can be based on one person's sketch or can be something completely new, or it can be a combination of your different sketches. You have to discuss this as a team and decide on a plan.

Don't delegate the drawing to one person; everybody should be drawing a part of the poster. You can use cartoons, stick figures, diagrams, any kind of drawing you want. And you can put in labels or captions or talk balloons to help explain what you are showing. But don't just draw a motorcycle or a helmet. You've got to show your thinking about the article, what you agree or disagree with. What would be good policies about helmets? OK—take seven or eight minutes to create your poster.

STEP 6   **Circulate and confer**   Especially the first time kids do these graphic responses, your coaching will be vital. You'll be lowering their art anxiety, urging kids to manifest reading responses in graphic form, and making sure everyone is holding a pen and using it. But you know what? Practically whatever kids draw can lead to great conversations when the gallery walk commences.

When groups are done, have them hang up their posters at well-spaced intervals around the room.

STEP 7 **Start the gallery walk**

Now, in your groups, you are going to go and look carefully at another group's poster, and talk over what they have created and how it responds to the article. Then, you'll write a response or comment for the authors to read later on. I want you to really shape those sentences together, not just delegate the work to one person. When you are done writing, your scribe will sign the entry with everyone's names and hang it right beside the poster you have been studying. Each time you switch posters, a new person should become your scribe and do the writing. Go alphabetically by last name.

STEP 8 **Explain the timing**

When we start, we'll take about two minutes for viewing and one minute for writing on each poster, and then we'll rotate clockwise around the room. But let's think ahead. The next poster you come to will have comments posted beside it, right? You need to read those ideas too, and maybe factor them into your response to the poster. So, at each stop, I'll give you a little more time for reading, talking, and writing.

Bring your copy of the article so you can refer to your own sketches and notes. Ready? Is there a poster that looks really interesting to you? Well, you better get to it—first come first served, and only one group at a poster at a time. Go!

STEP 9 **Monitor groups** As kids work, circulate and confer, coaching and questioning groups as needed. As always, you are looking for great quotes or examples that you can use to feed the discussion later.

STEP 10 **Regather and debrief** Once students have rotated through some or all of the posters—don't let the energy flag—have them return to their own posters. There, they should read and discuss all the written comments. Then, engage everyone in a standing whole-class discussion of the issues raised by the article. Try to dig out the agreements, controversies, and range of ideas that emerged from the various posters. Don't plod through every poster. Maybe just ask: *Was there a particular poster that really got you going? Which one made you think hardest or argue the most?* Let the responses spark an authentic conversation.

GALLERY WALK is used in Text Sets 4, 6, 8

Tips and Variations

■ **GET THE RIGHT ARTICLE** This activity lives or dies by the debatability of the article you choose, and its ability to put pictures in kids' heads as they read. This motorcycle topic sure delivers! Be ready for kids to ask for red markers as they draw their motorcycle crash pictures. Ugh. But just as we invite *graphic* responses (in both senses of the term), we recognize that sometimes students (read: boys) need to joke about life and death stuff, at least at first.

PUSH STUDENTS TO THINK DEEPLY ABOUT THE TOPIC Below are some questions that our students have come up with during gallery walks on this article. You can freeze people at any point in a gallery walk, and either toss out discussion topics or let kids volunteer them. Some questions that have engaged our students:

1. Who knows about the motorcycle helmet laws in our state? Are they appropriate?

2. Why do you think that car crashes have been going down and motorcycle crashes going up?

3. Why do you think that motorcycle riders love their sport so much?

4. Why do you think that so many motorcycle riders are against helmet laws?

5. Motorcycle riders have a saying: "There's only two kinds of riders, the ones that have been down, and the ones that are going down." What do you think that means?

6. Should people be able to do dangerous things if they want—like rock climbing, hang gliding, or riding a motorcycle without a helmet?

7. Is it fair for the public to pay the police, fire, and hospital costs of people who get injured doing dangerous things?

8. If you could ride or own a motorcycle someday, would you?

9. If there is a mandatory helmet law in a state, what should be the fine or punishment for ignoring it?

GOING DEEPER Another important, if distant, variation of Gallery Walk is the "science fair" version. We know, we know, most science fair projects are deadly, but hear us out. In this iteration, only three or four groups put up their posters at once, and the creators of each display stand beside their work and formally present it. The other students put their own posters aside and become the audience. At the teacher's signal, the audience distributes itself equally among the presenting groups.

The duty of each presenting team is to give a one-minute "spiel" or presentation on their thinking, explaining the graphic, and then answering questions from the visiting students. The visitors are required to pose questions and jot down what they are learning so they will be ready to report back later. This process takes five minutes max. Then the teacher calls for audience members to thank the presenters, move along to a different poster group, and repeat the cycle. Each group will present its poster twice, to two sets of visitors. Then everyone switches roles; the groups that have been serving as the audience post their charts, and the process repeats. Students don't hear a presentation from every group, but by both presenting and serving as an audience twice, they still get to delve more deeply into the topic.

If kids have engaged in a larger study, reading multiple sources, and dug more deeply into a topic, you can ramp up the gallery walk into a wonderful show-what-you-know event. When we use this variant, we also require each presenting group to create an attractive, engaging handout for all visitors—so their performance includes a prepared speech, answering questions on the spot, and writing a brochure.

Students create a poster

Motorcycle Helmet Use Laws

March 2010

Compared with cars, motorcycles are an especially dangerous form of travel. The federal government estimates that per mile traveled, the number of deaths on motorcycles in 2009 was about 37 times the number in cars. Motorcyclist deaths have been rising in recent years—more than doubling by 2008 from the record low in 1997. In 2008, more motorcyclists died in crashes than in any year since the National Highway Traffic Safety Administration (NHTSA) began collecting these fatal crash data. In contrast, passenger vehicle occupant deaths reached a record low in 2008.

In the event of a crash,

unhelmeted motorcyclists are three times more likely than helmeted riders to suffer traumatic brain injuries.

Motorcycles often have excessive performance capabilities, including especially rapid acceleration and high top speeds. They are less stable than cars in emergency braking and less visible to other motorists. Motorcyclists are more prone to crash injuries than car occupants because motorcycles are unenclosed, leaving riders vulnerable to contact with hard road surfaces.

Helmets decrease the severity of head injuries, the likelihood of death, and the overall cost of medical care. They are designed to cushion and protect riders' heads from the impact of a crash. Just like safety belts in cars, helmets cannot provide total protection against head injury or death, but they do reduce the incidence of both. The NHTSA estimates that motorcycle helmets reduce the likelihood of crash fatality by 37 percent. Helmets are highly effective in preventing brain injuries, which often require extensive treatment and may result in lifelong disability. In the event of a crash, unhelmeted motorcyclists are three times more likely than helmeted riders to suffer traumatic brain injuries.

Only 20 American states have laws requiring riders to wear helmets, while the rest have no laws or only require young riders (usually under 18) to wear helmets. Laws requiring motorcyclists to wear helmets are in effect in most countries outside the United States. Among them are Andorra, Argentina, Australia, Austria, Belgium, Brazil, Bulgaria, Canada, Czech Republic, Denmark, Finland, France, Germany, Hungary, India, Indonesia, Ireland, Italy, Japan, Latvia, Liechtenstein, Luxembourg, Malaysia, Netherlands, New Zealand, Norway, Poland, Portugal, Romania, Russia, San Marino, Singapore, Slovakia, South Africa, Spain, Sweden, Switzerland, Thailand, United Kingdom, and Venezuela.

STRATEGY LESSONS / MOVING CONVERSATIONS

Carousel Brainstorming

Strategy 20

- Time:
  40 minutes
- Grouping
  Sequence:
  Groups of 4 that
  also break down
  into pairs; whole
  class

Here's another up-and-about discussion structure that really gets kids thinking. Remember how we said in Strategy 2 that kids should *enter text thinking*? Carousel brainstorming is an excellent way for students to start engaging with a topic *before they read.*

Working in groups of four, students visit several different stations and record their reactions to specific prompts or questions on pieces of chart paper. With each group's comments identified by a different colored marker, kids read and discuss what previous groups have written, as well as add their own new ideas to the mix. Carousel brainstorming is great for introducing new topics or when understanding a text requires students to make consistent personal connections with their own experience and background knowledge.

MATERIALS NEEDED

Copy of article for each student, discussion prompts written on sheets of chart paper (see Step 2), different colored markers, projectable list of questions to prompt discussion.

Steps and Teaching Language

STEP 1 **Prepare the lesson** Decide on the size of the groups (four is recommended, three or five can work) and determine how many groups you will have altogether. Also decide on how the groups will be formed (already established groups, number off, etc.).

STEP 2 **Determine questions/prompts** Later in this lesson, kids will be reading an article about employers cracking down on employees who have bad health habits. So, to begin kids' thinking about that subject, create three or four questions, headings, or statements that have potential for prereading discussion. Here are some ideas:

- What foods do you eat that you think are unhealthy?

- If it's unhealthy, why do people smoke, eat fattening foods, and not exercise?

- What do you do for exercise?

- What would get people to eat healthier, stop smoking, and exercise?

Write each prompt on a separate sheet of chart paper. If you have more groups than prompts, make more than one chart for some of the prompts so that all groups can work at a different station during the brainstorming. Either post them on the walls around the room or spread them out on desks or the floor.

STEP 3 **Give carousel directions** Have students form into groups in the way you have determined and assign each group to a specific chart. As you pass out a different colored marker to each group, say: *As you work at each chart, read the prompt and talk about possible responses. Remember, brainstorming means thinking quickly and in quantity. Get down as many ideas as you can, and don't debate with each other. More is better. Have one person scribe the group's ideas on the chart with your marker. Do not move to another chart until I tell you.*

STEP 4 **Groups brainstorm at each chart** Give groups just a minute at the first chart, not so much time that all possibilities are exhausted. Rather than time each station exactly, monitor the groups carefully and decide when they've written enough and it's time to move on. When time is up, say:

Freeze. Stop writing and listen carefully. All groups need to move [indicate direction: left, right, clockwise, up the row, etc.] *to the next chart.*

From now on, you must not only read the prompt but also read and discuss the previous groups' responses. Try to use what's already on the chart to generate new ideas. This is called piggybacking ideas. Jot your group's new ideas on the chart below the previous responses. Also, make sure you use a different scribe at each station. Not only should I see your group's color on each chart, but I should also see different handwriting on each chart.

STEP 5 **Monitor groups** Continue monitoring the groups as they work through the charts and adjust the time accordingly. When groups get to their last chart, it will usually be much harder for them to add ideas to an already long list and, therefore, they will probably need less time toward the end of the carousel brainstorming.

STEP 6 **Students review charts** After the charts are completed, have students revisit the charts in a gallery walk (see Strategy 19) so that they have the chance to read the comments that were recorded in response to their own.

STEP 7 **Students read and annotate** After students have returned to their seats, pass out the article "Employers Get Tough on Health" and give instructions for annotating the text.

We spent the last few minutes brainstorming what people do or do not do to stay healthy. As you read this article, I want you to think about and look back at the charts. (Make sure charts are posted and can be seen from students' desks.) *Underline passages that stand out to you, and in the margin draw a connection between the underline and something that came up on one of the charts.*

CAROUSEL BRAIN-STORMING is used in Text Set 4

STEP 8 **Partners share**

Groups of four, split into pairs. Now turn to your partner and compare your annotations. What connections did you notice between our charts and the information in the article? What were some ideas that came up that no chart mentioned?

STEP 9 **Share with the whole class** Invite some of the pairs to share highlights and point out specific chart details that were particularly relevant to the reading.

Tips and Variations

■ **DON'T TRY THIS ON THE FIRST DAY OF SCHOOL** Carousel brainstorming depends on students being able to conduct themselves positively as they move in groups around the room. It tends to work much better a few weeks into the school year, when students have gotten to know each other and internalized your collaborative classroom norms.

■ **REDO CHARTS LATER** If you use carousel brainstorming to introduce important concepts for a unit of study versus an individual reading, save the initial charts. Using blank chart paper, repeat the brainstorming again at the end of the unit using the same prompts. Afterwards, compare the initial chart responses with those completed later. Your students will be amazed at how much more they know about the content topic at the end of the unit compared to when they started the study.

What foods do you think are unhealthy?

- McDonald's
- Pizza
- Cheese fries
- Coke
- **Candy**
- Bosco sticks
- Double cheeseburger
- Hot dogs

If it's unhealthy, why do people smoke, eat fattening foods, and not exercise?

- **Stress**
- No time to exercise
- **Exercise is work**
- McDonald's tastes good
- **Fast food is convenient**
- Friends
- **Play video games**

What do you do for exercise?

- Football
- Weightlifting
- **Aerobics**
- Dance
- Skateboard
- Bike
- **Nothing**
- Wii

What would get people to eat healthier, stop smoking, lose weight, and exercise?

- **Better fast food**
- Exercise buddy
- Time to exercise in school
- Time to exercise on job
- Better food in school cafeteria
- Low-calorie, good-tasting fast food
- **Weight Watchers**
- Stop-smoking programs

Carousel brainstorming example

Employers get tough on health
Some take punitive steps against smokers, overweight workers

By Tim Jones, *Chicago Tribune*
September 24, 2007

Get ready to say goodbye to the days of high-fat meals, junk food snacks and that after-work cigarette you always enjoy smoking -- at least if you intend to have a job and health insurance. The rules of the workplace are changing, and personal behavior and lifestyle habits -- those unrelated to what you do at work -- are now fair game for employers determined to cut health-care costs.

If you smoke, you may not get hired and you could get fired. If your cholesterol is too high, you can pay higher premiums for your insurance. The same goes for blood pressure, body mass and blood glucose levels. The requirements embraced by a growing number of companies are encroaching on privacy and raising questions about who will qualify for health insurance, as well as employment.

The Cleveland Clinic on Sept. 1 started nicotine testing in pre-employment physicals. If nicotine is found, applicants will not be hired.

At Weyco Inc., a company based in Lansing, Michigan, drew national attention in 2005 when it fired four employees who used tobacco. Weyco performs random testing every three months, usually of about 30 employees. Workers are summoned to blow into a Breathalyzer-like device that measures carbon monoxide levels. If the reading is high, employees take a urine test. If they fail the urinalysis twice they will be dismissed.

Although thousands of employers have put in place incentives for their workers to live healthier lifestyles, the vast majority of employers have not yet embraced the approach of penalizing employees who don't satisfy medical or behavioral dictates. But punitive measures are gaining a foothold in the workplace, according to lawyers and groups that follow insurance and employment trends, because health-care costs are growing at high-single-digit to double-digit rates annually.

Gary Climes, vice president of Meritain Health Michigan, which now owns Weyco, noted that the firings didn't violate Michigan law and that the 150 employees at the Okemos-based company have, over time, accepted the rules. "It really comes down to a personal choice as far as do you want to be employed here," Climes said. Since 2005 when Weyco instituted the wellness policy that includes the smoking ban, health insurance costs have increased by no more than 2 percent a year, well below the national average.

Handwritten annotations:

How can a job tell you what to eat? What if you work at McDonalds. Will they fire you if you eat their food? Will they pay for you to go to a gym?

Wow! Is this legal? Quitting smoking is hard - will unemployment help people quit? Does Weyco do anything to help people quit?

Jobs ar stressful as is and lots of people work long hours - that's why they eat fast food and don't exercise!

Plan works. How does average employee feel about Weyco? Are these people really healthier thanks to company policy?

Text annotation based on carousel brainstorming (shown on an earlier version of this article)

Chicago Tribune

Employers get tough on health

Some take punitive steps against smokers, overweight workers

September 24, 2007
By Tim Jones

Get ready to say goodbye to the days of high-fat meals, junk food snacks and that after-work cigarette you always enjoy smoking—at least if you intend to have a job and health insurance. The rules of the workplace are changing, and personal behavior and lifestyle habits—those unrelated to what you do at work—are now fair game for employers determined to cut health-care costs.

If you smoke, you may not get hired and you could get fired. If your cholesterol is too high, you can pay higher premiums for your insurance. The same goes for blood pressure, body mass and blood glucose levels. The requirements embraced by a growing number of companies are encroaching on privacy and raising questions about who will qualify for health insurance, as well as employment.

The Cleveland Clinic on Sept. 1 started nicotine testing in pre-employment physicals. If nicotine is found, applicants will not be hired.

Weyco Inc., a company based in Lansing, Michigan, drew national attention in 2005 when it fired four employees who used tobacco. Weyco performs random testing every three months, usually of about 30 employees. Workers are summoned to blow into a Breathalyzer-like device that measures carbon monoxide levels. If the reading is high, employees take a urine test. If they fail the urinalysis twice they will be dismissed.

Although thousands of employers have put in place incentives for their workers to live healthier lifestyles, the vast majority of employers have not yet embraced the approach of penalizing employees who don't satisfy medical or behavioral dictates. But punitive measures are gaining a foothold in the workplace, according to lawyers and groups that follow insurance and employment trends, because health-care costs are growing at high-single-digit to double-digit rates annually.

The rules of the workplace are changing,

and personal behavior and lifestyle habits—those unrelated to what you do at work—are now fair game for employers determined to cut health-care costs.

Gary Climes, vice president of Meritain Health Michigan, which now owns Weyco, noted that the firings didn't violate Michigan law and that the 150 employees at the Okemos-based company have, over time, accepted the rules. "It really comes down to a personal choice as far as do you want to be employed here," Climes said. Since 2005 when Weyco instituted the wellness policy that includes the smoking ban, health insurance costs have increased by no more than 2 percent a year, well below the national average.

Strategy 21 | # Tableaux

- Time:
  30 minutes
- Grouping
  Sequence:
  Groups of
  4 or 5

Have you ever seen the Iwo Jima Memorial or one of its reproductions around the country? It's a powerful image. You cannot help but be moved at the likenesses of six heroic GIs struggling to raise the American flag over a still-frenzied battlefield in WWII.

The Iwo Jima statue is a *tableau:* it's a frozen scene that communicates a huge amount of information and feeling.

We are always trying to get kids to visualize what they read, to make sensory images in their heads. Creating tableaux takes visualization a step further than the sketching we introduced in Strategy 5. Now, we ask students to reread and rethink text in order to create

Iwo Jima Memorial

their own living statues that represent meaning. Developing complex tableaux scenes demands that groups reconstruct information and ideas in a whole different medium from print. The physicality of tableaux is a fresh way to help students rehearse and remember information. And, since students get out of their seats and dramatically compose meaning, tableaux are especially appealing to movement-starved boys. And finally, because the actors in tableaux are motionless, this activity doesn't trigger the drama phobia of more theatrical activities.

MATERIALS NEEDED

Copy of article for each student, projectable image of the Iwo Jima Memorial or other dramatic statue.

Steps and Teaching Language

STEP 1 **Introduce the article and give reading instructions**

This article focuses on seven behaviors that prevent employees from doing well on the job. As you read this article, I want you to stop after each number and imagine a work scene that would illustrate the point. If you like, you can draw a quick sketch next to the point.

STEP 2 **Introduction to tableaux** As students finish up, give them the next instruction. *Today you are going to discuss what you read in a different way. You are going to work with your group to create a dramatic statue that depicts one of the points presented in the article.*

Now project an image of a dramatic statue, such as the Iwo Jima Memorial:

As you take a look at this famous statue, I want you to notice how it creates drama:

The figures are close together.

The figures stand at varying levels.

The gestures and facial expressions portray movement and tell a story.

STEP 3 **Form groups and explain the assignment** After they view the example, allow student groups to pick a section of the article to portray physically, or you can assign article sections yourself.

As you work to create your tableau, remember what makes a statue dramatic. Also, everyone in your group must be part of the statue. To create a good statue, you've got to experiment with different poses before you find what works best. That means you've got to get out of your seats and try out lots of stuff.

STEP 4 **Monitor group work** Give students five to seven minutes and warn them when they have just a couple minutes left. Cruise the room to keep students on task and give posing suggestions to those groups that seem stuck. Don't be surprised to see some pretty creative ideas take life. Expect to see another validation of the theory of multiple intelligences. Often, the kids you'd least expect will really take to this activity.

STEP 5 **Groups perform tableaux** Once time is up, all students should return to their seats for the performances. You may have groups perform in numerical order of the article points, or you may ask for volunteers. For best results, have audience members close their eyes briefly as each team sets up its tableau. Then upon opening their eyes, they see the completed scene frozen before them. If you are not going in article order, instruct groups to hold their pose while the rest of the class attempts to name which point the group is trying to illustrate.

TABLEAUX is used in Text Sets 9, 10

Tips and Variations

■ **SELECTING STATUES** Since kids will be creating tableaux in groups of four or five, complex, multifigure statues make the best examples. The classic general on horseback is not nearly as interesting or instructive as the Iwo Jima Memorial or Rodin's *The Burghers of Calais* (which portrays a city's leaders roped together, being led to their execution).

■ **SPEAKING STATUES** The statues do not necessarily have to be silent. You or another student can tap a statue figure lightly. This signals that the figure needs to explain what they're doing in the scene. You or audience members can even interview them.

■ **CLASSROOM ACTION STATUES** Instead of having students create a work scene tableau, ask them to figure out the classroom equivalent of each annoying behavior and enact that.

Sample tableau: Failing to follow through. This employee (seated) has made so many mistakes, his work is garbage and the project is in jeopardy, as evidenced by the looks of consternation by his supervisors.

Sample tableau: Asking too many questions. These clueless employees are giving their boss (seated) a headache!

Are You Driving Your Boss Crazy?

Seven Behaviors Bosses Dislike

By Robert Half International
msn.careerbuilder.com

In today's workplace, it's a good idea to remain on the boss's good side. Your relationship with this person can be a major factor in not only your on-the-job happiness but also your career success. Unfortunately, your manager may not always tell you if your behavior is driving him or her nuts. Here are seven actions to avoid:

1. Turning down new assignments.

Your supervisor comes to you to say that you'd be the ideal person to train a new staff member. She wants to know if you have the time to take on this task. You do, but you're not interested in the responsibility, so you decline the offer. Bad move. A pattern of "no's" can convince your manager to stop offering you opportunities, including ones you might be interested in.

2. Being "high-maintenance."

Do you require constant attention in order to remain productive? Your "high maintenance" may prevent your manager from attending to important tasks and impede his effectiveness.

3. Asking too many questions.

Repeatedly asking the same question is a surefire way to annoy your supervisor. Always listen carefully when your boss is speaking and try to seek clarification on new projects from the get-go.

4. Failing to follow through.

You're rushing to finish a presentation for your boss. After reviewing it, he notes a few typographical errors that you should have caught. Even when things are hectic, keeping a keen eye on every detail is necessary to impress your supervisor.

5. Refusing to admit your mistakes.

Creating an excuse to justify poor performance is dishonest and unprofessional. If you make a mistake, admit it and then go further by devising a plan for both correcting and avoiding similar incidents.

6. Waving the red flag after the ship has sunk.

Your manager has asked you to compile a complicated report by the end of the week. Friday afternoon, you realize you can't finish it in time and break the news to your boss. Let your supervisor know as soon as you sense a problem. With advance notice, your manager can often work with you to stave off disaster.

7. Fueling the rumor mill.

Above all, supervisors seek employees with a positive outlook. Enthusiasm is contagious, and these individuals are able to influence the attitudes of others. You don't want to be the one at the water cooler who spreads gossip or complains.

Quotation Mingle

Strategy 22

- Time:
  20 minutes
- Grouping
  Sequence:
  Rolling pairs,
  small groups,
  whole class

Have you done any mingling lately? You know—that social process where you wander around a gathering and spend a few moments with lots of different people? Mingling is exactly what we are usually trying to *prevent* in our classrooms, right? But for the following lesson, it's definitely legalized and lionized. Mingling rocks.

We're always trying to get kids engaged in a text—even before they read it. We want them predicting and hypothesizing, posing questions, and drawing inferences before they even open the book. Our buddy Jeff Wilhelm (2001) calls this "front-loading," or investing class time and activities in advance of reading to guarantee better comprehension later.

This strategy, also known as "Tea Party" (Beers 2006) is the most sociable form of front-loading we know. Mingling activities like this one get kids out of their seats, working purposefully and briskly with a succession of classmates. In this one, we expect kids to connect with eight to ten other kids in seven minutes. It's like a cocktail party without the cocktails.

MATERIALS NEEDED

Copy of article for each student, sentence cards or strips as described in Step 1.

Steps and Teaching Language

STEP 1 **Prepare the materials** Extract about eight interesting sentences from an engaging article and copy them onto index cards or paper strips. We have chosen some sentences from an article about the growing driving risks being taken by teenage girls (see page 136). You'll need one card or strip for each student in your class, so four copies each of eight sentences (counting on our fingers here) should yield thirty-two mini-texts. Yeah, a bit of prep, but these can be used for future classes.

STEP 2 **Describe the activity**

Today we are going to read a really interesting article, but for once I'm not going to tell you the topic beforehand. You'll have to guess. I've taken eight sentences from the article and copied them for you on these cards. We're going to have a "quotation mingle," where we take our cards and walk around the room and compare our quotes to ones other people have, one at a time.

You know what mingling is, don't you? Like when people arrive at a party or a wedding and everyone kind of walks around saying hi, making a little small talk with everyone, spending a minute or two with each person? Get it? So we're going to mingle and have some small talk about our sentences from the mystery article.

Your job is to figure out what this article is about by reading the sentence you have, and then hearing seven other sentences and talking with the people who have them. OK? With each person you talk to, discuss what the whole article might be about. The more people you talk to, the more quotes you'll see—plus your partners can tell you about other quotes they've seen. So as our quotation mingle goes on, you should be better and better able to figure out what the whole article is about.

When you need a partner, wave your card in the air, like this. When you find a partner, take turns reading your quotations aloud—then talk. Try to see ten people. There are only eight different quotations out there, so you may see some quotes twice. Ready? Let's mingle!

STEP 3 **Monitor and coach** Let kids mingle for six to eight minutes. Be in the crowd, urging kids to switch partners to keep it brisk and lively. Be a partner to lost or hiding kids.

STEP 4 **Call time** Have everyone freeze in place. Ask each pair to join up with another pair to form a group of four. Attach any stragglers, one at a time, making a couple of groups of five if needed

Now, in your groups of four, talk about what you think this mystery article will be about. Between the four of you, chances are you have heard all eight sentences, though you have only four on your own cards, right? Be sure and tell what you think will be the main points of the article. Go!

STEP 5 **Monitor** Allow three minutes of work time as kids discuss, still standing up. Circulate, confer, and look for interesting ideas or quotes you can call on later. When time is almost up, warn kids: *OK, we're going to get back together in one minute. Before we do, each group must come up with what you think will be the title or headline of this article, word for word. Figure out a good title and each of you write it down.* Allow two more minutes for this.

STEP 6 **Share with the whole class** Reconvene the class and invite discussion about the main predictions kids made while mingling. Then, ask each group to slowly and clearly read aloud its proposed title for the article. Both you and the other students can comment on titles, noting their overlaps and differences.

STEP 7 **Read the article** Now (at last!) it's time to reveal the text and let kids read it. Have students use text coding (especially the ✓ and **X**, as seen on page 47) to flag the spots where their predictions are confirmed or contradicted. Then, regather in small groups or as a class to talk, first about the content of the article, and then about how the predicting process worked.

QUOTATION MINGLE is used in Text Set 2

Tips and Variations

■ **WHEN KIDS FINALLY READ** What the quotation mingle accomplishes, in a sense, is getting kids primed to "read with a question in mind" (see Strategy 2). Expect to see some pretty active reading as kids gradually come to those familiar sentences in the text. You may even hear out-loud exclamations ("I knew it!") as kids find their predictions confirmed or contradicted. This is a great example of the payoff of front-loading and sociable interaction.

■ **MAKE YOUR OWN** The key to creating your own quotation mingles is to pick a mix of sentences that give good clues and context, but also ones that create more curiosity, or present puzzles or contradictions. Go for a range of sentence types: descriptions, quotations, statistics, and so on. Given a full set of six or eight sentences, a reasonable person should be able to reconstruct—oops, preconstruct—the gist of the piece. For another example, using a Civil War historical novel, see page 162.

■ **KEEP 'EM MOVING** One predictable and rather pleasant danger of mingling is that pairs get so absorbed in their conversations that they don't want to move on, thus clogging up the mingle. For this activity, the *quantity* of different contacts matters a lot, so that's why you need to be in the crowd, breaking things up and moving people around.

Chicago Tribune

Driving Risk Gap Between Teen Girls, Boys Narrows

February 17, 2010
By Julie Wernau
Tribune Newspapers

Molly Sutton finds it challenging to ignore a text message when she's driving. The 18-year-old high school senior said it's hard to wait until the next stoplight.

"I know it's not safe because there's proof with all the crashes and everything, but it's one of those things you don't think much of or you think you still have some control over," she said.

Her friend Claire Quinn, 18, finds it annoying when someone in front of her drives slowly, but she doesn't think she's a risky driver.

"Where do I start?" said Quinn's passenger, Matt Parilli, 17, cataloguing his friend's driving shortcomings. "She's crying in the car because there's snow on the ground, or she's in a rush to get to school."

Since the dawn of the automobile, teenage boys have been pegged as the more aggressive and risky drivers, with inflated insurance bills to prove it. But the gap in driving risks appears to be closing, according to insurance industry officials and a new report from a major insurer.

> *"I know it's not safe because there's proof with all the crashes and everything, but it's one of those things you don't think much of or you think you still have some control over."*

The Allstate Foundation, part of insurance giant Allstate Corp., says in a newly released "State of Teen Driving Report" that teenage girls admit to speeding, texting and acting aggressively behind the wheel more often than their male counterparts.

The trend hasn't translated into females becoming as big a risk behind the wheel as males, according to insurers. But if the trend continues, that could result in higher insurance rates down the road.

"Experience still shows female drivers are safer than boys at this age,"

Allstate spokesman Raleigh Floyd said. "Until those figures change, our rating isn't going to change."

"We've seen the difference between young men and young women getting smaller," DeFalco said. "There is still a gap, but it's getting smaller all the time."

According to the Allstate study, one in four teen girls reported frequently reading and writing texts and e-mails while driving, compared with 15 percent of boys.

We've seen the difference between young men and young women getting smaller. There is still a gap, but it's getting smaller all the time.

"They're bored while driving, so they try to find other things to do," said Kathy Clausen, co-owner of A-Adams School of Driving. "Most of them will tell you their parents do it."

Clausen said instructors preach to their teen drivers about the dangers of using a cell phone or texting while driving. "Texting is so insane," she said. "I can't believe people would think for a second they could handle that."

According to the National Association of Insurance Commissioners, gender-based insurance rates are a tradition in the insurance world. Higher insurance rates for young male drivers related to the fact that they drove more frequently and, therefore, had a greater risk of getting into a crash than young female drivers, a spokesman said.

"I think probably the biggest culprit is driver distraction," said Belden, adding that texting is a standout factor. "It's a trend with everybody, but teens tend to text more. Between DVD players and video game systems and things that people are putting into vehicles, there are lots of distractions, for teens in particular who are less experienced in driving."

Kristen Marzano, 17, has had her license for about five months and acknowledged that sometimes she puts on her makeup or fixes her hair in the car—or tries to fiddle with the adaptor for her MP3 player. "It's mostly I wait until the last minute to do everything," she said. "If I'm going to drive, I'm running out the door, dropping things. I guess it's just being disorganized."

In the Allstate study, 16 percent of teen girls admitted to aggressive behavior behind the wheel compared with 13 percent of teen boys, but Marzano disagreed.

"I have an older brother; he just turned 20. Driving with him before I got my license, he seemed to be more angry whenever someone cut him off or took his parking spot," she said. "He got pretty flustered."

Today, young men pay between 20 percent and 30 percent more than young women.

"Texting is so insane," she said.

Molly Sutton finds it challenging to ignore a text message when she's driving.

Teenage girls admit to speeding, texting and acting aggressively behind the wheel more often than their male counterparts.

"Where do I start?"
said Quinn's passenger, Matt Parilli, 17, cataloguing his friend's driving shortcomings.

"Most of them will tell you their parents do it."

But if the trend continues, that could result in higher insurance rates down the road.

"She's crying in the car because there's snow on the ground, or she's in a rush to get to school."

Strategy 23

Jigsaw

- Time:
  20 minutes

- Grouping
  Sequence:

  Pairs,
  whole class

One of the most pernicious myths in our school system is that all kids must study the exact same subject matter, at the same time, to the same depth. Often, learning has much more staying power when kids become *specialists* in a single, narrower subtopic. (If you missed it, revisit pages 23–26; we talked about this at some length in Chapter 1.)

This lesson gives kids basic practice in jigsawing, using just two articles and working in pairs. When we create jigsaw text sets about a topic, we are looking for multiple sources that work as proverbial puzzle pieces—five different versions of the topic, five attitudes or points of view, or five different examples—so that when kids blend their thinking, a rich, three-dimensional version of the topic becomes clear. In Text Set 1, for example, kids each choose to read about one of five different invasive species, from snakes to mollusks—but when they pool their learning, they discover the common underlying processes—how all alien species must arrive, survive, and thrive.

Once kids are good at jigsawing, you can hand them multiarticle text sets and ask them to dig out the overlaps, contrasts, and key ideas for themselves. But for this first time, we'll just use two articles and help kids build a list of things to watch for before they read. As this lesson unfolds, you will see that it incorporates elements of many other strategies introduced earlier.

MATERIALS NEEDED

Copy of both articles for each pair; projector for creating class lists, if desired.

Steps and Teaching Language

STEP 1 **Activate background knowledge**

Please form into pairs for this activity, and say hi to each other. Good. Today we are going to read a little bit about cloning. Has everyone heard that word? Have you ever read about it or studied it in school? Yes? Why don't you talk to each other for about two minutes and jot down a list of what you know or think you know about cloning.

Allow two minutes of work time, as you circulate and coach.

STEP 2 **Review background knowledge** Invite volunteers to share pieces of their background knowledge and make a list of this information. Probe thinking with questions like: *Where did you learn that? Do you think that it's reliable info? Anybody else have other ideas?* Be sure students understand that a clone is an exact genetic replica of the original creature.

STEP 3 **Help kids predict questions an article might answer**

In a minute we'll find out how much of your background knowledge is correct, and what else we can learn about cloning. Today I've brought two articles—one about cloning cats and one about cloning dogs. Do we have any dog lovers here today? Cat people?

Has anyone ever had a pet that was so good you'd like to have another one just like it? Or had a pet die, and the family wished they could have cloned it, so it would sort of live forever? Anyway, that's what these articles are about—the possibility of cloning cats and dogs. What do you think an article like this would probably include? What questions about dog or cat cloning would you want an article to answer?

Invite volunteers to help the class build a list, which will probably include items like these:

Class Question List on Cloning

1. How do they do it? What's the actual process of cloning?

2. What's the success rate? How effective is it?

3. Are the cloned animals normal?

4. Are they really identical?

5. Who's doing the cloning and why?

6. What are the uses of cloning? What's it good for?

7. Does anyone oppose it? Who and why?

8. Can we clone humans?

9. Is cloning right/ethical/OK?

Be sure to number and list the questions as kids offer them. If students do not come up with many of the items on this list, add some key questions yourself. For this first go-round with jigsawing, we want to give kids an explicit checklist of topics to look for as they read. When you've finished compiling the list, say: *OK, good. I'll keep this projected so you can refer to it as you read.*

STEP 4 **Kids choose and read articles** With students still in pairs, hand out one copy of each article to each pair. Let partners decide who will read which one. Then have students silently read their articles, using the class question list numbers to code the text. In other words, when a reader finds some information that answers question 1, they mark a 1 in the margin, and so forth (see Strategy 4, Text Coding).

STEP 5 **Pairs discuss** Now, have pairs talk about their dog and cat articles. They should use their text codes to remember where they found answers or information about some of the questions on the class list. Allow about five minutes for this as you circulate, listen, confer, and jot down teaching points. (See Strategy 1, Turn and Talk.)

STEP 6 **Share** Reconvene the class and ask students to share what they have learned about cat and dog cloning, following the list order. Make a two-column chart on the board, Dogs/Cats, and fill it out as a group. You can be pretty methodical about this: *How well does dog cloning work? How well does cat cloning work?* Make sure to emphasize when information overlaps—facts about cloning that are common—as well as differences between the two species. (See Strategy 6, Two-Column Notes.)

JIGSAW is used in Text Sets 1, 3, 4, 6, 7, 9

Tips and Variations

■ **THE THEORY OF JIGSAWING** As responsible teachers, we sometimes get nervous when we think of individual students learning different things—or everyone *not* learning the same things. Of course, there are some things all kids ought to know. And we have state tests that vigorously enforce the inclusion of these items.

But think how knowledge works in any setting other than the classroom. In real-life projects, a group's members tend to specialize, becoming experts in certain tasks or topics. In healthy organizations, it makes sense to jigsaw; everybody takes on a different piece of the puzzle. Then, when we put it all together, our result is better and smarter than if we all had tried to "specialize" in everything.

When we follow the dominant coverage model of curriculum, where we teachers essentially tell everything to students, kids end up with shallow knowledge on almost any given topic. With jigsawing, each kid slows down and goes deeper into a part of the topic, becoming a bit of a specialist. Then, the students teach each other about their chosen topics—at the time of need, at the point of use.

■ **ARTICLE SELECTION** When choosing tandem articles, be sure they are structurally similar. That is, try to find a pair where each covers many of the same subtopics, though differently.

■ **QUESTION LISTS** When helping kids create their question list, make sure each question is actually answered in the articles. If a kid offers a totally off-the-wall topic that you know is not addressed in the dog and cat pieces, diplomatically omit it so readers don't later go on a wild goose chase for nonexistent information.

■ **DEBATE AT THE END** You may want to save the ethical questions for last, because they will probably provoke the most lively discussion—and because kids will be better informed if they review all the factual information before launching into right-and-wrong debates. But now that we think of it, sometimes there's no way of holding those issues back!

Koreans produce world's first cloned dog

The Associated Press, March 8, 2006

Snuppy, the cloned Afghan hound

South Korea's pioneering stem cell scientist has cloned a dog, smashing another biological barrier and reigniting a fierce ethical debate—while producing a perky, lovable puppy.

The researchers, led by Woo-Suk Hwang, insist they cloned an Afghan hound, a resplendent supermodel in a world of mutts, only to help investigate human disease, including the possibility of producing stem cells for treatment purposes.

The researchers nicknamed their canine creation Snuppy, for "Seoul National University puppy," a reference to Hwang's lab. One of the dog's co-creators, Gerald Schatten of the University of Pittsburgh School of Medicine, described Snuppy, now 14 weeks old, as "a frisky, healthy, normal, rambunctious puppy."

But others immediately renewed calls for a global ban on human reproductive cloning before the technology moves any farther.

"Successful cloning of an increasing number of species confirms the general impression that it would be possible to clone any mammalian species, including humans," said Ian Wilmut, a reproductive biologist at the University of Edinburgh who produced the first cloned mammal, Dolly the sheep, from an adult cell nearly a decade ago. But Dolly died prematurely in 2003 after developing cancer and arthritis.

Researchers have since cloned cats, goats, cows, mice, pigs, rabbits, horses, deer, mules and gaur, a large wild ox of Southeast Asia. So far, efforts to clone a monkey or another primate with the same techniques have failed.

Wilmut and others complimented Hwang's achievement, but they said politicians and scientists must face the larger and more delicate issue — how to extend research without crossing the moral boundary of duplicating human life in the lab.

How they did it

On scientific terms, the experiment's success was mixed. Like Dolly, Snuppy was created using a method called somatic cell nuclear transfer. Scientists took a skin cell from the ear of a 3-year-old male Afghan hound and extracted genetic material from the nucleus. They transferred it to an unfertilized egg whose nucleus was removed. The reconstructed egg holding the DNA from the donor cell was zapped with an electric current to stimulate cell division.

They implanted 1,095 cloned embryos into 123 dogs and just three pregnancies resulted. That's a cloning efficiency rate lower than experiments with cats and horses. One fetus miscarried, and one puppy died of pneumonia 22 days after birth.

That left Snuppy. He was delivered by Caesarean section from his surrogate mother, a yellow Labrador retriever.

National Geographic News

Scientists Successfully Clone Cat

David Braun, February 14, 2002

Scientists in Texas have successfully cloned a cat, opening the way to replicating pets and other valued animals once the technique is perfected. The work was funded in part by a company that hopes to use the technology to provide commercial cloning of companion animals for pet owners.

Cloned kitty, "CC"

The kitten, called CC (the old typist's abbreviation for carbon copy) and now almost two months old, appears healthy and energetic, although she is completely unlike her tabby surrogate mother, Mark Westhusin and colleagues at Texas A&M University, College Station, announced in the February 21 issue of *Nature*.

The cat was cloned by transplanting DNA from Rainbow, a female three-colored (tortoiseshell or calico) cat, into an egg cell whose nucleus had been removed, and then implanting this embryo into Allie, the surrogate mother.

"CC's coat color suggests that she is a clone, and a genetic match between CC and the donor mother confirms this," the researchers say.

She is not, however, identical to her DNA donor. The reason for this is that the pattern on cats' coats is only partly genetically determined—it also depends on other factors during development.

Out of 87 implanted cloned embryos, CC is the only one to survive—comparable to the success rate in sheep, mice, cows, goats, and pigs, the scientists say. "If these odds can be improved and CC remains in good health, pet cloning may one day be feasible," the scientists reported.

How They Did It

In their first attempt, researchers obtained the cells used to make the clone from the skin cells of a "donor" cat. But it didn't work. "We did

188 nuclear-transfer procedures, which resulted in 82 cloned embryos that were transferred into seven recipient females," the scientists said. Only one cat became pregnant, with a single embryo. But this pregnancy miscarried.

In the next attempt, the scientists used cells from ovarian tissue to receive the DNA from the cat to be cloned. Five cloned embryos made in this way were implanted into a single surrogate mother. Pregnancy was confirmed by ultrasound after 22 days and a kitten was delivered by C-section on December 22, 2001, 66 days after the embryo was transferred.

Endangered Species Could Benefit

The Audubon Nature Institute welcomed the research. "Now we can take this technology and apply it for the preservation of endangered species," said their spokesman. "It proves that cloning can be applied not only to livestock but also to companion animals. Ultimately it will also be used for endangered species."

Humane Society Opposes Cloning

The Humane Society of the United States is opposed to the concept of cloning pets. "In the first place it is dangerous for the animals involved," said Brian Sodergren, who monitors the exploitation and abuse of companion animals for the society. "Take the cat that was cloned: The sheer amount of embryos it took is quite mind boggling."

"Secondly, cloning adds needlessly to the overpopulation of pets in the United States. There are millions of dogs and cats in shelters waiting to be adopted, looking for responsible owners and loving homes. About half of them will be euthanized because there are not enough homes for them."

Introduction to the Text Set Lessons

Back in Chapter 2, we explained how we put these text sets together, how they support common curricular topics, and how they can be scheduled and taught. Now that you are about to jump into the ten lessons, a few quick notes:

■ Each text set offers an **initial 45- to 50-minute lesson,** designed to fit into a standard middle or high school class period, or half of a 90-minute block.

■ Lessons 3, 4, 7, 8, 9, and 10 offer one or more **extensions that build on the initial lesson**, add further articles, and deepen kids' thinking. The extensions are presented in sequence; each one builds upon the previous activities. In effect, we are providing you with multiday lessons (almost teaching units) for many of these topics. The extensions run from **20 to 100 minutes**; we show the time required for each.

■ Every text set lesson is **built upon a sequence of reading strategies** from the strategy lessons section of the book. These are listed at the start of the lesson; the relevant strategies are also noted in the margin at point of use, both for easy cross-referencing and because we don't re-explain strategies here.

■ As in the strategy lessons, we present these lessons through a combination of **explanation** (numbered steps, set in roman type) and direct **teacher talk** (in italics, in a sans serif font)—the kind of language we actually use with kids. You can try on our wording or make up your own.

■ The **articles vary in difficulty.** When a text set offers harder and easier reading choices, we'll identify the easier one(s) for you at the start of the lesson. But also keep in mind our chart "What Makes Reading Easier" (page 21). In these lessons, we provide maximum "comprehensibility" by choosing interesting and relevant texts, and then using them in a highly supportive, structured, and sociable context.

■ Just about anything you need to **project visually** is ready for use on our website, www.heinemann.com/textsandlessons, and you will see this icon in the margin.

■ Unlike the more generic strategy lessons at the front of the book, the text set lessons are more **closely tied to commonly taught school subjects.** Under "Curriculum Connections," we share some of the ways in which our lesson can launch or enrich units you are already teaching across the curriculum. Our connections are just samples; you'll likely think of many more. We also recommend classic and contemporary books (and occasionally, video resources) that correlate with the subject matter. We didn't clutter up this section with citations; in this high-tech age, all you need is the book title to search out publication info.

■ We present these ten lessons **in order of complexity**. Simpler, shorter ones come first; then, as you move through the collection, lessons tend to have more steps, incorporate more strategies, and have more extensions and variations.

■ The **directions pack a lot of information** into a small amount of space. We prefer the terms *elegant* or *sophisticated*, but there's no doubt: the lessons require careful reading. With our tongue only slightly in cheek, we'll say: you have to use your best proficient-reader strategies to understand these lessons. Start by visualizing a class of your own going through the steps, and let that movie play in your head as you read. Monitor your comprehension; stop, think, and react as you go. Slow down your reading rate, reread, ask questions of the text, annotate the lesson, make marks in the margin. You know the drill.

■ Most states have signed on to the Common Core State Standards, as promulgated by the National Governor's Association and the Council of State School Officers (2010). States that haven't done so already usually have comparable home-grown standards that define content-area literacy, what skills should be taught and when. Our text set **lessons are closely aligned with the letter and spirit of those standards**; each one addresses at least a handful.

■ Even though these ten lessons are content-specific, they are highly adaptable. Their underlying structures and teaching language can be applied to countless other topics and texts. **Make these lessons your own**. Revise, replace, build on, expand, or toss out the articles we have chosen. Find images to go with an article and articles to go with images; add videos and primary sources; collect interviews and surveys; scour websites and wikis. Once you get started, tweaking these lessons is pleasantly addictive. Enjoy!

Invasive Species

Grouping Sequence:

Pairs, groups of 5, whole class

Smokey fondly remembers Nayetsy, whom he taught in sixth grade a couple of years ago:

"One day she came up to me, kind of out of the blue, and asked: 'Do you know that there have only ever been five species of tigers in the world?'

Taken a little aback, I replied, honestly, 'No, I really didn't know that.' Nayetsy went on, 'And two of those species are already extinct.' By the time she finished that sentence, her eyes had filled with tears."

All kids, from elementary through high school (and maybe all people), have a lingering curiosity about animals. Maybe we're not all as intense as Nayetsy, but it's one of those topics that everyone cares about and has opinions about. Of course, in elementary school, little kids get to learn about all the cute and cuddly critters—jungle animals, farm animals, our finny friends under the sea. But with the bigger kids, we like to study some problem creatures, some animal "delinquents" instead.

Invasive alien species are becoming a huge problem all around the world. In this lesson, we provide examples of a mollusk, a fish, a snake, two insects, and a mammal, all of which have become destructive in their newly adopted homes. Despite the differences in their phyla, all of these critters had to achieve the same underlying processes: they had to somehow arrive, survive, and thrive in a new habitat. This highly conceptual lesson is designed to help kids deduce from five examples what conditions favor the takeover of habitats by non-native species.

TEXTS IN ORDER OF USE

"Outback Steakhouse" (for the think-aloud)

"Scientists Fear Spread of Exotic Snakes" (easier)

"Fire Ants" (easier)

"Killer Bees"

"Zebra Mussels"

"Asian Carp and the Great Lakes"

CURRICULUM CONNECTIONS

Science: Biology, zoology, ecosystems, biomes, evolution.

Social Studies: Geography, transportation.

Math: Calculating population densities and growth rates.

Literature: The World Without Us (what would happen if the world's most invasive species—humans—suddenly disappeared).

English Language Arts: Draw inferences from text, analyze multiple articles on related topics, practice discussion skills, utilize note-taking strategies.

STRATEGIES USED

Think Aloud, Turn and Talk, Text Coding, Jigsaw

MATERIALS NEEDED

One set of all five articles for each group; projectable images of species, if desired, from www.images.google.com or other site (suggested links are on the website); large chart paper (for Step 11).

Steps and Teaching Language

Strategy 8: **THINK ALOUD**

Strategy 1: **TURN AND TALK**

STEP 1 **Introduce the topic** Often with text sets, we like to lead off with a captivating news item that allows us to build engagement and get kids eager to read. Here's how we might do this with alien species:

I read the most amazing article this weekend. I couldn't believe it. Let me ask you something: Where do you think camels live? In the Middle East, right, in desert countries? Uh-huh. Well, guess what? There are more than a million camels running loose in Australia. Australia! Who knew?

STEP 2 **Think aloud a section of the article**

Let me read you a little of this article from Atlantic *magazine.*

Read the first three paragraphs of "Outback Steakhouse" aloud, stopping to share your reactions, connections, and questions as you go. If possible, project a picture of the Ozzie feral camels while you read this. Search on "camels Australia," and you'll find abundant images.

STEP 3 **Kids read and talk** Hand out copies of "Outback Steakhouse" and let kids read the rest of the article silently; then invite pairs to talk and react. Encourage discussion and speculation about how camels were used in Australia, why people would even consider shooting them now, how hunters would dispose of the bodies—whatever catches the kids' attention.

STEP 4 **Reconvene the whole class and offer more information** The opportunity to define invasive alien species should arise naturally from the kids' pair conversations.

According to InvasiveSpecies.org (and they should know): "an invasive species is one that does not naturally occur in a specific area and whose introduction does or is likely to cause economic or environmental harm or harm to human health."

OK, so some organisms become destructive when they move from their homes (or native range) to new habitats. Camels aren't native to Australia, but as we just learned, they were brought there in the 1840s as a means of desert transportation in the arid outback. But eventually they were replaced by trucks and trains, turned loose, and have now become a huge environmental problem.

STEP 5 **Get kids questioning**

So let's think about this. When a species somehow gets to some other habitat, what happens? It might immediately die out. But some species make a happy home. What's the difference between the two? What favors a species taking hold? Let's read about it.

STEP 6 **Kids choose articles** Arrange kids in groups of five and hand each group a stack of the five different articles. *Today, you're each going to get a chance to specialize in one particular species. In a minute you'll read an article about one of five different creatures: Burmese pythons, zebra mussels, killer bees, fire ants, or Asian carp. I am giving each group one copy of each article and you can decide who wants to read about which one. Go ahead and decide that now.* Assign articles to any slowpokes.

STEP 7 **Explain coding**

Strategy 4: **TEXT CODING**

So to help you read these articles, I'm going to suggest a special version of our text coding strategy. To become invasive, an alien species must do three things: arrive, survive, and thrive.

*First, they have to get to a new location; they have to somehow **arrive** there to even have a chance of invading. Then, they have to **survive**. They have to find a place to live, find something to eat, and be able to keep living. Think about this: you could theoretically "arrive" on Mars, but you could not survive for one minute unless you had oxygen, food, and shelter, right? And finally, to become invasive, an alien species needs to **thrive**—which means it has to take over a niche, reproduce effectively, and perhaps come to dominate or drive out other species.*

*So as you read, if you come across something that tells how the critter arrived, code that with an **A** in the margin. Then if your article explains how the species survived, mark that information with an **S**. Finally, when you see information about how one of these species has come to really take over a habitat, mark that section with a **T** for thrive. OK? Happy reading, everyone.*

STEP 8 **Monitor and coach** Help kids to apply the codes to their articles. There is plenty of information about arrival, survival, and "thrival" in each piece, so this should be doable.

STEP 9 **Invite discussion**

OK, now your teams can meet for six or seven minutes. Your job is to look at these three stages of invasiveness, and talk about how each of your creatures accomplished those stages. Pool your information. You may find things they did in common and things they did differently. Start by comparing notes on how each different creature arrived, then move on to how they survived, and finally about how each one came to thrive, if it did.

Visit and confer as kids work, making sure that they mark information in all three categories.

STEP 10 **Add a second question**

*OK, hang onto your thoughts about how species arrive, survive, and thrive. Now let's look at invasiveness from a slightly different angle. What are the **conditions that favor the success** of what we might call a "wannabe invasive species"? It might be something about the critter itself, or its behaviors, or about the new habitat, that make it more likely to eventually thrive. Make a list of those factors, and we'll compare notes in a few minutes.*

Allow three or four more minutes for talking and listing.

STEP 11 **Share with the whole class** Back as a whole class, have groups contribute their information, and make a large chart of findings as the discussion unfolds. By layering on information from the two stages of discussion, you'll get a rich picture of the invasion process, including the huge part that we hapless and reckless humans too often play in the process. One class's chart included these factors:

What Helps Alien Species Thrive

- people bring you there

- arriving at a place over and over

- being highly aggressive

- having a high reproduction rate

- not being picky about temperature, humidity, etc.

- not having any predators in the new location

- lots of food

- good weather

- feels like home

- not much competition for food or homes

Tips and Variations

■ **USE EXPERT GROUPS** This takes a little extra time but is so worth it. After Step 8, have everyone stand up and go meet with a few other students who have read the same article. This stage allows kids to confirm the most important aspects of their creature, compare notes on the article, and return to their heterogeneous groups with refined expertise for the discussions.

■ **INCLUDE REGIONAL SPECIES** If there is a local invasive species that kids might know about, replace one of our articles with one about a more familiar invader. While developing this lesson, we worked in some schools in North Dakota where Japanese beetles (similar to ladybugs) were imported to eat the aphids off soybean crops. The trouble was, they became a rampaging nuisance that overwintered in people's houses and emerged in spring to—guess what—bite people! Some ladybugs.

■ **SHOW KIDS SOME VIDEO FROM YOUTUBE.** Nothing drives home the overwhelming nature of alien species like seeing hundreds of Asian carp leaping out of the water or thousands of Africanized honey bees on a stinging rampage.

■ **ONE MORE STEP** Here's a great final proposition to debate (or even use as a research topic): "Human beings are the most destructive invasive species on the planet." Discuss that! (And perhaps have kids read segments of Alan Wiseman's excellent book, *The World Without Us.*)

■ **REPLICATE THE STRUCTURE** This lesson can be applied to countless other topics: it simply offers several different examples of a phenomenon, system, or paradigm, and lets students deduce from a few examples what the common features are for *all* versions.

the Atlantic

Outback Steakhouse

Australia's bush meat is tasty, healthy, and enviro-friendly.
But can you get people to eat it?

Marina Kamenev, April 2010

Garry Dann nudged the steak in the rusty electric frying pan at his meat store in Alice Springs, a town in central Australia far from everything except desert. He pushed aside the bottle of canola oil next to the pan. "It's a great cut. You don't need to add anything, just cook it in its own fat," he said.

It tasted like a juicier version of beef. But the meat in question was camel—freshly slaughtered at Dann's abattoir, Centralian Gold, which he has been running, off and on, since 1986. In that time, the population of Australian camels has escalated to plague proportions, and Dann believes that selling their meat could become a multimillion-dollar industry.

Camels were first brought to Australia from the Canary Islands in the 1840s as beasts of burden. They carried goods across the harsh, Martian-red desert. As roads were built, they were gradually released into the wild. Now Australian camels make up the largest wild herd in the world, numbering about a million. With no natural predators, they are expected to double in population every decade.

Like most foreign species introduced into Australia's delicate ecosystem, camels have

> **"It's a good meat, low in cholesterol. I would hate to see it go to the worms."**

wreaked havoc. They feed on roughly 80 percent of Australia's plant species, and have pushed some to the brink of extinction. In their search for water, they soil Aboriginal drinking holes, destroy everything from fences to air conditioners, and cause more than $12 million worth of damage each year. In response, the Australian government plans to cull 349,000 of them, at a cost of $17 million.

Dann thinks this is a waste of potentially valuable meat. He concedes that camel is still a novelty in Australia, but he sees a lucrative market in the Middle East, where it's widely accepted. If he wins government approval to export, he aims to up the number of animals he slaughters each week from 20 to 300. "It's a good meat, low in cholesterol," he said. "I would hate to see it go to the worms."

The camel-meat sector faces its own economic challenges. The market price of the meat is too low to support the cost of transporting it across the country, according to Gordon Grigg of Queensland University. And many camels roam in remote locations accessible only by air, which makes them costly to herd for slaughter.

San Francisco Chronicle

Scientists Fear Spread of Exotic Snakes

United Press International, Feb. 24, 2008

WASHINGTON—Scientists fear that Burmese pythons, already known to be breeding in South Florida, could spread through much of the southern United States.

According to the new US Geological Survey report, the python would find about one-third of the United States—including much of California—to be comfortable for its expansion. "Although other factors, such as type of food available and suitable shelter, also play a role, Burmese pythons and other giant constrictor snakes have shown themselves to be highly adaptable to new environments," the report says.

The snakes weigh up to 250 pounds and slither at a rate of 20 miles per month, according to USGS zoologist Gordon Rodda. They are not staying put. One of them has already slithered about 100 miles westward from its breeding colony in Arkansas. "We have not yet identified something that would stop their spreading all the way to San Francisco," Rodda said. If pet pythons were introduced into the wild in California by irresponsible pet owners, as happened in Florida, they could become established here even faster, without need of a cross-country journey.

What could stop the huge snakes? They'd have to get past Florida's alligators first,

> The snakes weigh up to 250 pounds and slither at a rate of 20 miles per month... They are not staying put.

although it's a complicated relationship—while alligators do eat pythons, pythons can also eat alligators. But once out of Florida, there aren't any free-roaming African lions and tigers between Florida and San Francisco. So the absence of major predators outside Florida could help the snakes on their journey west.

While there are no recorded attacks on humans by Burmese pythons in the wild, they have killed children in their native range, Southeast Asia. Pet pythons sometimes kill their owners, probably because they have mistaken the human for food and are unable to stop their instinctive reaction to coil and squeeze. In Florida, they eat bobcats, deer, alligators, raccoons, cats, rats, rabbits, muskrats, possum, mice, ducks, egrets, herons and song birds. They grab with their mouth to anchor the prey, then coil around the animal and crush it to death before eating it whole.

Fire Ants

Red Fire Ants Information, www.fireant.net

Who Are These Fiends?

Fire ants are known for their lively and aggressive behavior, swarming over anyone or anything that disturbs their nest, often attacking wild animals, pets or people, in some instances, even killing them. 20 million people a year are stung by fire ants.

When these pesky critters invade an area, they come in enormous numbers, which can dramatically reduce populations of native ants, other insects, and even ground-nesting wildlife. They invade homes, school yards, athletic fields, golf courses, and parks. They will damage crops and electrical equipment, costing humans huge amounts of money each year in repairs and eradication.

Red Imported Fire Ant

The red fire ant was accidentally introduced into the United States in 1929, when a cargo ship that had used soil as ballast arrived in Mobile, Alabama, from South America. In recent years, the fire ant has spread as far west as California and as far north as Kansas and Maryland, covering 300 million acres and growing all the time. Although fire ants keep marching farther and farther, northerners don't have to worry because fire ants cannot survive in areas where soil temperatures drop to near freezing for more than 2 to 3 weeks.

Facts About Fire Ants

Fire ants are not picky eaters. They are omnivores and will eat almost any plant or animal material, including other insects, ground-nesting animals, mice, turtles, snakes, and other vertebrates, young trees, seedlings, plant bulbs, saplings, fruit and grass.

Fire ants are extremely organized. With an anthill population of 100,000–500,000, they need to be. Young fire ants help the queen deliver her eggs and tend to the larvae. Tunnel diggers dig new tunnels as the population grows, making room for increased traffic and new rooms for eggs and larvae. Guard fire ants stay near the entrance of the mound, blocking strangers from entering. Winged male and female fire ants go on mating flights in the spring and summer and start new colonies. Shortly after mating, the male dies and the female becomes a queen. She flies anywhere from 100 feet to 10 miles to start a new colony. And the foragers, the oldest of the colony, constantly search for food.

TEXT SET LESSONS / INVASIVE SPECIES

Smithsonian Institution

Killer Bees

Department of Systemic Biology, National Museum of Natural History, Smithsonian Institution

Description: The general appearance of killer bees (Africanized bees) is the same as common honey bees, but there are some distinctive physical differences between the two. To analyze the differences, a laboratory has to measure and compare some 20 different structures. Another way to check is to analyze the specimen's DNA and enzymes.

Distribution: **Honey bees are not native to the Western Hemisphere.** European settlers brought most honey bees to the Americas approximately 400 years ago. In 1956, some colonies of African honey bees were imported into Brazil, with the idea of cross-breeding them with local populations of honey bees to increase honey production. In 1957, twenty-six African queens, along with swarms of European worker bees, escaped from an experimental apiary about 100 miles south of Sao Paulo. They've been spreading ever since. These African bee escapees have since formed hybrid populations with European honey bees, both feral and from commercial hives. They have gradually spread northward through South America, Central America, and eastern Mexico, progressing some 100 to 200 miles per year. In 1990, killer bees reached southern Texas, appeared in Arizona in 1993, and found their way to California in 1995. They are expected to form colonies in parts of the southern United States.

Damage done: Africanized honey bees (killer bees) are dangerous because they attack intruders in numbers much greater than European honey bees. Since their introduction into Brazil, they have killed some 1,000 humans, with victims receiving ten times as many stings as from the European strain. They react to disturbances ten times faster than European honey bees, and will chase a person a quarter of a mile. Africanized honey bees will attack when unprovoked, and they respond rapidly and in large numbers to disturbances that European honey bees would ignore. Both types of bee die shortly after leaving their stings and ends of their abdomen in their victim.

Other concerns with Africanized honey bees are the effects on the honey industry (with an annual value of 140 million dollars) and general pollination of orchards and field crops (with an annual value of 10 billion dollars). Interbred colonies of European and Africanized honey bees may differ in pollination efforts, be more aggressive, excessively abandon the nest, and not survive the winters.

Control: Two primary solutions have been considered. The first is termed drone-flooding, which involves maintaining large numbers of common honey bees (originally from Europe) in areas where commercially reared queen bees mate. This process would limit the mating possibilities between Africanized drones and European queens. The second strategy is requeening frequently, where the beekeeper replaces the queen of the colony, thus assuring that the queens are European honey bees and that mating has also occurred with European drones.

| Article | Discussion | Read | Edit | View History |

Zebra Mussels

Wikipedia, http://en.wikipedia.org/wiki/Zebra_mussel

The **Zebra mussel**, *Dreissena polymorpha*, is a bivalve mussel native to freshwater lakes of southeast Russia. Zebra mussels are filter feeders. When in the water, they open their shells to admit food. Zebra mussels get their name from the striped pattern on their shells, though not all shells bear this pattern. They are usually about the size of a fingernail, but can grow to a maximum length of nearly two inches. Its native distribution is the Black Sea and Caspian Sea. Zebra mussels are considered an invasive species in North America, Great Britain, Ireland, Italy, Spain, and Sweden.

Scientific Classification	
Kingdom:	Animalia
Phylum:	Mollusca
Class:	Bivalvia
Subclass:	Heterodonta
Order:	Veneroida
Superfamily:	Dreissenoidea
Family:	Dreissenidae
Genus:	Dreissena
Species:	D. polymorpha

Effects: Zebra mussels are a great nuisance to people. Since colonizing the Great Lakes, they have covered the undersides of docks, boats, and anchors. They can grow so densely that they block pipelines, clogging water intakes of municipal water supplies and hydroelectric companies.

They also cleanse the waters of inland lakes, resulting in increased sunlight penetration and growth of native algae at greater depths. This proves beneficial for fish most of the time, helping the fish live in better conditions. They may also decrease the recreational value of inland lakes because once the mussels have devoured all the microorganisms in the water, weeds proliferate.

Reproduction: An adult female zebra mussel is one of the most reproductive organisms in the world. It may produce between 30,000 and 1 million eggs per year.

Spread: In the U.S., they were first detected in the Great Lakes in 1988. It is believed they were inadvertently introduced into the lakes in the ballast water of ocean-going ships traversing the St. Lawrence Seaway. Since adult zebra mussels can survive out of water for several days or weeks if the temperature is low and humidity is high, boats provide temporary refuge for clusters of adult mussels that could easily be released when transoceanic ships drop anchor in freshwater ports.

From their first appearance in American waters in 1988 zebra mussels have spread to a large number of waterways, disrupting the ecosystems, killing any local mussels (primarily by outcompeting native species for food, and damaging harbors, boats, and power plants). The cost of fighting the pests at power plants and other water-consuming facilities is $500 million a year in the U.S., according to the Center for Invasive Species Research at the University of California, Riverside.

A common inference made by scientists predicts that the zebra mussel will continue spreading passively, by ship and by pleasure craft, to more rivers in North America. Since no predator or combination of predators has been shown to significantly reduce zebra mussel numbers, such spread would most likely result in permanent establishment of zebra mussels in many North American waterways.

Recent Additions   Contact Us   Search: ○ All EPA ○ This Area

Asian Carp and the Great Lakes

U.S. Environmental Protection Agency, www.epa.gov/glnpo/invasive/asiancarp

> Asian carp are a significant threat to the Great Lakes because they are large, extremely prolific, and consume vast amounts of food. They can weigh up to 100 pounds, and can grow to a length of more than four feet.

Asian carp have been found in the Illinois River, which connects the Mississippi River to Lake Michigan. Due to their large size and rapid rate of reproduction, these fish could pose a significant risk to the Great Lakes Ecosystem.

To prevent the carp from entering the Great Lakes, the U.S. Army Corps of Engineers, U.S. EPA, the State of Illinois, the International Joint Commission, the Great Lakes Fishery Commission, and the U.S. Fish and Wildlife Service are working together to install and maintain a permanent electric barrier between the fish and Lake Michigan.

The Chicago Sanitary and Ship Canal, where the barrier is being constructed, connects the Mississippi River to the Great Lakes via the Illinois River. Recent monitoring shows the carp to be in the Illinois River within 1 mile of Lake Michigan.

How did Asian carp get so close to the Great Lakes?

Two species of Asian carp—the bighead and silver—were imported by catfish farmers in the 1970's to remove algae and suspended matter out of their ponds. During large floods in the early 1990s, many of the catfish farm ponds overflowed their banks, and the Asian carp were released into local waterways in the Mississippi River basin.

The carp have steadily made their way northward up the Mississippi, becoming the most abundant species in some areas of the River. They outcompete native fish, and have caused severe hardship to the people who fish there. When approached by a powerboat, these fish often jump in the air, and can seriously injure boat occupants. The carp have little economic value, as most Americans consider them inedible.

What effects might Asian carp have on the Great Lakes?

Asian carp are a significant threat to the Great Lakes because they are large, extremely prolific, and consume vast amounts of food. They can weigh up to 100 pounds, and can grow to a length of more than four feet. They are well-suited to the climate of the Great Lakes region, which is similar to their native Asian habitats.

Researchers expect that Asian carp would disrupt the food chain that supports the native fish of the Great Lakes. Due to their large size, ravenous appetites, and rapid rate of reproduction, these fish could pose a significant risk to the Great Lakes Ecosystem. Eventually, they could become a dominant species in the Great Lakes.

TEXT SET LESSONS / INVASIVE SPECIES

Post-traumatic Stress Disorder (PTSD)

Grouping Sequence:

Mingling pairs, groups of 4, small groups based on article choice

Though it is getting plenty of headlines these days, post-traumatic stress disorder among soldiers is nothing new. Under other names, this kind of trauma has probably been around since warfare began. In the American Civil War, the symptoms were known as "soldier's heart"; in World War I, "shell shock"; in World War II, "battle fatigue." Today, as diagnosis improves, 35 percent of American soldiers returning from the Middle East are being identified as suffering from PTSD. The more tours they have been through, and the more intense the battles they've experienced, the more likely they are to be affected.

On TV, in movies, and while playing video games, our students see (and often virtually participate in) countless simulations of war and battle. Few of these are realistic; fewer still portray any of the real human costs of warfare. In school we have also traditionally taught and even celebrated "great wars"— but without focusing on the individual lives, sacrifices, and potential lifelong suffering of the soldiers who survive war. This lesson turns those tables, for an hour. If you have PTSD sufferers among your students or their family members, please see our cautions under Tips and Variations.

TEXTS IN ORDER OF USE

Excerpt from *Soldier's Heart,* by Gary Paulsen

A Soldier's Letter Home from WWII

"The Forever War of the Mind"

"Post-traumatic Stress Disorder (PTSD)"

Blog post: "Daddy's Home"

CURRICULUM CONNECTIONS

Social Studies: Current events. All wars and battles, especially the U.S. Civil War, WWI, WWII, Vietnam, Iraq, Afghanistan.

Science and Technology: Physics of weapons and warfare.

Literature: Compare fiction versus nonfiction accounts of events: *Hiroshima, Ghost Soldiers, The Things They Carried, The Hurt Locker.*

Biology: Psychology, the brain, hormones, stress, neurology.

English Language Arts: Gather information from fiction and nonfiction sources; evaluate details of a text in order to build defensible interpretations; use appropriate note-taking strategies to enhance comprehension; work with partners to build knowledge.

STRATEGIES USED

Quotation Mingle, Turn and Talk, Text Annotation

MATERIALS NEEDED

Sentence strips for mingle (see Step 1); copy of the *Soldier's Heart* excerpt for each student; ample copies of the four articles that students choose from in Part 2, Step 1.

Steps and Teaching Language

PART 1   QUOTATION MINGLE AND CONVERSATION *(20 minutes)*

STEP 1   **Prepare the materials** This lesson begins "cold," without preannouncing the topic. The first activity is a quotation mingle. In preparation, print several copies of the sentences from Gary Paulsen's *Soldier's Heart* provided on page 161. Cut up enough so each student will receive one sentence; place on index cards if you wish. This means eight different quotes will be circulating among the class.

STEP 2   **Give quotation mingle instructions**

In a few minutes we are going to read an important selection from a book. To help you better understand it, I've prepared a "preview" by cutting out just eight sentences from the longer piece. I'm distributing these randomly. Let kids pick a sentence out of a hat or box.

Now everyone has one piece of the puzzle. If you could see all the sentences other people have, you could probably make a good prediction as to what the whole thing is about. But to do that, you'd have to get a look at other people's sentences, right? That's just what we are going to do now.

Strategy 22: **QUOTATION MINGLE**

STEP 3   **Commence the mingle** Invite kids to join in a pairs mingle, following the instructions on page 131. Their job is to try to figure out what the larger text means by recurrently forming pairs, looking at each other's sentence strips, and talking about them.

Try to compare your quote with at least ten other people's sentences in the next five or six minutes. Go!

Insert yourself in the crowd; monitor and keep kids mingling.

STEP 4   **Form discussion groups and give instructions** Have kids sit down in groups of four.

Based on what you saw and heard during the mingle,

- *What do you think the passage is going to be about?*

- *What time and place are depicted?*

- *Any guesses about who wrote this?*

To answer these questions, everyone has to pool their knowledge—and between the four of you, you probably saw all eight quotes. Take about five minutes—have a good conversation.

STEP 5 **Monitor and support** Circulate and coach groups as they work, being alert for good examples or quotes you can bring up in the later discussion.

STEP 6 **Invite volunteers to share** The sentences used in this mingle are quite explicit, so students should have little trouble predicting the battle scene. Push students to see if they can figure what war this passage describes, and what clues in the text help them determine this (e.g., the capitalized word *Rebel*). If there are any Gary Paulsen fans in the group, they may well identify him as the author. If not, the pleasure is yours.

STEP 7 **Read the full selection** With kids still sitting in their groups of four, hand out the full excerpt from *Soldier's Heart. Now you can read the whole thing—it's one page from the novel—and see how accurate your predictions and inferences were.* Allow a few minutes for reading, then share a few comments from groups.

If Charley survived the war—which we cannot tell from this passage—how do you think he would do? Would he be able to go right back to normal life, or do you think he might have had to struggle with his memories? Do you think he might suffer from post-traumatic stress disorder? Do you know what that is? Here's how the Mayo Clinic defines it:

> Post-traumatic stress disorder (PTSD) is a type of anxiety disorder that's triggered by a traumatic event. You can develop post-traumatic stress disorder when you experience or witness an event that causes intense fear, helplessness or horror. In some cases the symptoms can get worse or last for months or even years. Sometimes they may completely disrupt your life. In these cases, you may have post-traumatic stress disorder.

So, do you think Charley would or would not suffer from this condition? Try to base your prediction on facts in the text.

Strategy 1: **TURN AND TALK**

Allow two or three minutes of turn-and-talk time in their groups. Take comments from a few volunteers. If kids get intrigued by the discussion, remind them that they can read Paulsen's 104-page book to find out what happens to Charley. (He does survive the war, but suffers from multiple injuries and a crippling case of "soldier's heart." He succumbs to these afflictions at age twenty-three.)

STEP 1 **Introduce the texts** Be sure to have plenty of copies of each text, since not all selections will be appropriate for all students. *Now everyone is going to get a chance to read an article of their own choice to learn more about PTSD. Today we have four choices. The first two are very intense accounts from a battlefield—you should consider your sensibilities before choosing one of those options.*

A Soldier's Letter Home from WWII: This was written by an American GI serving in the Pacific, graphically telling his parents about the combat casualties he had seen.

"The Forever War of the Mind": Max Cleland, who served as head of the Veterans Administration, recounts how he lost an arm and both legs in battle—and describes the mental anguish that accompanied his physical wounds.

"Post-traumatic Stress Disorder (PTSD)": Basic problems associated with PTSD, from the U.S. Veterans Administration.

Blog Post—"Daddy's Home": Written by the wife of a decorated soldier who suffers from PTSD, this article offers tips for families in the same situation.

STEP 2 **Give reading instructions** Once students have chosen their articles, have them sit down with small groups of kids who have picked the same piece. Keep these groups to three to five members; split bigger groups. If only one or two kids pick an article, grab a copy and join them yourself.

Strategy 3: **TEXT ANNOTATION**

As you read, mark up your article using the text annotation strategy. Be sure to stop, think, and jot your thoughts in the margin as you go.

Allow seven or eight minutes for reading and note-taking.

STEP 3 **Start discussions**

Take a few minutes in your groups and talk about what struck you about the piece you chose. Use your annotations to locate important topics to discuss.

Circulate and confer with kids as they talk. After about three minutes, add these two targeted questions:

Now, here is a discussion question for people with one of the first two, battlefield-oriented articles. Having read this, do you think you might suffer from PTSD if you found yourself in such a situation? Be specific as to why or why not, realizing that, of course, we can never predict exactly how we might respond in an unknown situation. Jot down a few key quotes you hear from group members as they answer this question.

And for the readers of the other two articles, will you please talk about this question: What are some things that family members and friends can do to help someone suffering from PTSD? Make a list of specific actions.

STEP 4 **Share learnings** Reconvene the whole class and, first, invite volunteers to report some key facts and information they have learned about PTSD. Then ask a few students to share their thinking from the specialized discussion questions.

How many readers of the battlefield articles thought you might suffer from PTSD, and what were your reasons for thinking so? And, among those who read the symptoms-and-treatment articles, what did you come up with for ways to help someone with PTSD?

Tips and Variations

■ **BE AWARE OF PTSD SUFFERERS IN YOUR CLASS** When teaching this lesson, be mindful that some of your students may have a parent or sibling who has suffered some form of military-related PTSD. This can be a sensitive problem to gracefully tiptoe around—or it can be a huge asset, if the student or family member chooses to share his or her experience. Some PTSD sufferers are eager to get their story out—it is often a tale of woefully inadequate services. If you teach high school, you may also have students in class who are getting ready to enlist in the armed forces, and again, these kids can contribute an important perspective, and should be involved carefully and respectfully.

More broadly, anyone can suffer from PTSD symptoms as the result of accidents, injuries, displacement following a natural disaster, or even family strife. Be sensitive to these possibilities also. Incorporate kids' stories where appropriate. If this lesson reveals a student with what might be undiagnosed PTSD-related problems, be sure to inform the school counselor or nurse.

Finally, we'll reiterate that the two battlefield articles are quite graphic; think about which kids, if any, should read either of these choices.

Bullets flew past him with evil little snaps and snickers as they cut the air.

Make it stop now, Charley thought.

It was impossible to see or understand anything.

It was like a blade cutting grain.

Next to him Massey's head suddenly left his body and disappeared.

Many were torn apart, hit ten or twelve or more times before they had time to drop.

I'm not supposed to be here.

Charley aimed in the general direction of the Rebels and pulled his trigger, firing blind.

Excerpt from *Soldier's Heart*

by Gary Paulsen

Make it stop now, Charley thought, or thought he was thinking until he realized he was screaming it: "Make it all stop now!"

Death was everywhere, nowhere. Bullets flew past him with evil little snaps and snickers as they cut the air. Next to him Massey's head suddenly left his body and disappeared, taken by a cannon round that then went through an officer's horse, end to end, before plowing into the ground.

This can't be, he thought. I can't be here. A terrible mistake. I'm not supposed to be here.

He had forgotten to fire. The officers had marched them out into a field in perfect order and told them where to aim and fire and he had raised his rifle and then the whole world had come at him. The Rebel soldiers were up a shallow grade a hundred yards away, behind some fallen trees, and they had opened on Charley and the others before anyone else could fire.

It was like a blade cutting grain. He heard the bullets hitting the men—little thunk-slaps—and saw the men falling. Some of them screamed as they fell. Most were silent. Many were dead before they hit the ground. Many were torn apart, hit ten or twelve or more times before they had time to drop.

The men left standing with Charley fired, then the survivors of that round reloaded and fired again, and Charlie aimed in the general direction of the Rebels and pulled his trigger, firing blind.

The black powder smoke clouded from the rifles and the rebel guns on the hill and it was impossible to see or understand anything.

I don't know anything, Charley thought—the words jerked through his mind before he thought them.

A Soldier's Letter Home from WWII

April 29, 1945

Dearest Folks,

This letter will undoubtedly seem queer to you because I am going to give forth with the news. My outfit hit the beach on Okinawa about three hours after the first wave on Easter Sunday. Then we moved on and dead bodies appeared. Along the road were arms, legs, heads, torsoes, blood and guts scattered everywhere. The stink and smell of dead bodies in the air everywhere. Dried up blood and bones are strewn around, and wounded people straggling around.

When I get home I want to forget about all I have seen. Like the way I found two of my buddies. They weren't dead but dying, tied and staked to the ground, their guts cut open and their tongues cut out and their private parts stuck in their mouths. Now I ask you Mom and Dad, can you blame a man for feeling bitter?

I'm sorry that this is such a gruesome letter but it's the truth, something you rarely hear in the papers. I wish you'd read this letter to your friends so they will know what it is really like over this way, and so they will not be misled by the papers.

Lots and lots of love to the best parents in the world,

JOHNNIE

Pfc. John W. Taussig, Jr. USMC

Regimental Y&S Brty

15th Marines, 6th Marine Division

c/o F.P.O. San Francisco, California

The New York Times

The Forever War of the Mind

November 7, 2009
By Max Cleland

War is haunting. Death. Pain. Blood. Dismemberment. A buddy dying in your arms. Imagine trying to get over the memory of a bomb splitting a Humvee apart beneath your feet and taking your leg with it. The first time I saw the stilled bodies of American soldiers dead on the battlefield is as stark and brutal a memory as the one of the grenade that ripped off my right arm and both legs.

No, the soldier never forgets. But neither should the rest of us.

When I was wounded, post-traumatic stress disorder did not officially exist. It was recognized as a legitimate illness only in 1978, during my tenure as head of the Veterans Administration under President Jimmy Carter. Today, it is not only recognized, but the Army and the V.A. know how to treat it. I can offer no better testament than my own recovery.

There are estimates that 35 percent of the soldiers who fought in Iraq will suffer post-traumatic stress disorder. I'm sure the numbers for Afghanistan are similar. Researchers have found that nearly half of those returning with the disorder have suicidal thoughts. Suicide among active-duty soldiers is on pace to hit a record total this year. More than 1.7 million soldiers have served in Iraq and Afghanistan. Imagine that some 600,000 of them will have crippling memories, trapped in a vivid and horrible past from which they can't seem to escape.

> *More than 1.7 million soldiers have served in Iraq and Afghanistan. Imagine that some 600,000 of them will have crippling memories, trapped in a vivid and horrible past from which they can't seem to escape.*

We have a family Army today, unlike the Army seen in any generation before. We have fought these wars with the Reserves and the National Guard. Fathers, mothers, soccer coaches and teachers are the soldiers coming home. Whether they like it or not, they will bring their war experiences home to their families and communities.

Post-traumatic Stress Disorder (PTSD)

PTSD is a condition that can develop after you have gone through a life-threatening event. If you have PTSD, you may have trouble keeping yourself from thinking over and over about what happened to you. You may try to avoid people and places that remind you of the trauma. You may feel numb. You may startle easily and you may feel on guard most of the time. Other symptoms may include:

Depression: Depression involves feeling down or sad more days than not. If you are depressed, you may lose interest in activities that used to be enjoyable or fun. You may feel low in energy and be overly tired. You may feel hopeless or in despair, and you may think that things will never get better. Depression is more likely when you have had losses such as the death of close friends. If you are depressed, at times you might think about hurting or killing yourself. For this reason, getting help for depression is very important.

Self-blame, guilt, and shame: Sometimes in trying to make sense of a traumatic event, you may blame yourself in some way. You may think you are responsible for bad things that happened, or for surviving when others didn't. You may feel guilty for what you did or did not do. Most of the time, that guilt, shame, or self-blame is not justified.

Anger or aggressive behavior: Trauma can be connected with anger in many ways. After a trauma, you might think that what happened to you was unfair or unjust. You might not understand why the event happened and why it happened to you. These thoughts can result in intense anger. Although anger is a natural and healthy emotion, intense feelings of anger and aggressive behavior can cause problems with family, friends, or co-workers. If you become violent when angry, you just make the situation worse.

Alcohol/drug abuse: Drinking or "self-medicating" with drugs is a common, and unhealthy, way of coping with upsetting events. You may drink too much or use drugs to numb yourself and to try to deal with difficult thoughts, feelings, and memories related to the trauma. While using alcohol or drugs may offer a quick solution, it can actually lead to more problems. If someone close begins to lose control of drinking or drug use, you should try to get them to see a health care provider about managing their drinking or drug use.

TEXT SET LESSONS / PTSD

Daddy's Home

by Heather Hummert, wife of an Operation Iraqi Freedom veteran and Purple Heart recipient

Daddy's home. Daddy's gone. Daddy's home. Daddy's gone. Daddy's home. Daddy's gone.

This is the life your child has known up until now. There have been piles of upheaval and adjustments they make with a relative ease even you can't fathom. Despite the "here today, gone tomorrow" father of military homes, our children build connections with him and love him and crave for him to be near.

Then he comes home and everything seems beautiful. But Daddy is different. He doesn't want to play trains and tea party anymore. He doesn't take them to the park or tickle them to make them laugh. And while this is breaking your heart, it's bewildering to your children.

And they think:

What did I do? Daddy doesn't love me anymore. I'm not "good enough" for Daddy. I'm scared of Daddy. Things will NEVER be good again. Sound familiar? Like the soundtrack running in your own brain? Guess what, they need reassurance too.

Will Daddy be okay again? They worry about things getting "normal" again just like you. They need reassurance that if Daddy gets the help he needs, he will be okay.

It's all YOUR fault. Daddy's angry. I didn't do anything wrong. It's MOM's fault. It's not your fault. You didn't do it. PTSD did it.

It's all MY fault. Daddy is always angry at me and I don't know what I did wrong, but him being angry MUST be my fault. It's not their fault. It's PTSD.

But how do you describe this to your teenager?

Your children definitely know what is going on and they might be angry at how your spouse treats you. Let them know how you feel gently. Explain that yes, it makes you angry too but you know Daddy can get better when he gets help. Encourage them to participate in activities that are important to them. Do not take these away as a punishment. This is the age when they really need to be learning self-discipline. Many children, when given the choice, will punish themselves harsher than you would have and the punishment will seem fairer to everyone.

Encourage children who want to do something about this to get active in politics. There may be a debate team at school or a local political campaign they want to participate in. Encourage them to be solid thinkers and to explain to the world clearly and concisely what the needs of the veteran community are. They might even do a paper in school on the subject.

Country X

Grouping Sequence:

Base groups and expert groups of 5 each, research teams of 3 to 5

Are GPS units killing the study of geography? In the old days, if you got lost, you looked at a map. Now, little talking boxes sit on our dashboards telling us where to turn, as if we were babies. But we are still in charge. If we get tired of hearing that grumpy American Lady voice say, "Recalculating, recalculating…" we can swap her out for the more easygoing, less irascible Australian Guy.

The trouble is, when our little boxes fail altogether (and they always do), then we're really lost—because we no longer carry a map in the car, and we probably couldn't read it if we did.

In this lesson, kids work with six maps of an imaginary country, depicting natural vegetation, summer and winter temperature, altitude, rainfall, landforms and more. As students study and discuss these maps, we ask them to infer or imagine what kinds of human habitations might have arisen there, and in doing so, they inductively discover a host of key principles about human and economic geography.

Reading maps is just one example of the importance of "reading" graphic displays of information—tables, charts, graphs, timelines, diagrams, matrices, and the like. From the front page of the daily paper to websites throughout the Internet, vital information and materials are arrayed in a variety of such graphic forms. Our kids really need this experience.

Here's the bonus: "Country X" is not imaginary. It is actually a stylized version of the former Soviet Union, flipped upside down and placed in the Southern Hemisphere. So after students have made all their prognostications about how this country might develop, we can compare their hypothetical outcomes to the actual nation, circa 1989. There really are some right answers—as well as some big surprises—in terms of where large cities developed, what crops were grown, and what kind of culture evolved.

TEXTS IN ORDER OF USE

Six maps of Country X (all of equal difficulty); one map of the Soviet Union

1. Basic map of Country X
2. Types of vegetation
3. Altitude (elevation)
4. Rainfall
5. January mean temperature
6. July mean temperature
7. Political map of the USSR, circa 1989

CURRICULUM CONNECTIONS

Social Studies: Human and economic geography, climate, economics, history, agriculture, transportation, migration patterns, culture, understanding and applying key principles of geography to a novel situation, the Cold War.

Biology: Ecology, biomes, animals, evolution, adaptation.

Literature: Tolstoy, Dostoyevsky, Akhmatova; *The World Without Us.*

English Language Arts: Evaluating content presented in visual displays, building academic vocabulary, posing and pursuing research questions, subdividing and monitoring tasks within a collaborative team.

STRATEGIES USED

Reading a Visual Image, Jigsaw

MATERIALS NEEDED

Copies of maps 1–6 for all students, maps 1–7 downloaded for projection (available on the website); for the extension, list of research topics (also on the website).

Steps and Teaching Language

STEP 1 **Prepare and introduce the lesson** Grab all the maps from our website and be ready to project them when needed. Determine where kids will be working at each step of the lesson, and form them into initial groups of five. This number is important because there are five informational maps about the country. You'll be asking each group to have one member specialize in one of the five maps. In a numbers pinch, you can have a couple groups of four or six, which will mean omitting or duplicating one article.

Over the next couple of classes, we are going to be "reading" five maps of an imaginary country. We are going to use these maps to try and figure out how people might live in this place, where they might settle, what they might eat, how they would get around, how they would adapt to the conditions, and even what kinds of industries, cultures, or religions might evolve in this country.

STEP 2 **Distribute and explain materials** Each student should have printed copies of all six maps in front of them. Project map 1, the basic view of the country, to start. *OK, let's all look at map 1 together. What do you notice about the country right away?* Kids will offer ideas like: "It's got mountains and lowlands," "It is surrounded by oceans," and "It is really big." Make a point of how we use the *scale*, a common feature of maps, to calculate the size of an area (this one is huge, more than four thousand miles wide). Confirm other valuable observations. Talk with the class about what each of the maps depicts, defining terms like *vegetation, elevation*, and *mean temperature*. Be sure kids notice that this whole region is in the Southern Hemisphere—the temperature maps are a giveaway.

STEP 3 **Form expert groups**

OK, now each person pick one of the five informational maps—maps 2 through 6—that you want to specialize in and study further with some classmates. You each have to pick a different map, no duplicates, OK? Ready? (Assign maps if kids are slow or hesitant.) *Now we are going to form ourselves into "expert groups." That means everyone who has the July isotherms map is going to meet together, and the people with the January isotherms will be another group, and so on.* Direct kids to specific locations if need be. *Get settled. Now your job is to read and talk about your chosen map, and determine what it shows about the country. You are welcome to use the books and computers in the room for help.*

Strategy 7: **READING A VISUAL IMAGE**

After ten minutes, each expert group will give a two-minute report to the class about how your map helps us understand the country. Each group member must give part of the oral report, so you need to decide who's doing what, and make some notes to guide your presentation. You might want to give your report as a series of three or four points that you can show us directly on the map.

STEP 4 **Monitor** While kids are working, circulate, confer, and coach.

STEP 5 **Reconvene and take reports** Kids remain sitting in their five expert groups. Invite two-minute reports from each group, being sure that all members of each group take a part. Invite other students to ask questions and toss in questions of your own, making sure that everyone is getting a sharper picture of this country.

Strategy 23: **JIGSAW**

STEP 6 **Return to base groups and create summaries** Now have kids return to their original "base groups" of five. Each group will now have an "expert" on each of the five informational maps.

Now that we have heard all this specific information, we want to come up with a summary, a general description of what kind of country this is. Using all the information you have learned from all the maps and reports, please create a one-sentence description of this country. We want a statement that is concise, but full of details. Take two minutes. Write down your statement so you can read it aloud when we come back together.

STEP 7 **Allow work time and then reconvene** Ask groups to read their summaries aloud to the class, in turn. Have kids keep track of what each different summary adds to the big picture—and check to be sure that each detail is supported by the maps. What we are hoping for are statements like this: "This big, complicated country has some warm and probably fertile areas, but lots of really cold and dry places that don't look too good for people."

STEP 8 **Reveal the surprise** If you are not continuing with the extension, be sure to tell kids that these maps depict the former Soviet Union, flipped upside down in the Southern Hemisphere. Project the map of the USSR circa 1989 and let them make comparisons. If you *are* going on with the extension, keep the Soviet Union thing secret for now.

EXTENSION

EXTENSION INQUIRY CIRCLES *(50–100 minutes)*

STEP 1 **Prepare for the extension** Now, the kids have studied Country X's geography for one class period. Hopefully, at this point they will be curious and a little bit puzzled. This open-ended extension is based on Smokey's recent work with Stephanie Harvey in *Comprehension and Collaboration: Inquiry Circles in Action* (2009). Coming up, you'll have small, peer-led teams choose and investigate topics of interest in the curriculum, with guidance and modeling from the veteran learner in the room—that's you!

Decide how much class (and perhaps homework) time to allot to this next stage, in which small groups of kids will pick an investigation topic from the list below (or develop their own). Then you'll support them in researching and sharing their learning.

STEP 2 **Introduce the research project and offer topic choices**

Now I want you all to find something about this mysterious country that you would like to investigate further. In different ways, we are all going to think about how this country might have developed over time. Here are some topics you might look into:

On the Web

Possible Country X Investigation Topics

- Where would the three largest cities develop, and why?

- What areas of this region would have the highest populations and why? The least?

- What would be the main foods eaten by the people in this region? How would diet differ by location?

- If there were major wars or ongoing conflicts in this region, where might they have occurred and what issues might have sparked them?

- How would the modern economic development of the area look? What would be the three or four major industries and where would they be located?

- Over time, what would be the three biggest problems working against the development of this country?

- We have been referring to this area as a country—but this large area might well have turned out to be several different countries. What can you say about the political development of this space? What tribes, clans, states, or other forms of organization might have arisen?

- Assuming that the human species did not originally evolve here, when and how do you think people first arrived in this region? Were they apes, modern people, or something in between? Where did they settle first?

- Say the initial human settlement was established at the foot of the potato-shaped lake in the northeastern area. As population grew and people needed more living space, where would people migrate to and why?

- Pick any spot on the map and make a detailed prediction of how human activities would have developed there. No fair picking the icecap and saying "none."

Form kids into groups of three to five, based on their topic choice. For more control, you can even have kids submit a written ballot with their top five choices, and then form the groups from that information.

The kids' job is to combine the information given on the maps with their knowledge about the ways climate and landscape limit or potentiate human activity (including what they have learned in school). Then they must develop supportable interpretations. Of course, these projects will have a speculative aspect; after all, the kids cannot look up the right answers or expert opinions about Country X! But these topics should lead students to searching and studying concepts like migration, population density, birth rates, carrying capacity, the water cycle, arctic wildlife, and many more.

STEP 3 **Allow work time and provide support** Give students at least an hour of class time to develop their predictions and supports. Make sure they know what form is required, and how the resulting reports will be shared—in writing, as posters, as oral reports.

While teams work, you can help them in two important ways: (1) by listening to their ideas, challenging assumptions, or reminding them of factors they may have overlooked; (2) by sitting down at a computer with a group and doing a "search-aloud" with them, modeling how you'd look for information on their topic.

STEP 4 **Share reports** Provide time for each group to share its prognostications with the whole class. Be sure that listeners have a job to do as audience members, making notes or preparing follow-up questions.

STEP 5 **Reveal the "secret"**

Has anyone been suspecting that this might not be a completely imaginary country? Yes? Well, you're right. What we have been calling Country X is actually a simplified map of the old Soviet Union, turned upside down and placed in the Southern Hemisphere. Look at this map of the USSR in 1989 and see what similarities you notice. Project the USSR map (map 7).

STEP 6 **Study and react** Give kids time to study the map and talk with each other about what they are noticing. A few "right answers" will pop right off the map—like whether big cities actually developed in the spots where kids predicted. But many contrasts will require more research—so what *are* the main crops of this region? Is fishing as big a food source as predicted? What was the Soviet Union anyhow, and how does its history fit into kids' predictions about tribes, regions, migration, and governments?

Tips and Variations

■ **THIS CONTENT REALLY MATTERS** Kids inductively encounter many valuable ideas about human geography from this exercise. What are the constraints that nature places upon us? What are resources and how do we use them? How do size and distance affect human life? It is obvious from this activity that geography powerfully shapes, but does not completely control, human habitation. Sometimes people can adapt to unpromising circumstances; other times we humans seem to ignore better geographic possibilities that stand right before us, and of course, geography is always changing, requiring us to adapt or move on.

■ **SPEND MORE TIME WITH THE IMAGE** In Step 3 of the main lesson, you can insert the quadrant-viewing exercise explained on pages 58–61. Have kids fold their chosen maps in quadrants and study each section slowly. Then, when they sit down with other kids in an expert group, they will bring more "noticings" to the table.

■ **THE MORE THE MERRIER** In the extension, it is fine for several groups to take on the same inquiry question if they want. This gives rise to some of the most interesting reports and conversations later on—for example, when two groups differ about the location of major cities. But as teams with the same question work, make sure they don't just imitate each other and come up with the same answers.

■ **A POSSIBLE FURTHER EXTENSION** Once kids have seen the USSR map—and if time allows—encourage the groups to search for more information and create a final report in which they compare their predictions to the realities.

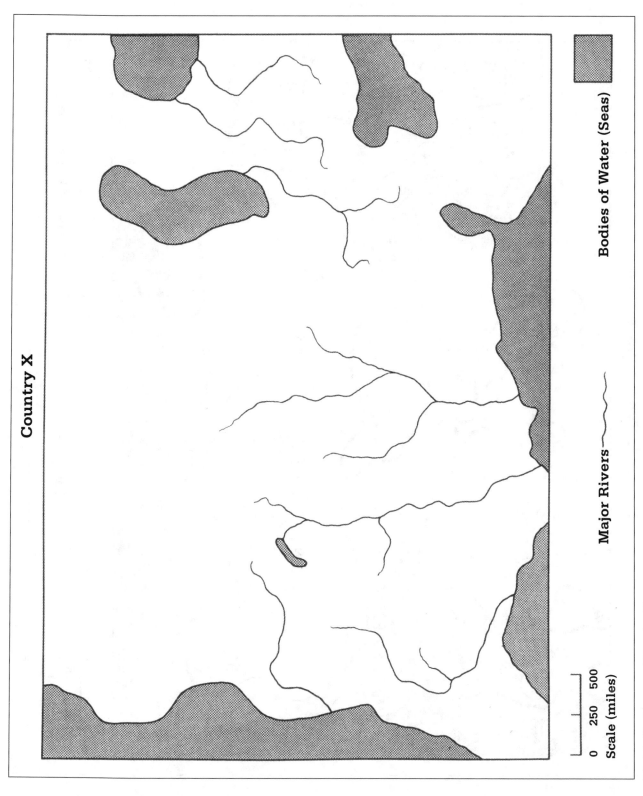

Map 1: Basic map of Country X

Country X: Types of Vegetation

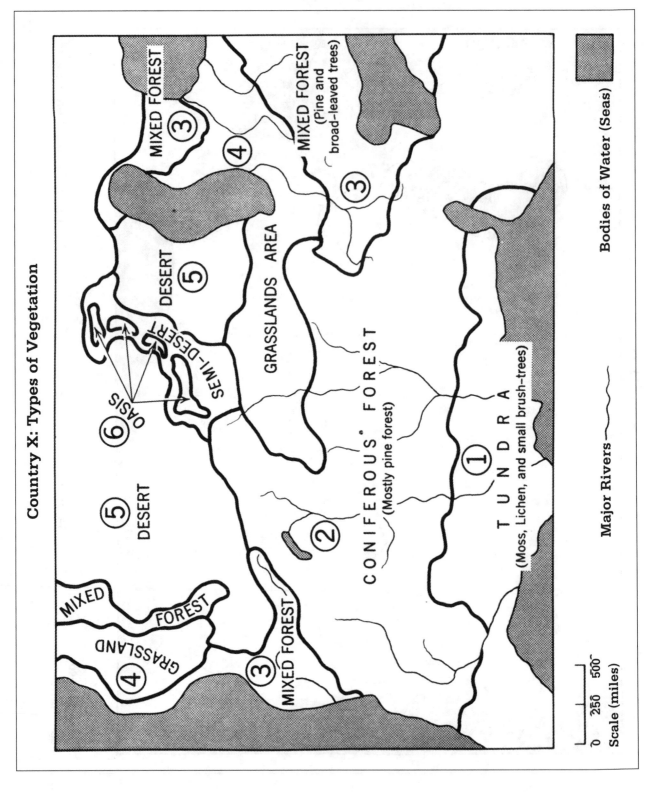

Bodies of Water (Seas)

Major Rivers ⌇⌇⌇

Scale (miles)
0   250   500

Map 2: Types of vegetation

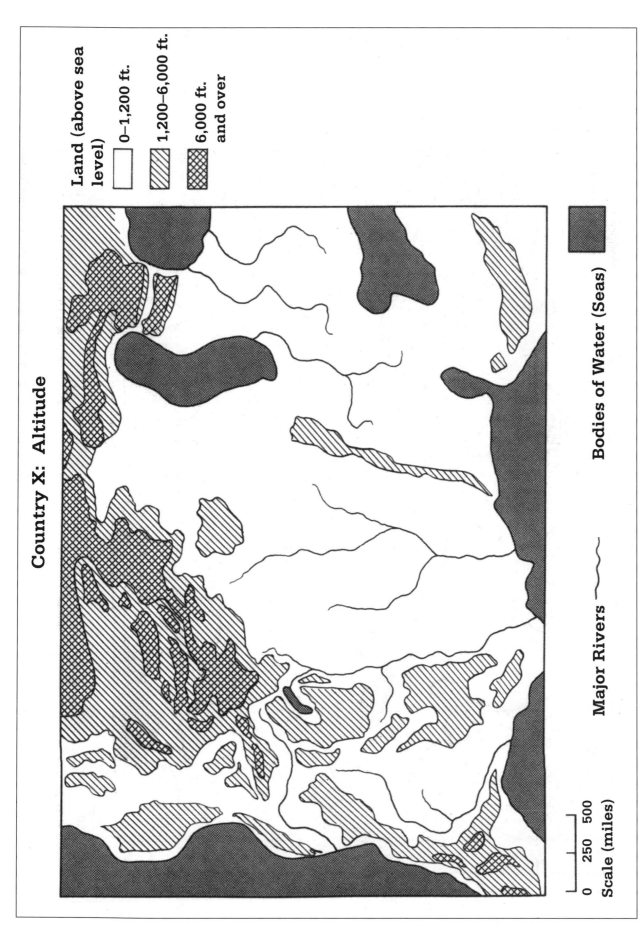

Country X: Altitude

Land (above sea level)

☐ 0–1,200 ft.

▨ 1,200–6,000 ft.

▨ 6,000 ft. and over

Bodies of Water (Seas) ■

Major Rivers ∿

Scale (miles)

0 250 500

Map 3: Altitude (elevation)

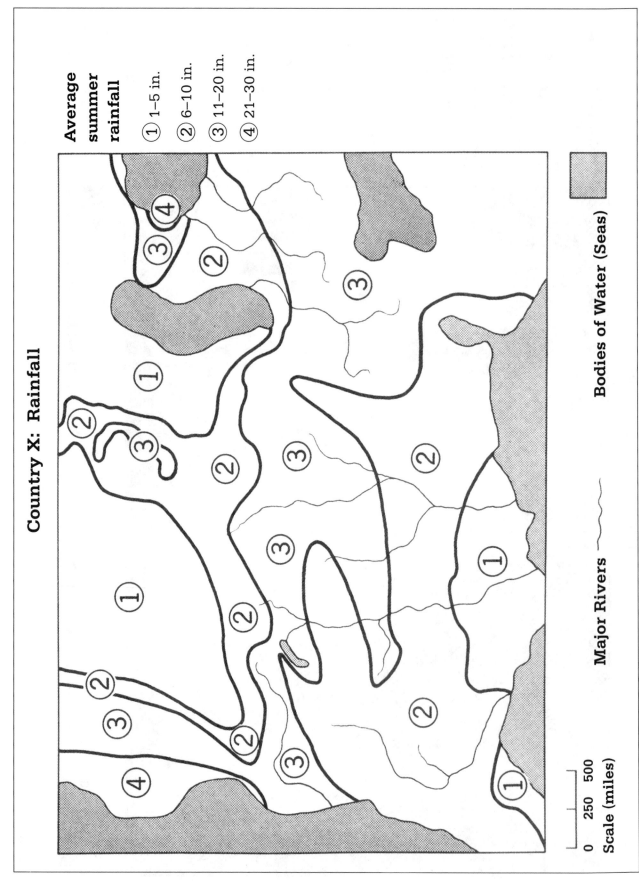

Country X: Rainfall

Average summer rainfall

① 1–5 in.

② 6–10 in.

③ 11–20 in.

④ 21–30 in.

Bodies of Water (Seas)

Major Rivers

0   250   500

Scale (miles)

Map 4: Rainfall

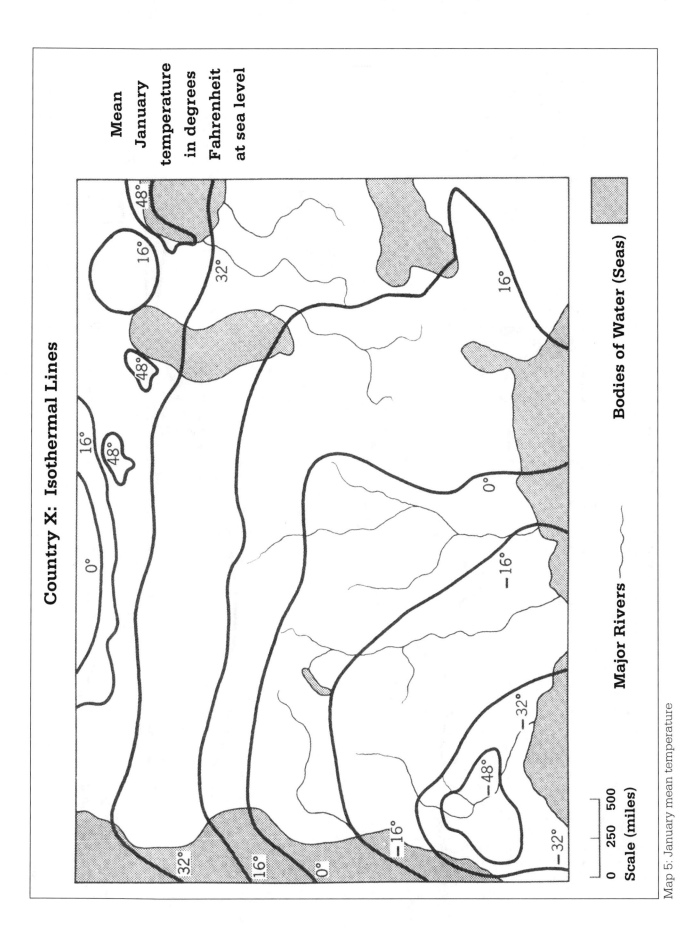

Country X: Isothermal Lines

Mean January temperature in degrees Fahrenheit at sea level

Major Rivers

Bodies of Water (Seas)

Scale (miles)
0   250   500

Map 5: January mean temperature

Country X: Isothermal Lines

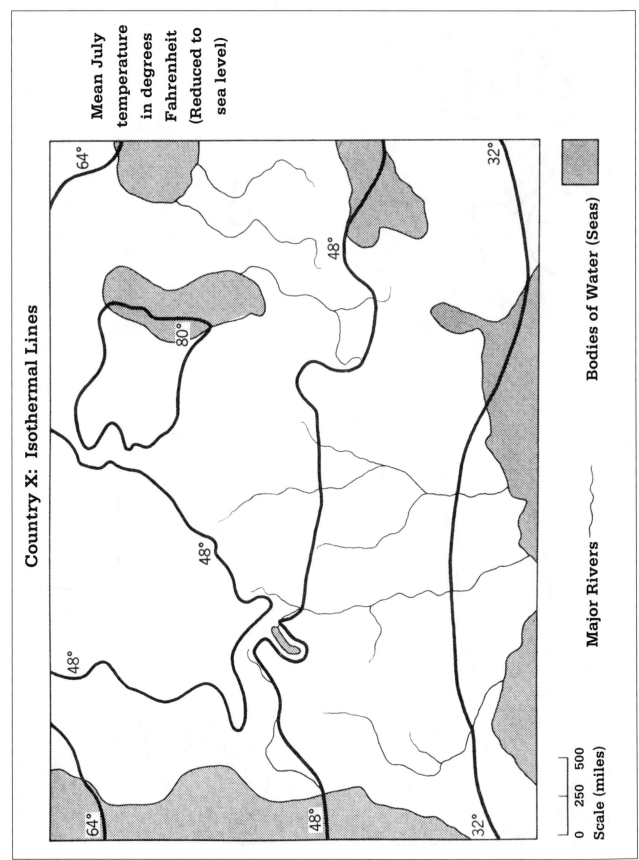

Mean July temperature in degrees Fahrenheit (Reduced to sea level)

Bodies of Water (Seas)

Major Rivers

Scale (miles)

0   250   500

Map 6: July mean temperature

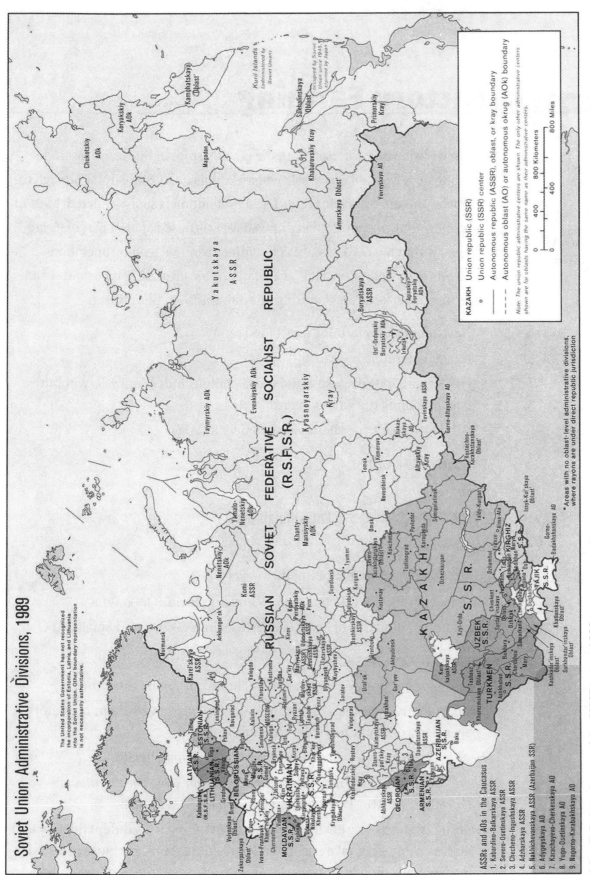

Soviet Union Administrative Divisions, 1989

The United States Government has not recognized the incorporation of Estonia, Latvia, and Lithuania into the Soviet Union. Other boundary representation is not necessarily authoritative.

RUSSIAN SOVIET FEDERATIVE SOCIALIST REPUBLIC (R.S.F.S.R.)

Yakutskaya ASSR

Kuril Islands (administered by Soviet Union)

Occupied by Soviet Union since 1945, claimed by Japan

Kamchatskaya Oblast'

Koryakskiy AOk

Chukotskiy AOk

Magadan

Sakhalinskaya Oblast'

Khabarovskiy Kray

Amurskaya Oblast'

Yevreyskaya AO

Primorskiy Kray

Chita

Aginskiy Buryatskiy AOk

Buryatskaya ASSR

Ust'-Ordynskiy Buryatskiy AOk

Irkutsk

Tuvinskaya ASSR

Gorno-Altayskaya AO

Evenkiyskiy AOk

Krasnoyarskiy Kray

Taymyrskiy AOk

Yamalo-Nenetskiy AOk

Khanty-Mansiyskiy AOk

Nenetskiy AOk

Komi ASSR

Altayskiy Kray

Kemerovo

Tomsk

Novosibirsk

Omsk

Tyumen'

Kurgan

Sverdlovsk

Perm'

Komi-Permyatskiy AOk

Kirov

Arkhangel'sk

Murmansk

Karel'skaya ASSR

Vostochno-Kazakhstanskaya Oblast'

Semipalatinsk

Pavlodar

Tselinograd

Karaganda

Kokchetav

Kustanay

K A Z A K H   S. S. R.

Kyzyl-Orda

Aktyubinsk

Ural'sk

Gur'yev

Mangyshlak

Taldy-Kurgan

Alma-Ata

Frunze

Issyk-Kul'skaya Oblast'

KIRGHIZ S.S.R.

Osh

Gorno-Badakhshanskaya AO

TAJIK S.S.R.

Dushanbe

Leninabad

Namangan

Fergana

Tashkent

UZBEK S.S.R.

Bukhara

Samarkand

Kashkadarinskaya Oblast'

Surkhandarinskaya Oblast'

Khatlonskaya Oblast'

Chardzhou

Mary

Ashkhabad

TURKMEN S.S.R.

Krasnovodsk

Kara-Kalpakskaya ASSR

Syrdarinskaya Oblast'

Dzhambul

Chimkent

ASSRs and AOs in the Caucasus
1. Kabardino-Balkarskaya ASSR
2. Severo-Osetinskaya ASSR
3. Checheno-Ingushskaya ASSR
4. Adzharskaya ASSR
5. Nakhichevanskaya ASSR (Azerbaijan SSR)
6. Adygeyskaya AO
7. Karachayevo-Cherkesskaya AO
8. Yugo-Osetinskaya AO
9. Nagorno-Karabakhskaya AO

Bashkirskaya ASSR

Chelyabinsk

Orenburg

Ufa

Tatarskaya ASSR

Kazan'

Udmurtskaya ASSR

Mariyskaya ASSR

Chuvashskaya ASSR

Kuybyshev

Ul'yanovsk

Penza

Saratov

Volgograd

Mordovskaya ASSR

Tambov

Lipetsk

Voronezh

Rostov

Astrakhan'

Kalmytskaya ASSR

Stavropol'skiy Kray

Krasnodarskiy Kray

Dagestanskaya ASSR

Baku

AZERBAIJAN S.S.R.

ARMENIAN S.S.R.

GEORGIAN S.S.R.

Tbilisi

Abkhazskaya ASSR

Vologda

Kostroma

Yaroslavl'

Ivanovo

Vladimir

Gor'kiy

Ryazan'

Tula

Orel

Kursk

Belgorod

Kaluga

Bryansk

Smolensk

Kalinin

Moscow

MOSCOW

Leningrad

Novgorod

Pskov

ESTONIAN S.S.R.

Tallinn

LATVIAN S.S.R.

Riga

LITHUANIAN S.S.R.

Vilnius

Kaliningrad (R.S.F.S.R.)

Brest

Grodno

Minsk

BELORUSSIAN S.S.R.

Mogilev

Gomel'

Vitebsk

UKRAINIAN S.S.R.

Kiev

Chernigov

Sumy

Khar'kov

Poltava

Cherkassy

Kirovograd

Dnepropetrovsk

Donetsk

Voroshilovgrad

Zaporozh'ye

Kherson

Nikolayev

Odessa

Krym Oblast'

Vinnitsa

Zhitomir

Rovno

Volynskaya Oblast'

L'vov

Ivano-Frankovsk

Ternopol'

Khmel'nitskiy

Zakarpatskaya Oblast'

Chernovtsy

MOLDAVIAN S.S.R.

Kishinev

Legend

KAZAKH — Union republic (SSR)

○ Union republic (SSR) center

—— Autonomous republic (ASSR), oblast, or kray boundary

– – – Autonomous oblast (AO) or autonomous okrug (AOk) boundary

Note: The union republic administrative centers are shown. The only other administrative centers shown are for oblasts having the same name as their administrative centers.

*Areas with no oblast-level administrative divisions, where rayons are under direct republic jurisdiction

0   400   800 Kilometers

0   400   800 Miles

Map 7: Political map of the USSR, circa 1989

Factory Farming

Grouping Sequence:

Groups of 5, whole class; for the extension, pairs or groups of 4

On the Web

When we bring home a roast from the grocery store or bite into a fast food hamburger, how often do we ask: where did this meat come from? Though we probably picture a bucolic family farm, that notion is sadly outdated. Most of the meat that graces our plates nowadays was raised at least part of its life-span within the confines of a concentrated animal feeding operation (CAFO). By definition, CAFOs are large, typically raising thousands of animals in a single location. Some big questions arise in this text set:

- How does factory farming affect food safety?
- Is factory farming humane?
- How can a CAFO dispose of the waste of thousands of animals without contaminating the environment?
- Would you want your house located near a CAFO?

TEXTS IN ORDER OF USE

Main Lesson:

"Boss Hog"—Parts 1–5 (all of equal difficulty)

Extension:

"The Superbug in Your Supermarket"—Parts 1–2

Fact Sheet #13B: CAFO Requirements for Large Swine Operations

Regulatory Definitions of Large CAFOs, Medium CAFOs, and Small CAFOs

CURRICULUM CONNECTIONS

Science: Agriculture, environmental pollution, antibiotic resistance.

Social Studies: Economies of food production, how government regulatory agencies work, how food reflects culture.

Health: Connection between food supply and human health.

Literature: The Jungle, Fast Food Nation, Chew on This, The Omnivore's Dilemma, The Way We Eat: Why Our Food Choices Matter.

English Language Arts: Read complex informational texts independently and discuss with peers; take and defend a position; represent ideas in visual media; draw upon important details to create a synthesis of text.

Carousel Brainstorming, Gallery Walk, Jigsaw, Text Annotation, Two-Column Notes, Save the Last Word for Me, Read with a Question in Mind, Where Do You Stand, Turn and Talk

MATERIALS NEEDED

For the main lesson, one projectable version of "Boss Hog" for each group, five projectors, poster paper, colored markers, tape, projectable list of discussion questions for class share. For the extension, copies of the four articles (see Step 1), labels for the room corners.

Steps and Teaching Language

PART 1 CAROUSEL BRAINSTORMING *(15 minutes)*

STEP 1 **Prepare materials** Before beginning the lesson, determine how you will have students form groups of five. Of course, no class has exactly fifteen or thirty students, so you may have some groups of four. However, the more groups you have, the more stations you will need, which in turn means more preparation work for you! Also, the more groups you have, the longer this activity will take. Prepare poster paper charts equal to the number of groups, each with a different heading/question:

• Favorite Fast Foods

• Reasons for Eating Meat

• Reasons for Being a Vegetarian

• How Do You Think Food Animals Are Raised?

Try to have all groups respond to only three or four prompts. For a large class, use the same prompts twice but post them on opposite sides of the room. Once groups are in place, send half of the class to one side of the room and the rest to the other side.

Strategy 20: **CAROUSEL BRAIN-STORMING**

STEP 2 **Introduce carousel brainstorming**

Today before we read, we're going to do some carousel brainstorming. As you walked in, you probably noticed the charts on the wall. After you form your groups, I am going to give each group a different colored marker. Your group will visit each chart for a couple of minutes. When you are at a chart, I want you to talk about the topic with your group and jot down on the chart as many ideas or examples as you can. As you might have guessed, today we're going to be reading about food.

STEP 3 **Finish assignment instructions and monitor brainstorming**
Situate groups at the various charts and explain to the class that they will be switching to a new chart when you call time. Give groups just a minute at each chart. That way, no one group will have time to jot down every idea they can think of—and the other groups will then get a shot at adding something new when they arrive. Also, when students get to the "fast food" chart, tell them to add new favorites but also place voting checks by the foods already listed that are their favorites.

Strategy 19: **GALLERY WALK**

STEP 4 **Conduct a gallery walk** Once groups have circled through all the charts, open the class up to a gallery walk. *Now that the groups have jotted ideas on all the topics, I want you to take a quick look at all the charts. Pay attention to what got added after you visited a chart. Notice the ideas that your group didn't think of.* Give students just enough time to read through the charts and then have them return to their seats.

STEP 5 **Share with the whole class** Open the class up for a quick share. *What were some interesting ideas that you noticed on the charts? What common ingredients do a lot of your favorite fast foods contain? Meat, right?*

PART 2 JIGSAWING ARTICLES USING TWO-COLUMN NOTES
(30 minutes)

Strategy 23: **JIGSAW**

STEP 1 **Introduce the topic and jigsaw text**
When we talked about your favorite fast foods, lots of you mentioned some kind of meat: chicken, beef, or pork (the bacon on that cheeseburger). Most of the animals used for fast food meat are raised in large numbers at locations called concentrated animal feeding operations; the acronym for this is CAFO. The text we're going to read today is from Rolling Stone *magazine; it's an article about how pigs are raised—and some problems that can come up when they are grown in CAFOs. Since the original article was pretty long, I broke it into five parts that are all about the same length. Each of your groups needs to gather around a different screen and I'll show you which section number your group will be reading.*

STEP 2 **Give instructions for reading**
I think you're going to find these articles interesting; actually, there are parts that are kind of gross or shocking. I bet if we were to text-code some of these passages, we would all probably put the same code next to them: OMG!

Strategy 3: **TWO-COLUMN NOTES**

Anyway, before we start reading, take out a piece of paper, fold it "hot dog" style, and label the columns "Information" and "Reactions/Questions." As you silently read your group's section, I want you to do two things. In the left-hand column of your paper, write down information from the article that seems particularly gross or shocking. Then jot down a response or a conversation question about the information you've noted: something that will really get your group talking about this passage..

STEP 3 **Monitor reading** Circulate, confer, and assist. Remind students to follow the instructions you outlined. If you notice students finishing early, prompt them to go back and add to their thoughts and questions.

STEP 4 **Form new groups and give instructions for group discussion**

Strategy 10: **SAVE THE LAST WORD FOR ME**

Everybody stand up and hold up your right hand. Now signal what section of the article you just read by holding up that many fingers. Look around and see who has what sections. Quickly form new groups of five. Each member should have read a different section of the article. Once seated, turn to your group to share and discuss your notes. Go in the numbered order of the articles. When it's your turn, read aloud the most gross or shocking information, and then "save the last word." Instead of immediately explaining why you picked it, let the other members of your group say something first. They can explain how your information relates to something else in another part of the article. Or they can explain how your passage connects with an idea on one of our posted charts. After everyone has contributed, add any ideas that didn't already get mentioned or ask one of your questions—whatever you think will best keep the conversation going.

As groups discuss, monitor for following the directions and remembering to use the Save the Last Word strategy. As soon as you see discussion winding down, call time.

STEP 5 **Share with the whole class** Call groups back to order for a quick large-group share framed around these questions:

- How does factory farming affect food safety?

- Is factory farming humane?

- How can a CAFO dispose of the waste of thousands of animals without contaminating the environment?

- Would you want your house located near a CAFO?

EXTENSION

JIGSAW *(40 minutes)*

STEP 1 **Prepare the lesson** This jigsaw can be done in groups of either two or four. If using pairs, copy the two articles on CAFOs back to back and the two parts of "The Superbug in Your Supermarket" back to back. If using groups of four, run each piece on a separate page so that you have four choices. Prepare signs to label room corners "strongly agree," "agree," "disagree," and "strongly disagree."

when your groups discussed "Boss Hog," I heard in the sharing that most of you noticed that antibiotics are necessary to keep animals healthy in a CAFO environment.

Today in your group [or pair] you're going to have to negotiate who's reading what. Two of the articles are government-written guidelines for CAFOs; the other two articles are about how the antibiotics used on livestock are starting to affect us.

Strategy 2: **READ WITH A QUESTION IN MIND**

STEP 3 **Give instructions for reading** Pass out the articles and allow groups to negotiate who is reading what. *As you read, I want you to think about the following questions* [project or write on the board]:

- Are CAFOs the best way to raise animals for food? Why?

- What food safety and environmental problems might CAFOs be creating?

- Who is the intended audience for each of these articles and how might the text influence that audience?

- After reading these articles, are you likely to increase or decrease your consumption of animal products? Why?

- Would you ever consider becoming a vegetarian? Why?

- Is eating vegetables safer than eating meat?

STEP 4 **Determine the discussion prompts you will use** Next, choose three prompts for the class to respond to from the possibilities listed or use ones you've created. Use only three—more than that diminishes the impact and kids may get distracted.

- I'm thinking about eating less meat.

- I'm thinking about becoming a vegetarian.

- CAFO operations are animal cruelty.

- I wouldn't mind living near a CAFO.

- The EPA needs to redefine CAFO regulations so that they do not pollute.

- I am concerned about the overuse of antibiotics in raising livestock.

- I would be willing to pay more for my fast-food favorites if I knew the animals were treated humanely.

- I would be willing pay more for my fast-food favorites if I knew that the way the livestock was raised was not polluting the environment or endangering us with antibiotic overuse.

Strategy 18: **WHERE DO YOU STAND?**

STEP 5   **Begin Where Do You Stand?** After students have finished reading: *Instead of having another small-group discussion about the reading, we are going to get up and physically show our thoughts. I'm going to give you a statement and you have to decide whether you strongly agree, agree, disagree, or strongly disagree. Then you're going to walk to that spot in the room. You are voting with your feet. You cannot be neutral or abstain. Everybody stand up and listen to the first statement.* Read one of the prompts you previously chose. *Based on the information in the article you just read, move to the corner label—"strongly agree," "agree," "disagree," or "strongly disagree"—that best reflects your reaction to this statement.*

Strategy 1: **TURN AND TALK**

STEP 6   **Give discussion instructions** Give students time to move into position—vote with their feet. *Now quickly find a partner and interview each other on your reasons for why you strongly agree, agree, disagree, or strongly disagree. Be sure to work with your partner to defend your opinion with facts from the texts you've read.*

STEP 7   **Share with the whole class** After a minute, call on one pair from each opinion category to explain their reasoning. If the class seems particularly engaged, you might invite pairs to attempt to persuade a different opinion group to defect to their side. Once the whole-class share is concluded, offer the next prompt and repeat. Remember: use only three prompts total, unless kids are really into it.

Tips and Variations

■   **LET KIDS DEVELOP STATEMENTS** In Step 4 of the extension, we offer some ready-made statements for the "Where Do You Stand?" activity. But, if you'd rather have your students think of their own statements, have them brainstorm this prompt with their groups or in pairs: *What does knowing more about factory farms make you think about? How might this knowledge change your attitude or eating behavior? Brainstorm two or three statements and write them on the index cards I've passed out. Use one index card per group.* We suggest using index cards rather than creating a master list because this will save time as well as create a bigger surprise for the rest of the class when a group's statement is chosen.

Rolling Stone

Boss Hog—Part 1

America's top pork producer churns out a sea of waste that has destroyed rivers, killed millions of fish and generated one of the largest fines in EPA history. Welcome to the dark side of the other white meat.

JEFF TIETZ

Dec. 14, 2006

Smithfield Foods, the largest and most profitable pork processor in the world, killed 27 million hogs last year. Hogs produce three times more excrement than human beings do. The 500,000 pigs at a single Smithfield farm generate more fecal matter each year than the 1.5 million inhabitants of Manhattan. The best estimates put Smithfield's total waste discharge at 26 million tons a year. That would fill four Yankee Stadiums.

Smithfield's pigs live by the hundreds or thousands in warehouse-like barns, in rows of wall-to-wall pens. Sows are artificially inseminated and fed and delivered of their piglets in cages so small they cannot turn around. Forty fully grown 250-pound male hogs often occupy a pen the size of a tiny apartment. They trample each other to death. There is no sunlight, straw, fresh air or earth. The floors are slatted to allow excrement to fall into a catchment pit under the pens.

The temperature inside hog houses is often hotter than ninety degrees. The air, saturated almost to the point of precipitation with gases from feces and chemicals, can be lethal to the pigs. Enormous exhaust fans run twenty-four hours a day. The ventilation systems function like the ventilators of terminal patients: If they break down for any length of time, pigs start dying.

From Smithfield's point of view, the problem with this lifestyle is immunological. Taken together, the immobility, poisonous air and terror of confinement badly damage the pigs' immune systems. They become susceptible to infection, and in such dense quarters microbes or parasites or fungi, once established in one pig, will rush spritelike through the whole population.

Accordingly, factory pigs are infused with a huge range of antibiotics and vaccines, and are doused with insecticides. Without these compounds—oxytetracycline, draxxin, ceftiofur, tiamulin—diseases would likely kill them. Thus factory-farm pigs remain in a state of dying until they're slaughtered. When a pig nearly ready to be slaughtered grows ill, workers sometimes shoot it up with as many drugs as necessary to get it to the slaughterhouse under its own power. As long as the pig remains ambulatory, it can be legally killed and sold as meat.

The drugs Smithfield administers to its pigs, of course, exit its hog houses in pig feces. Industrial pig waste also contains a host of other toxic substances: ammonia, methane, hydrogen sulfide, carbon monoxide, cyanide, phosphorous, nitrates and heavy metals. In addition, the waste nurses more than 100 microbial pathogens that can cause illness in humans, including salmonella, cryptosporidium, streptocolli and girardia. Each gram of hog feces can contain as much as 100 million fecal coliform bacteria.

> **Forty fully grown 250-pound male hogs often occupy a pen the size of a tiny apartment. They trample each other to death. There is no sunlight, straw, fresh air or earth.**

Rolling Stone

Boss Hog—Part 2

America's top pork producer churns out a sea of waste that has destroyed rivers, killed millions of fish and generated one of the largest fines in EPA history. Welcome to the dark side of the other white meat.

JEFF TIETZ

Dec. 14, 2006

Smithfield's feces holding ponds—the company calls them lagoons—cover as much as 120,000 square feet. The area around a single slaughterhouse can contain hundreds of lagoons, some of which run thirty feet deep. The liquid in them is not brown. The interactions between the bacteria and blood and urine and excrement and chemicals and drugs turn the lagoons pink.

The lagoons themselves are so viscous and venomous that if someone falls in it is foolish to try to save him. A few years ago, a truck driver in Oklahoma was transferring pig feces to a lagoon when he and his truck went over the side. It took almost three weeks to recover his body. In 1992, when a worker making repairs to a lagoon in Minnesota began to choke to death on the fumes, another worker dived in after him, and they died the same death. In another instance, a worker who was repairing a lagoon in Michigan was overcome by the fumes and fell in. His fifteen-year-old nephew dived in to save him but was overcome, the worker's cousin went in to save the teenager but was overcome, the worker's older brother dived in to save them but was overcome, and then the worker's father dived in. They all died in pig feces.

> **Studies have shown that lagoons emit hundreds of different volatile gases into the atmosphere, including ammonia, methane, carbon dioxide and hydrogen sulfide.**

Studies have shown that lagoons emit hundreds of different volatile gases into the atmosphere, including ammonia, methane, carbon dioxide and hydrogen sulfide. A single lagoon releases many millions of bacteria into the air per day, some resistant to human antibiotics. Hog farms in North Carolina also emit some 300 tons of nitrogen into the air every day as ammonia gas, much of which falls back to earth and deprives lakes and streams of oxygen, stimulating algal blooms and killing fish.

Looking down from a plane, we watch as several of Smithfield's farmers spray their hog feces straight up into the air as a fine mist: It looks like a public fountain. Lofted and atomized, the feces is blown clear of the company's property. People who breathe the feces-infused air suffer from bronchitis, asthma, heart palpitations, headaches, diarrhea, nosebleeds and brain damage.

TEXT SET LESSONS / FACTORY FARMING

Rolling Stone

Boss Hog—Part 3

America's top pork producer churns out a sea of waste that has destroyed rivers, killed millions of fish and generated one of the largest fines in EPA history. Welcome to the dark side of the other white meat.

JEFF TIETZ

Dec. 14, 2006

Each of the company's lagoons is surrounded by several fields. Pollution control at Smithfield consists of spraying the pig feces from the lagoons onto the fields to fertilize them. The idea is borrowed from the past: The small hog farmers that Smithfield drove out of business used animal waste to fertilize their crops, which they then fed to the pigs. Smithfield says that this, in essence, is what it does—its crops absorb every ounce of its pig feces, making the lagoon-sprayfield system a zero-discharge, nonpolluting waste-disposal operation. In fact, Smithfield doesn't grow nearly enough crops to absorb all of its hog waste. The company raises so many pigs in so little space that it actually has to import the majority of their food, which contains large amounts of nitrogen and phosphorus. Those chemicals—discharged in pig feces and sprayed on fields—run off into the surrounding ecosystem. At one point, three hog-raising counties in North Carolina were producing more nitrogen, and eighteen were producing more phosphorus, than all the crops in the state could absorb.

Many studies have documented the harm caused by hog-waste runoff; one showed the pig feces raising the level of nitrogen and phosphorus in a receiving river as much as sixfold. In eastern North Carolina, nine rivers and creeks in the Cape Fear and Neuse River basins have been classified by the state as either "negatively impacted" or environmentally "impaired."

To appreciate what this agglomeration of hog production does to the people who live near it, you have to appreciate the smell of industrial-strength pig feces. To get a really good whiff, I drive down a narrow country road of white sand and walk up to a Smithfield lagoon. There is an unwholesome tang in the air, but there is no wind and it isn't hot, so I can't smell the lagoon itself. I walk the few hundred yards over to it. It is covered with a thick film; its edge is a narrow beach of big black flies. Here, its odor is leaking out. I take a deep breath.

> **The smell at its core has a frightening, uniquely enriched putridity, both deep-sweet and high-sour.**

I fight an impulse to vomit. I've probably smelled stronger odors in my life, but nothing so insidiously and instantaneously nauseating. The smell at its core has a frightening, uniquely enriched putridity, both deep-sweet and high-sour. I back away from it and walk back to the car but I remain sick—it's a shivery, retchy kind of nausea—for a good five minutes. That's apparently characteristic of industrial pig feces: It keeps making you sick for a good while after you've stopped smelling it. It's as if something has physically entered your stomach.

Boss Hog—Part 4

America's top pork producer churns out a sea of waste that has destroyed rivers, killed millions of fish and generated one of the largest fines in EPA history. Welcome to the dark side of the other white meat.

JEFF TIETZ

Dec. 14, 2006

Studies show that those who live near hog lagoons suffer from abnormally high levels of depression, tension, anger, fatigue and confusion. Sometimes the stink literally knocks people down: They walk out of the house to get something in the yard and become so nauseous they collapse. When they regain consciousness, they crawl back into the house.

That has happened several times to Julian and Charlotte Savage, an elderly couple whose farmland now abuts a Smithfield sprayfield—one of several meant to absorb the feces of 50,000 hogs. Sitting in the kitchen, Charlotte tells me that she once saw Julian collapse in the yard and ran out and threw a coat over his head and dragged him back inside. Before Smithfield arrived, Julian's family farmed the land for the better part of a century. He raised tobacco, corn, wheat, turkeys and chickens. Now he has respiratory problems and rarely attempts to go outside.

A river that receives a lot of waste from an industrial hog farm begins to die quickly. Toxins and microbes can kill plants and animals outright; the waste itself consumes available oxygen and suffocates fish and aquatic animals; and the nutrients in the pig feces produce algal blooms that also deoxygenate the water.

> **They walk out of the house to get something in the yard and become so nauseous they collapse. When they regain consciousness, they crawl back into the house.**

The biggest spill in the history of corporate hog farming happened in 1995. The dike of a 120,000-square-foot lagoon owned by a Smithfield competitor ruptured, releasing 25.8 million gallons of waste into the headwaters of the New River in North Carolina. It was the biggest environmental spill in United States history, more than twice as big as the Exxon Valdez oil spill six years earlier. The sludge was so toxic it burned your skin if you touched it, and so dense it took almost two months to make its way sixteen miles downstream to the ocean. From the headwaters to the sea, every creature living in the river was killed. Fish died by the millions.

It's hard to conceive of a fish kill that size. The kill began with turbulence in one small part of the water: fish writhing and dying. Then it spread in patches along the entire length and breadth of the river. In two hours, dead and dying fish were mounded wherever the river's contours slowed the current. Within a day dead fish completely covered the riverbanks. The smell of rotting fish covered much of the county; the air above the river was chaotic with scavenging birds. There were far more dead fish than the birds could ever eat.

Boss Hog—Part 5

America's top pork producer churns out a sea of waste that has destroyed rivers, killed millions of fish and generated one of the largest fines in EPA history. Welcome to the dark side of the other white meat.

JEFF TIETZ

Dec. 14, 2006

Corporate hog farming contributes to another form of environmental havoc: Pfiesteria piscicida, a microbe that, in its toxic form, has killed a billion fish and injured dozens of people. Nutrient-rich waste like pig feces creates the ideal environment for Pfiesteria to bloom: The microbe eats fish attracted to algae nourished by the waste. Pfiesteria is invisible and odorless—you know it by the trail of dead. The microbe degrades a fish's skin, laying bare tissue and blood cells; it then eats its way into the fish's body. After the 1995 spill, millions of fish developed large bleeding sores on their sides and quickly died. Fishermen found that at least one of Pfiesteria's toxins could take flight: Breathing the air above the bloom caused severe respiratory difficulty, headaches, blurry vision and logical impairment. Some fishermen forgot how to get home; laboratory workers exposed to Pfiesteria lost the ability to solve simple math problems and dial phones; they forgot their own names. It could take weeks or months for the brain and lungs to recover.

Several state legislatures have passed laws prohibiting or limiting the ownership of small farms by pork processors. In some places, new

> **The volumes of concentrated pig waste produced by industrial hog farms are plainly not containable in small areas. The land "just can't absorb everything that comes out of the barns."**

slaughterhouses are required to meet expensive waste-disposal requirements; many are forbidden from using the waste-lagoon system. North Carolina, where pigs now outnumber people, has passed a moratorium on new hog operations and ordered Smithfield to fund research into alternative waste-disposal technologies. South Carolina, having taken a good look at its neighbor's coastal plain, has pronounced the company unwelcome in the state. The federal government and several states have challenged some of Smithfield's recent acquisition deals and, in a few instances, have forced the company to agree to modify its waste-lagoon systems.

These initiatives, of course, come late. Industrial hog operations control at least seventy-five percent of the market. According to Dr. Michael Mallin, a marine scientist at the University of North Carolina at Wilmington who has researched the effects of corporate farming on water quality, the volumes of concentrated pig waste produced by industrial hog farms are plainly not containable in small areas. The land, he says, "just can't absorb everything that comes out of the barns."

The Superbug in Your Supermarket Part 1

A potentially deadly new strain of antibiotic-resistant microbes may be widespread in our food supply

Stephanie Woodard, August 2009

You've probably heard of people contracting certain strains of MRSA in hospitals, where it causes many illnesses: postsurgical infections, pneumonia, bacteremia, and more. Others encounter different types of the bug in community centers such as gyms, where skin contact occurs and items like sports equipment are shared; this form causes skin infections that may become systemic and turn lethal.

Then in 2008, a new source and strain of MRSA emerged in the United States. Researcher Tara Smith, PhD, an assistant professor of epidemiology at the University of Iowa, studied two large Midwestern hog farms and found the strain, ST398, in 45% of farmers and 49% of pigs.

You may not have the same close contact with meat that a processing plant worker has, but scientists warn there is reason for concern: Most of us handle meat daily, as we bread chicken cutlets, trim fat from pork, or form chopped beef into burgers. Cooking does kill the microbe, but MRSA thrives on skin, so you can contract it by touching infected raw meat when you have a cut on

MRSA thrives on skin, so you can contract it by touching infected raw meat when you have a cut on your hand.

your hand, explains Stuart Levy, MD, a Tufts University professor of microbiology and medicine. MRSA also flourishes in nasal passages, so touching your nose after touching meat gives the bug another way into your body, adds Smith.

MRSA is so common in the United States that it accounts for more than half of all soft-tissue and skin infections in ERs. The CDC estimates that invasive MRSA infections (those that entered the bloodstream) number more than 94,000 a year. People who get MRSA need ever more powerful medication. "Staph-related infections have become serious illnesses that can require hospitalization and stronger drugs," says Georges C. Benjamin, MD, executive director of the American Public Health Association (APHA).

Scientists know that antibiotic overuse in humans caused ordinary staph to become resistant, says Levy. And they know the large amounts of meds used by agriculture caused other bacteria, such as E. coli and Salmonella, to develop resistance. "Now we're looking at the relationship between antibiotic use on farms and MRSA," he says.

The Superbug in Your Supermarket Part 2

A potentially deadly new strain of antibiotic-resistant microbes may be widespread in our food supply

Stephanie Woodard, August 2009

Animals consume nearly 70% of antibiotics, perhaps more than 24 million pounds a year, says the Union of Concerned Scientists. The drugs compensate for the often unsanitary conditions in the country's 19,000 factory farms—also called concentrated animal feeding operations, or CAFOs—where about half our meat is produced. Long gone are many family farms with animals grazing on pastureland, says Bob Martin, senior officer of the Pew Environment Group. "Instead, they're packed into cramped quarters, never going outdoors, living in their waste." A swine CAFO may house thousands of hogs; a poultry operation, hundreds of thousands of chickens. "As a result, you need to suppress infection," he says.

The large amounts of antibiotics used in CAFOs include drugs critical to curing human illnesses, he says. Premixed animal feed can contain medications you may have taken, such as tetracycline and cephalosporin (Keflex is a familiar brand); you can also buy a 50-pound bag of antibiotics at a feed store to add to your animals' chow—no prescription necessary, confirms Amy Meyer, executive director of the Missouri Farmers Union.

> *The near constant exposure to less-than-therapeutic levels of antibiotics allows the resistant bacteria to survive; they can then be transferred to people.*

The near constant exposure to less-than-therapeutic levels of antibiotics allows the resistant bacteria to survive; they can then be transferred to people, he says. This needless use of medication is what docs try to avoid when they don't prescribe antibiotics for a simple cold.

In the areas surrounding CAFOs, docs see first-hand how MRSA impacts the community. Philip McClure, DO, practices in Trenton, MO, which is home to many hog farms. MRSA infections have risen as the number of pigs has grown, he says. "Both CAFO workers and others get them," says McClure, who treats a MRSA-related skin problem every month. That may be because you can pick up MRSA and not show symptoms for years. Meanwhile, you can pass it to others by something as simple as sharing a towel. Kim Howland, 44, a former hog CAFO worker in Oklahoma, fears she did just that, when in 2007, her husband and daughter developed MRSA skin infections. "My coworkers told me about lumps they had and I realized I could have become a carrier," she says. Howland, who left her job, wasn't tested at the time, so she'll never know if she gave MRSA to her family.

Livestock and Poultry Environmental
Stewardship (LPES) curriculum

CAFO Fact Sheet series

Fact Sheet #13B: CAFO Requirements for Large Swine Operations

By Don Jones, Purdue University; Glenn Carpenter, USDA–NRCS; Karl VanDevender, University of Arkansas; and Peter Wright, Cornell University

In December 2002, EPA released new rules defining and clarifying the Concentrated Animal Feeding Operation (CAFO) regulations.

Requirements for Swine Operations

The CAFO program for swine applies only to those confined feeding operations that have a one-time capacity of 2,500 head (each weighing more than 55 pounds) or 10,000 swine (each weighing less than 55 pounds).

Common Manure-Handling Systems—Liquid Manure Storage

Most swine manure is handled as a liquid. Manure typically falls through a slotted floor into either a gutter or a concrete storage pit. Four- to ten-foot-deep storage pits, typically providing from 3 to 12 months of manure storage, are usually located directly under the slotted floor. In some operations, the manure falls through the slotted floor into a shallow gutter and is periodically removed to a larger outside storage. Storage is usually sized large enough to hold at least six month's accumulation, preventing the need to apply manure during the crop-growing season or when weather conditions are unsuitable.

Stored liquid manure must be agitated thoroughly to make the manure nutrient content more uniform from load to load when it is hauled to the field for application.

Note: Take precautions when agitating an underslat storage unit or unit connected to the building through the drain system. Even in low concentrations, the hydrogen sulfide gas released during agitation is toxic.

When a deep pit is agitated, animals on a slotted floor over the pit should be removed if possible. Ventilation fans should be operated at high capacity, and humans should stay out of the building. These precautions are especially important during the first 10 to 20 minutes of agitation. Pipes or drain openings between rooms and the outside storage should be gas trapped or sealed.

Liquid manure is either surface applied or incorporated into the soil. Spray irrigation is an efficient method of land application. However, since odor emissions can be significant with spray or surface application, it should be avoided in populated areas.

Regulatory Definitions of Large CAFOs, Medium CAFOs, and Small CAFOs

A large CAFO confines at least the number of animals described in the table below.

A medium CAFO falls within the size range in the table below and either:

• has a manmade ditch or pipe that carries manure or wastewater to surface water; **or**

• the animals come into contact with surface water that passes through the area where they're confined.

A small CAFO confines fewer than the number of animals listed in the table **and** has been designated as a CAFO by the permitted authority as a significant contributor of pollutants.

Animal Sector	Size Threshold (number of animals)		
	Large CAFOs	**Medium CAFOs[1]**	**Small CAFOs[2]**
cattle or cow/calf pairs	1,000 or more	300–999	less than 300
mature dairy cattle	700 or more	200–699	less than 200
veal calves	1,000 or more	300–999	less than 300
swine (weighing over 55 pounds)	2,500 or more	750–2,499	less than 750
swine (weighing less than 55 pounds)	10,000 or more	3,000–9,999	less than 3,000
horses	500 or more	150–499	less than 150
sheep or lambs	10,000 or more	3,000–9,999	less than 3,000
turkeys	55,000 or more	16,500–54,999	less than 16,500
laying hens or broilers (liquid manure handling systems)	30,000 or more	9,000–29,999	less than 9,000
chickens other than laying hens (other than liquid manure handling systems)	125,000 or more	37,500–124,999	less than 37,500
laying hens (other than liquid manure handling systems)	82,000 or more	25,000–81,999	less than 25,000
ducks (other than liquid manure handling systems)	30,000 or more	10,000–29,999	less than 10,000
ducks (liquid manure handling systems)	5,000 or more	1,500–4,999	less than 1,500

[1] Must also meet one of two "method of discharge" criteria to be defined as a CAFO or may be designated.
[2] Never a CAFO by regulatory definition, but may be designated as a CAFO on a case-by-case basis.

Child Labor

As students pass through American schools, they get taught about slavery several times, usually in connection with the Civil War. But it's a tricky topic. To kids, it can seem so ancient—all those black-and-white pictures, battle accounts, names of generals. It's also uncomfortable; who wants to talk about white people holding black folks in bondage, especially when the descendants of slaves and slave owners might be sitting in the same room? But this topic is too important to ignore, not just because it is central to American history but because human bondage afflicts the whole world, right this minute.

In this lesson, kids study contemporary images (provided by the U.S. State Department) of child slavery across many countries. We know that using visual texts can help us differentiate instruction and invite all students into the circle of comprehension. But this isn't just about accommodating your English language learners, kids with special needs, and striving readers. "Reading" pictures is just as vital as reading print. Indeed, in today's world, images sometimes seem even more important, given the vast visual exposure we get from screens all day long. Kids need to know how to read an image; to slow down and go deeper into visual information, just as we have been teaching them to do with print.

TEXTS IN ORDER OF USE (photos of equal difficulty)

Girl making bricks

Boys tending ship

Boy making jewelry

Girl selling flowers

Brothel waiting room

Girls weaving

Social Studies: Child labor, forced labor, U.S. slavery and the Civil War, the United Nations; industry, production and distribution of goods, economics, capitalism, globalization, the "flat" world; social justice.

Literature: Beloved, Holes.

Art: Photojournalism, documentary photography.

Language Arts: Use proficient-reader strategies to view and understand images; use note-taking tools matched to the genre of text at hand; work with others to develop nuanced understandings of public affairs issues.

STRATEGIES USED

Turn and Talk, Support Your Position, Reading a Visual Image

MATERIALS NEEDED

Quiz questions ready to project or hand out, cutout masking tool, child labor photographs. For best results you should project these images, which you can find on the U.S. State Department website at http://www.gtipphotos. state.gov/gtip.cfm?galleryID=562&id=9. A link is also on our website. Note that the photos we have chosen appear in a different order on the website, so rearrange them first and divide image 6 into quadrants.

If using printed pictures, you'll need to make a cutout masking tool for each student. Cut a piece of paper exactly the size of the pictures, and then cut out one quadrant. By flipping and inverting this tool, you can mask any three quadrants at a time to focus on just one. For a quick review of this framing activity, see Strategy 7, page 58.

Steps and Teaching Language

Strategy 1: **TURN AND TALK**

STEP 1 **Form groups and introduce the topic**

There is a problem that is causing increasing outrage and concern around the world today, and that is child slavery, sometimes called child labor or exploitation. Have you heard about this on the news, maybe? Let's get into groups and share what we know, or think we know, about this issue. Have a recorder jot down your background knowledge.

Project the words *child labor* if possible. Visit groups briefly as they discuss.

STEP 2 **Groups report out** Invite a few groups to share highlights of their prior knowledge. Be sure kids understand the difference between actual slavery and having chores, like making your bed, feeding the chickens before school, or working at McDonald's on the weekend. Later in the lesson, kids will probably return to this distinction, trying to figure out where the line is between slavery and being born into a "primitive" culture where children work from dawn to dusk.

STEP 3 **Give the quiz**

Now let's look at child labor another way. I have a two-question quiz that I created from information on the United Nations International Children's Emergency Fund (UNICEF) website. I'm going to put up the first question, and you take a minute in your groups to figure out the answer.

What proportion of the world's children, aged 5 to 17, are in forced labor?

A 1 in 1000

B) 1 in 100

C) 1 in 20

D) 1 in 12

E) 1 in 6

Strategy 12: **SUPPORT YOUR POSITION**

Your group has two minutes to decide on the right answer and be ready to explain your thinking.

When kids are ready, call them back and take each group's answer, asking each to defend their thinking briefly. Encourage groups to challenge each other's reasoning. Reveal that the correct answer is E, 1 in 6. Invite discussion about how that surprising statistic could be true. Encourage kids to piggyback on each other's ideas and questions.

STEP 4 **Present the second question**

What percentage of children in forced labor are girls?

A) 10%

B) 35%

C) 52%

D) 71%

E) 90%

STEP 5 **Repeat the process and let groups determine the answer**
Take responses. The correct answer is E, 90 percent. Have kids discuss how this great disparity could be. (The main reasons trace to the devaluing of females in many countries; girls have lower rates of school attendance than boys and may be sold into prostitution or domestic service.)

STEP 6 **Introduce images** By this time kids should be puzzled, agitated, confused—and ready (even eager) to read. But this time, they'll read pictures rather than paragraphs.

I am going to show you some pictures of kids in child labor around the world. As we look at these, let's talk out loud about what we think we are seeing, what kind of work is being done, what questions we have.

Strategy 1: **TURN AND TALK**

Spend about thirty seconds on each of the images on pages 200 and 201, letting kids think and talk quietly about them in their groups. If kids are just staring, prod them to talk out loud.

STEP 7 **Go deeper with one image** Now project Image 6, of the child weavers. After about thirty seconds, tell the kids:

With this image, we are going to dig a little deeper. Get a blank sheet of paper. We need to divide it into quadrants, or four equal sections. So just fold the paper vertically (hot dog style) and then fold it again horizontally (hamburger style) and unfold. Voila, quadrants!

I have divided this image into four sections also. As I show you each one, I'm going to invite you to jot down notes, just words or phrases, about what you are noticing in that part of the picture. Make your notes in the corresponding quadrant.

Strategy 7: **READING A VISUAL IMAGE**

Here is the upper left section of the picture. Say these instructions in a quiet, slightly hypnotic voice. *As you look into this part of the picture, I invite you to patiently and thoughtfully notice what's in the foreground . . . and what's in the background. What details do you see? If you were in this place, what sounds might you hear? What might you sense or smell? If anything in the picture could talk, what would it say? If you were there, what would you do or ask? As you look more deeply into the picture, what do you wonder? What questions are coming into your mind?*

Give kids a good full minute to jot notes. Circulate through the room, making sure that everyone has several items written before you move to the next quadrant.

Now here is the lower left section of the picture. Repeat the instructions above. For the third and fourth quadrants, you can shorten the instructions or omit them if kids seem fully engaged. However, do not

Student quadrant notes example

project the prompts; this can break the spell of concentration. Show the final two quadrants one at a time, leaving one full minute of viewing and writing time for each.

Now you are going to reveal the whole picture once more. Many kids say that after viewing the four sections, when they see the whole image again, it just pops out, "like going into 3-D." So do this with some ceremony.

OK, we have looked really closely at all four sections. Now I am going to show you the whole picture again. Ready?

As you show the whole picture again, say: *Now you may want to take a minute to add to your notes in some way.*

STEP 8 **Groups meet** Have groups talk over the following three questions, or discuss them immediately with the whole class.

So, what do you think? You've studied this picture really hard.

• What's going on here?

• Where are they?

• What's the relationship between the girls and the man?

Let different kids and groups share and support their ideas. Encourage a range of responses. There are no right answers, but there are more or less well-supported hypotheses.

STEP 9 **Move into the curriculum** At this point, kids will be primed and prepared to view, read, and think further about slavery. You might go directly to a text set of recent articles about child labor around the world. There is a ton of material on the UNICEF and U.S. Departments of Labor and State websites. Or, you can bridge directly to texts about American slavery, the slave trade, the middle passage, the plantation economy, or the U.S. Civil War.

Tips and Variations   ■   **HOW TO MAKE YOUR OWN DIVIDED IMAGES** If you want to use this powerful viewing comprehension strategy for any topic, start with www.images.google.com or other image searching site. Capture an image you want to work with (a photo, painting, or other artwork). It should have high resolution and interesting details in every quadrant. Now dump it into PowerPoint, select the picture, and choose Picture Tools. Use the cropping tool to cut the image down to one quadrant. Expand this image to fill the whole screen and save it. Repeat with the other three sections. Be sure to place the whole image before and after the quadrants. This masking idea is highly flexible: you can also cut circles out of images, focusing kids on a small portion of the image at a time, with no obligation to show it all.

Image 1

Image 2

Image 3

Image 4

Image 5

Image 6

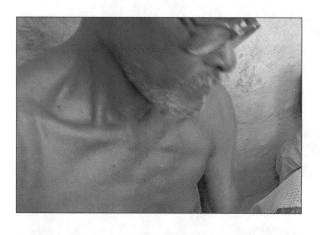

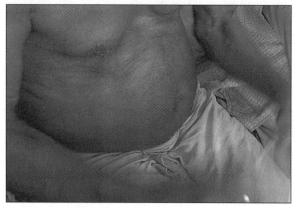

E-Waste

Have you ever run across dusty old electronic stuff in your attic or garage? Like a cell phone the size of a cinderblock, a cassette tape player, a CB radio, an old TV monitor, an Apple II computer, a bag of drained batteries? Well, you and everybody else. Isn't it amazing how fast we acquire and discard these tools, toys, whatever they are?

We are surrounded by our own e-junk. The used-up, worn-out, tossed-aside detritus of our material lives is piled up all around us—or tucked just out of sight. Those stashes of e-junk aren't such a big problem in our own basements or attics—but around the world, day by day, humanity is increasingly imperiled by the production, use, and discarding of these electronic gizmos.

This lesson makes use of a survey, a map, and various nonfiction texts to help students explore their understanding of e-waste. First, we engage kids by reminding them of their own dependence on electronics. Then we ask them to ponder some big questions:

- Do these electronic devices improve our quality of life?
- Is our rapid consumption of electronic consumer goods necessary?
- How concerned should we be about the disposal of these products?
- What is the connection between being "plugged in" 24/7 and the accumulating space junk orbiting the earth?

TEXTS IN ORDER OF USE

Electronics Use Survey, Parts 1 and 2

Choice 1: "Types of Satellites" and "Space Junk Cleanup Needed" (easier), copied back to back

Choice 2: "E-Waste Facts and Figures"

Choice 3: "Following the Trail of Toxic E-Waste" (two pages) and the map "Who Gets the Trash," copied and stapled together

CURRICULUM CONNECTIONS

Chemistry: Toxic substances in common electronic products.

Physics: How satellites communicate.

Earth/Space Science: Eco-space effects of e-waste, improving environmental citizenship.

Social Studies: Geography of e-waste, economics of e-waste.

Literature: Science fiction; *High Tech Trash: Digital Devices, Hidden Toxics, and Human Health.*

Language Arts: Annotating text; drawing information from multiple sources; taking and supporting a position; representing ideas in drawing; working with others to develop a synthesis.

STRATEGIES USED

Turn and Talk, Jigsaw, Text Coding, Support Your Position, Sketching Through the Text, Gallery Walk

MATERIALS NEEDED

Copy of survey for each student, one set of the other texts for each group of three, white 8½-×-11-inch paper, projectable list of discussion prompts, poster paper, markers, tape. Copying instructions for the three text sets are given under "Texts in Order of Use." It is least confusing for the students if you number the choices 1, 2, and 3 or duplicate each choice in a different color.

Steps and Teaching Language

PART 1 · ELECTRONICS USE SURVEY *(10 minutes)*

STEP 1 · **Complete the survey** Arrange kids in groups of three and pass out the Electronics Use Survey. Read the Part 1 directions aloud to the class and ask if there are any questions. Give students a few minutes to complete Part 1 individually. As students finish, tell them to read the directions for Part 2 and complete it as well. Circulate and answer individual questions as students work.

STEP 2 · **Groups discuss**

Strategy 1: **TURN AND TALK**

You will work with your group to compare your answers to Part 1 of the survey. Be sure to talk about the following:

- *What are the most popular electronic devices that everyone has?*

- *Which devices seem to get replaced most often?*

- *What is the most common way that members of your group deal with the old ones? In other words, were the members of your group most likely to dispose, recycle, or store old electronic products?*

STEP 3 · **Whole class shares** As groups finish up, gather some quick responses to the questions posed using a quick show of hands. Try to determine what the most common answers were.

STEP 4　**Groups discuss Part 2 of the survey**

Now turn back to your group for a moment and compare your answers on Part 2. Observe groups and continue discussions until on-topic conversation diminishes. *Take another look at this list and see if your group can figure out what all these items have in common.*

STEP 5　**Whole class shares**　After another minute, take some guesses and suggestions from the groups. In the end, be sure kids realize that all of these devices/services depend on space satellites in order to function. *These communication and information satellites are increasing as our use of electronic devices increases. And as our e-waste is accumulating on earth, our waste from broken or outmoded satellites is cluttering up space.*

PART 2　**JIGSAW** *(40 minutes)*

Strategy 23: **JIGSAW**

STEP 1　**Introduce text selections**　Pass out a complete text set to each group.

Today each person in your group will be reading some different information related to e-waste or space waste. Let me give you a preview.

Choice 1: "Types of Satellites" explains how we depend on satellites in the course of our daily lives; "Space Junk Cleanup Needed" (on the back) describes how more and more space junk is going to interfere with our lives.

Choice 2: "E-Waste Facts and Figures" gives some hard and fast figures about e-waste.

Choice 3: "Following the Trail of Toxic E-Waste" tells a story about how toxic and dangerous it is for the people who recycle our discarded electronics; on the back, "Who Gets the Trash?" shows where these recyclers live.

STEP 2　**Groups negotiate**

Now decide who is going to read which articles. I wouldn't worry about getting a bad one; they're all pretty interesting.

STEP 3　**Give instructions for reading**

Strategy 4: **TEXT CODING**

Now that you've chosen your articles, I want you to read with some coding in mind. As you read, please underline, code, and annotate for three things:

★　*Information that is particularly important. Underline that passage, mark with a star, and jot a quick note on what you were thinking.*

!　*Information that is new or surprising. Underline that passage, mark with an exclamation point, and jot a quick note on what you were thinking.*

∞　*Information that connects back to the survey we took at the beginning of class. Underline that passage, mark with chain links, and jot a quick note on what you were thinking.*

STEP 4 **"Expert groups" meet and discuss articles** As kids finish, call time. *Everybody stand up and stretch. Pick up your article and pen. Now you are going to gather by articles.* Hold up texts one set at a time. *If you've got the "Satellite" pair, gather in this corner; if you have the "Facts and Figures" article, meet in that corner; the "Trail of Waste" people, gather over here. Go!* Give everyone a minute to move.

Now that you are with all the others who read the same article, I want you to break into groups of three and compare what you annotated, and then decide what the most important two or three pieces of information or connections are. Be sure to write down your conclusions so you'll remember them. When you return to your original group, you will be the expert on this article, so make sure you are prepared.

Give students about five minutes for discussion and then tell them to return to their original groups.

STEP 5 **Jigsaw groups share and discuss information**

Strategy 12: **SUPPORT YOUR POSITION**

Now that you are back in your original groups, you need to first share your information. Take a few minutes for each member to explain the highlights of his or her article, as you determined them in your expert groups. When it is your turn, remember to support your position and give specific facts or quotes in your explanation.

Monitor carefully and end discussion as soon as groups appear to be finished. Allow five or six minutes for this stage.

STEP 6 **Groups discuss answers to prompts**

Since everyone is done sharing, I want your groups to take the discussion a step further and come up with some answers to these questions:

- *Do these electronic devices really improve our quality of life?*

- *Is our rapid consumption of electronic consumer goods necessary?*

- *How concerned should we be about the disposal of these products?*

- *What is the connection between being "plugged in" 24/7 and the accumulating space junk orbiting the earth?*

STEP 7 **Group members sketch discussion highlights** Pass out blank pieces of white 8½-×-11-inch paper. *To summarize something your group discussed related to these questions, each member should draw a quick sketch that is a visual representation of something you talked about.* Allow kids to sketch for five minutes.

Strategy 5: **SKETCHING THROUGH THE TEXT**

STEP 8 **Group members share sketches and display them** *Turn back to your group, show your picture, and share your thoughts. After everyone has shared, tape your pictures to this piece of poster paper.* Pass materials around as you explain and monitor—or have a student from each group serve as materials handler. *At the bottom write a caption that captures the important ideas from all three sketches. Once you are finished, post your drawings on the wall.*

Strategy 19: **GALLERY WALK**

STEP 9 **Gallery walk** Once all pictures are posted, say: *With your group, take a quick gallery walk and look at all of the drawings. Stop and discuss what other groups' drawings have in common with yours and also notice how each group's drawings and ideas were different.*

STEP 10 **Share with the whole class** End with a quick whole-class discussion. *As you looked at all the drawings, what were some key ideas that really stood out?*

Tips and Variations

■ **NOT ENOUGH TIME?** Part 2 of this lesson is somewhat lengthy. If you do not have the time for all of the steps, here are some ways to shorten this segment.

- Skip the drawing completely and end the text study with a whole-class discussion after groups have completed their jigsaw conversations.

- Rather than a Gallery Walk on the day of reading, students can quickly share some ideas from their drawings and then post the art around the classroom in the last couple of minutes for later perusal.

- Use pairs instead of trios and eliminate the "Facts and Figures" handout.

- Pairs can also eliminate the search for an "expert group," if your desks are arranged in rows or if students are sitting four to a table. Shoulder partners should each read a different article and the face partners will work together as expert pairs. (See Strategy 17, Arguing Both Sides, for an explanation of how face partners and shoulder partners are used.)

Electronics Use Survey: Part 1

DIRECTIONS: Complete the following survey. Place a check in each box that applies. Read the complete definition of each survey category before beginning.

Currently use: Which of the following electronic devices do you currently use/possess/can be found in your home?

Replaced when broken/new model available: Have you ever replaced this device when it broke or a newer model with more features came out?

Discarded old model: You threw away the old model; it went out with the trash.

Recycled/reused old model: You took the device to Best Buy or someplace else that officially recycles electronic waste. Or you gave the device to another person or organization.

Store old model: You kept the device you no longer use and still have it stored in your house.

Electronic Device	Currently use	Replaced when broken/ new model available	Discarded old model	Recycled/ reused old model	Store old model
Cell Phone					
Smart Phone					
Laptop Computer					
Desktop Computer					
Television					
DVD Player					
Gaming System					
Digital Camera					
Video Camera					
iPad					
e-Reader (e.g., Kindle)					

Electronics Use Survey: Part 2

DIRECTIONS: Read the list of electronic devices and services below and check off any that you have ever used.

☐ Cell phone

☐ Smart phone

☐ Wireless gaming

☐ Cable/Satellite TV

☐ XM/Sirius radio

☐ Internet

☐ GPS

☐ Google Maps

☐ Air travel

☐ Weather.com/ Weather Channel

Types of Satellites and Their Uses

http://www.satellite-orbits.info/articles/satellites/types-of-satellites.php

Many types of satellites are in constant orbit around the Earth. Each has a specific job, whether it's as a storm-tracker, communications station or as part of our nation's military surveillance operations. Any object that orbits another is technically a satellite. Natural satellites include the moon, as it orbits Earth, and the Earth as it orbits the sun. Artificial satellites are those that are manmade and provide useful information for everyday use and scientific advancement as they orbit Earth.

Different Types of Satellites

Communications satellites are vital to our everyday lives. They're responsible for beaming signals around the world for a host of correspondence devices, including:

- computers
- fax machines
- pagers
- telephones
- television

Military satellites provide a number of services to the government and private sector. They do act as spy satellites and perform reconnaissance missions within their orbits. These satellites can also:

- observe land and sea transport movements
- offer navigational assistance
- provide top-secret communications on secure channels
- track weather

Navigational satellites have been around for many years. They provide location data to ships and planes. Vehicles now incorporate global positioning systems (GPS) and even individuals can carry handheld systems to avoid getting lost.

Scientific or research satellites operate in several different ways. They may focus on the Earth or can be catapulted into space to study the universe. Scientific satellites' uses are numerous and include:

- crop studies
- freshwater depletion tracking
- locating pollution sources

Weather satellites relay real-time information to meteorologists and databases around the world. They provide instant information that individuals can access through most means of communications. These satellites are capable of assessing atmospheric conditions and can collect information through infrared or standard cameras. Weather satellites are also vital in following the paths of storms, including hurricanes and cyclones.

NATIONAL GEOGRAPHIC NEWS

Space Junk Cleanup Needed, NASA Experts Warn

January 19, 2006, Stefan Lovgren

Space is filling up with trash, and it's time to clean it up, NASA experts warn. A growing amount of human-made debris—from rocket stages and obsolete satellites to blown-off hatches and insulation—is circling the Earth. Scientists say the orbital debris, better known as space junk, poses an increasing threat to space activities, including robotic missions and human space flight. "This is a growing environmental problem," said Nicholas Johnson, the chief scientist and program manager for orbital debris at NASA in Houston, Texas.

The U.S. Space Surveillance Network is currently tracking over 13,000 human-made objects larger than four inches (ten centimeters) in diameter orbiting the Earth.

Johnson and his team have devised a computer model capable of simulating past and future amounts of space junk. The model predicts that even without future rocket or satellite launches, the amount of debris in low orbit around Earth will remain steady through 2055, after which it will increase. While current efforts have focused on limiting future space junk, the scientists say removing large pieces of old space junk will soon be necessary.

Since the launch of the Soviet Union's Sputnik I satellite in 1957, humans have been generating space junk. The U.S. Space Surveillance Network is currently tracking over 13,000 human-made objects larger than four inches (ten centimeters) in diameter orbiting the Earth. These include both operational spacecraft and debris such as derelict rocket bodies. "Of the 13,000 objects, over 40 percent came from breakups of both spacecraft and rocket bodies," Johnson said.

In addition, there are hundreds of thousands of smaller objects in space. These include everything from pieces of plastic to flecks of paint. Much of this smaller junk has come from exploding rocket stages. Stages are sections of a rocket that have their own fuel or engines. These objects travel at speeds over 22,000 miles an hour (35,000 kilometers an hour). At such high velocity, even small junk can rip holes in a spacecraft or disable a satellite by causing electrical shorts that result from clouds of superheated gas.

Three accidental collisions between catalogued space-junk objects larger than four inches (ten centimeters) have been documented from late 1991 to early 2005. The most recent collision occurred a year ago. A 31-year-old U.S. rocket body hit a fragment from the third stage of a Chinese launch vehicle that exploded in March 2000.

Johnson believes it may be time to think about how to remove junk from space. Previous proposals have ranged from sending up spacecraft to grab junk and bring it down to using lasers to slow an object's orbit, causing it to fall back to Earth more quickly. Given current technology, those proposals appear neither technically feasible nor economically viable. "Space junk is like any environmental problem," Johnson said. "It's growing. If you don't tackle it now, it will only become worse, and the remedies in the future are going to be even more costly."

TEXT SET LESSONS / E-WASTE

E-Waste Facts and Figures

How Much Electronic Waste Is Being Discarded? Whether trashed or recycled, what are we getting rid of each year in the US? (See next section for what we stockpile.)

EPA Report on E-Waste in 2007—Was It Trashed or Recycled?

Products	Total Disposed** (millions of units)	Trashed (millions of units)	Recycled (millions of units)	Recycling Rate (by weight)
Televisions	26.9	20.6	6.3	18%
Computer Products*	205.5	157.3	48.2	18%
Cell Phones	140.3	126.3	14	10%

*Computer products include CPUs, monitors, notebooks, keyboards, mice, and "hard copy peripherals," which are printers, copiers, multis and faxes.

**These totals don't include products that are no longer used, but stored.

41.1 million desktops & laptops

The EPA (in report summarized above) estimates that 29.9 million desktops and 12 million laptops were discarded in 2007. That's over 112,000 computers discarded per day!

31.9 million computer monitors

The EPA report (above) estimates that 31.9 million computer monitors were discarded in 2007—both flat panel and CRTs.

400 million units of e-waste

In a 2006 report, the International Association of Electronics Recyclers projects that with the current growth and obsolescence rates of the various categories of consumer electronics (a broader list than the EPA used above, including DVDs, VCRs, mainframes), somewhere in the neighborhood of 3 billion units will be scrapped during the rest of this decade, or an average of about 400 million units a year.

Over 3 million tons of e-waste disposed in 2007 in USA

In 2007, we generated 3.01 million tons of e-waste in the US. Of this amount, only 410,000 tons or 13.6% was recycled, according to the EPA. The rest was trashed—in landfills or incinerators.

Selected consumer electronics include products such as TVs, VCRs, DVD players, video cameras, stereo systems, telephones, and computer equipment.

20 to 50 million metric tons of e-waste disposed worldwide each year

According to the 2006 United Nations Environment Programme report, "Some 20 to 50 million metric tons of e-waste are generated worldwide every year, comprising more than 5% of all municipal solid waste. When the millions of computers purchased around the world every year (183 million in 2004) become obsolete they leave behind lead, cadmium, mercury and other hazardous wastes. In the US alone, some 14 to 20 million PCs are thrown out every year. In the EU the volume of e-waste is expected to increase by 3 to 5 per cent a year. Developing countries are expected to triple their output of e-waste by 2010."

E-waste is still the fastest growing municipal waste stream in the US

The category of "selected consumer electronic products" grew by almost 6% from 2006 to 2007, from 2.84 million tons to 3.01 million tons. While it's not a large part of the waste stream, e-waste shows a higher growth rate than any other category of municipal waste in the EPA's report. Overall, between 2005 and 2006, total volumes of municipal waste increased by only 1.2%, compared to 8.6% for e-waste.

Only 13.6% of disposed e-waste is recycled

According to the EPA, only 13.6% of the consumer electronic products generated into the municipal waste stream (meaning, that people tossed out) were "recovered" for recycling in 2007.

How Much Electronic Waste Gets Stored or Stockpiled?

68% of consumers stockpile

A Hewlett Packard survey revealed that "68 percent of consumers stockpile used or unwanted computer equipment in their homes."

235 million units in storage as of 2007, including 99 million TVs

The EPA estimates the following quantities of electronics were in storage by 2007 (not including cell phones):

Televisions: 99.1 million

Desktop computers: 65.7 million

Desktop monitors: 42.4 million

Notebook computers: 2.1 million

Hard copy peripherals: 25.2 million

(printers, copiers, faxes, multis)

TOTAL: 234.6 million units in storage

FOLLOWING THE TRAIL OF TOXIC E-WASTE

60 Minutes Follows America's Toxic Electronic Waste as It Is Illegally Shipped to Become China's Dirty Secret

60 MINUTES CBSNews.com, August 30, 2009

60 MINUTES is going to take you to one of the most toxic places on Earth. It's a town in China where you can't breathe the air or drink the water, a town where the blood of the children is laced with lead and much of this poison is coming out of the homes, schools and offices of America. This is a story about recycling—about how your best intentions to be green can be channeled into an underground sewer that flows from the United States and into the wasteland.

Computers may seem like sleek, high-tech marvels. But what's inside them? Lead, cadmium, mercury, chromium, polyvinyl chlorides. All of these materials have known toxicological effects that range from brain damage to kidney disease to mutations, cancers. E-waste is the fastest-growing component of the municipal waste worldwide. In the United States alone we throw out about 130,000 computers every day and over 100 million cell phones are thrown out annually.

At a recycling event in Denver, *60 Minutes* found cars bumper-to-bumper for blocks, in a line that lasted for hours. They were there to drop off their computers, cell phones, TVs and other electronic waste. Most folks in line were hoping to do the right thing, expecting that their waste would be recycled in state-of-the-art facilities that exist here in America. But really, there's no way for them to know where all of this is going. The recycling industry is exploding and, as it turns out, some so-called recyclers are shipping the waste overseas, where it's broken down for the precious metals inside.

Executive Recycling, of Englewood, Colo., which ran the Denver event, promised the public on its Web site: "Your e-waste is recycled properly, right here in the U.S.—not simply dumped on somebody else." Executive does recycling in-house, but *60 Minutes* was curious about shipping containers that were leaving its Colorado yard. *60 Minutes* found one container filled with monitors. They're especially hazardous because each picture tube, called a cathode ray tube or CRT, contains several pounds of lead. It's against U.S. law to ship them overseas without special permission. *60 Minutes* took down the container's number and followed it to Tacoma, Wash., where it was loaded on a ship. When the container left Tacoma, *60 Minutes* followed it for 7,459 miles to Victoria Harbor, Hong Kong. It turns out the container that started in Denver was just one of thousands of containers on an underground, often illegal smuggling route, taking America's electronic trash to the Far East.

Our guide to that route was Jim Puckett, founder of the Basel Action Network, a watchdog group named for the treaty that is supposed to stop rich countries from dumping toxic waste on poor ones. Puckett runs a program to certify ethical recyclers. And he showed *60 Minutes* what's piling up in Hong Kong. It's literally acres of computer monitors. "This is absolutely illegal, both from the standpoint of Hong Kong law

FOLLOWING THE TRAIL OF TOXIC E-WASTE

60 MINUTES | **CBSNews.com**, August 30, 2009

but also U.S. law and Chinese law. But it's happening," Puckett said.

60 Minutes followed the trail to a place Puckett discovered in southern China—a sort of Chernobyl of electronic waste—the town of Guiyu. "This is really the dirty little secret of the electronic age," Jim Puckett said. Greenpeace had been filming around Guiyu and caught the recycling work. Women were heating circuit boards over a coal fire, pulling out chips and pouring off

Women were heating circuit boards over a coal fire, pulling out chips and pouring off the lead solder. Men were using what is literally a medieval acid recipe to extract gold. Pollution has ruined the town. Drinking water is trucked in.

the lead solder. Men were using what is literally a medieval acid recipe to extract gold. Pollution has ruined the town. Drinking water is trucked in. Scientists have studied the area and discovered that Guiyu has the highest levels of cancer-causing dioxins in the world. They found pregnancies are six times more likely to end in miscarriage, and that seven out of ten kids have too much lead in their blood. The recyclers are peasant farmers who couldn't make a living on the land. Destitute, they've come by the thousands to get $8 a day.

Back in Denver, we told Brandon Richter, CEO of Executive Recycling that we'd

tracked his container to Hong Kong. "This is a photograph from your yard, the Executive Recycling yard," our correspondent, Scott Pelley, told Richter, showing him a photo we'd taken of a shipping container in his yard. "We followed this container to Hong Kong. The Hong Kong customs people opened the container . . . and found it full of CRT screens which, as you probably know, is illegal to export to Hong Kong," Pelley said.

"No, absolutely not. It was not filled in our facility," Richter said. But that's where *60 Minutes* filmed it. And we weren't the only ones asking questions. It turns out Hong Kong customs intercepted the container and sent it back to Executive Recycling, the contents listed as "waste: cathode ray tubes." U.S. customs x-rayed the container and found the same thing. *60 Minutes* showed Richter this evidence, and later his lawyer told us the CRTs were exported under Executive Recycling's name, but without the company's permission.

But here's one more fact: the federal Government Accountability Office set up a sting in which U.S. investigators posed as foreign importers. Executive Recycling offered to sell 1,500 CRT computer monitors and 1,200 CRT televisions to the GAO's fictitious broker in Hong Kong. But Executive Recycling was not alone. The GAO report found that another 42 American companies were willing to do the same. Since *60 Minutes* first broadcast this story, federal agents executed a search warrant at the Executive Recycling headquarters as part of an ongoing investigation.

Who gets the trash?

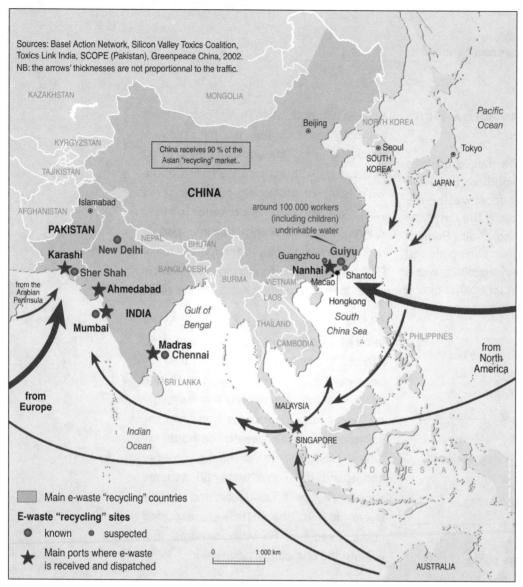

Sources: Basel Action Network, Silicon Valley Toxics Coalition, Toxics Link India, SCOPE (Pakistan), Greenpeace China, 2002. NB: the arrows' thicknesses are not proportionnal to the traffic.

KAZAKHSTAN

MONGOLIA

Beijing

NORTH KOREA

Pacific Ocean

KYRGYZSTAN

Seoul

Tokyo

SOUTH KOREA

TAJIKISTAN

China receives 90 % of the Asian "recycling" market..

JAPAN

CHINA

AFGHANISTAN

Islamabad

around 100 000 workers (including children) undrinkable water

PAKISTAN

NEPAL

Karashi

New Delhi

BHUTAN

Guangzhou

Guiyu

Sher Shah

BANGLADESH

Nanhai

Shantou

Macao

from the Arabian Peninsula

Ahmedabad

BURMA

VIETNAM

Hongkong

INDIA

Gulf of Bengal

LAOS

South China Sea

Mumbai

THAILAND

CAMBODIA

PHILIPPINES

Madras

Chennai

from North America

SRI LANKA

from Europe

Indian Ocean

MALAYSIA

SINGAPORE

I N D O N E S I A

Main e-waste "recycling" countries

E-waste "recycling" sites

● known   ● suspected

★ Main ports where e-waste is received and dispatched

0   1 000 km

AUSTRALIA

Source: United Nations Environment Programme/GRID–Arendal, http://maps.grida.no/go/graphic/who-gets-the-trash

Crash

Grouping
Sequence:
Whole class,
pairs, whole
class. For the
extension: pairs,
whole class

The relationship between American teenagers and cars is emotional and complex. Even though getting your driver's license doesn't seem to have the urgency of yore (see page 40), most kids still see it as a rite of passage and the ticket to a kind of freedom that's not obtainable otherwise. You've got to get away from those parents, the more literally and rapidly the better. Smoking tires preferred. But car crashes are also the leading cause of death among American teens. Sad but true, in 2010, over 5,000 kids lost their lives in cars, and 350,000 were seriously injured in automobile accidents.

While this text set does not focus on death and destruction, it does give kids a chance to understand the physics, psychology, and sociology of driving while distracted. The lesson makes use of graphs, charts, and text to help students explore the choices and possible consequences of using their phones to talk or text while driving. Big questions to consider include:

- How do weight and speed affect a car's stopping distance?
- What kinds of activities distract drivers from paying attention to their driving?
- How are car accidents and distracted driving connected?
- What is the best way to prevent distracted driving?

TEXTS IN ORDER OF USE

Main Lesson:

"Stopping Distance" (text and chart; easier)

"Study: Distractions Cause Most Car Crashes" (easier)

Extension:

"Texting While Driving: How Dangerous Is It?" (text and charts)

"New Data from VTTI Provides Insight into Cell Phone Use and Driving Distraction" (text and chart)

CURRICULUM CONNECTIONS

Physics: Force and motion.

Biology: Nervous system, neural pathways, eye-hand coordination.

Health: Personal safety.

Driver Education: Avoiding distractions that cause accidents.

Social Studies: Federal, state, and local laws; law enforcement; how laws evolve as technology changes.

Language Arts: Read and understand information presented in charts and tables; use text annotation to deepen understanding; connect nonfiction text to one's own life experience; meet in small, peer-led groups to discuss and debate readings.

STRATEGIES USED

Turn and Talk, Read with a Question in Mind, Conversation Questions, Save the Last Word for Me, Jigsaw, Text Coding

MATERIALS NEEDED

For the main lesson, copies of the Stopping Distance chart and "Distractions" article for each student; for the extension, copies of the additional two articles for each pair plus some extra copies of "Texting While Driving"; whiteboard or projector for brainstorming.

Steps and Teaching Language

 PART 1 INTRODUCE THE DYNAMICS OF STOPPING DISTANCE
(20 minutes)

STEP 1 **Introduce the concept of force and motion** *Anybody ever ride in a car while the driver was using a cell phone?* Note the show of hands. *Just about everybody. How much do you think the average car weighs?* Listen to volunteer estimates. *The average car weighs between 3,000 and 5,000 pounds. Pick-up trucks and SUV's are even heavier. How do you think the weight of a car affects its ability to stop?* Listen to ideas. Answer: *The heavier the car is, the longer it takes to stop. What else would affect the stopping distance of a car besides its weight?* Listen to responses. Answer: *The speed at which it is traveling. Of course, the condition of your brakes and pavement are going to make a difference as well. But the two biggest factors that affect stopping distance are weight and speed.*

How fast do you think a car can travel in one second at a given speed, say 70 miles per hour? Listen to guesses. *Actually, there's a formula that can give you a rough estimate. First take the speed, 70 miles per hour, and divide it in half. What's the answer? Yes, 35. Then take that number, 35, and multiply it by three. What's the answer? Yes, 105. That means that a car moving at 70 mph travels 105 feet every second. How many feet would that car travel in three seconds? Yes, 315 feet. How long is a football field? Remember, 100 yards equals 300 feet. So in three seconds, a car going 70 miles per hour travels further than the length of a football field.*

STEP 2 **Discuss the stopping distance chart** Pass out the stopping distance handout.

Any time you try to stop a car, two things come into play. First is the driver's reaction distance. That's the distance the car travels between the moment a driver recognizes a danger and the moment the driver actually hits the brake pedal. The braking distance is the distance traveled by the car after the brakes are applied and until the vehicle comes to a complete stop.

Take a look at this chart. What is the connection between stopping distance and speed? (The faster a car travels, the greater the stopping distance.)

Notice that this chart estimates the stopping distance of cars on dry, level pavement. Besides speed, what else could increase stopping distance? Take responses (rain, snow, gravel, traveling downhill, heavier vehicle, slower reaction time).

STEP 3 **Pairs discuss reaction time** Students form pairs (self-chosen or teacher determined).

Strategy 1: **TURN AND TALK**

All of those definitely could lengthen stopping distance. Let's think about reaction time. This chart assumes that the driver is paying total attention to the road conditions and traffic. What kinds of things might lengthen reaction time by distracting the driver? Turn to your partner and make a quick list.

Give students a minute or two to brainstorm and jot answers.

Now, with your partner, go back through the list and prioritize your items. Which is most distracting? The most likely to keep your eyes off the road? Number the circumstance that is most likely to lengthen reaction time #1 and then continue numbering according to importance.

STEP 4 **Share reasons for lengthened reaction time** Give pairs another minute to prioritize their lists. Before sharing, choose a volunteer recorder to write the items on the board or in a projectable form.

As I call on each pair, I want you to give us your #1 item. If that's taken, give us your #2; if that's taken, give us your #3; and so on. Any questions? If I get to you and all of your ideas are taken, give us your #1 and we'll put a check by it on the list. As we create our master list, I want everyone to copy it down because you'll need to refer to this list for the next activity.

Go around the room and get one idea from each pair. After creating the list, take a moment to discuss what the top reaction time extenders are. (The following example shows one class's final ranking.)

Possible Distractions

1. Texting

2. Talking on cell phone

3. Eating

4. Reaching for something

5. Listening to iPod

6. Talking to passenger

7. Putting on make-up

8. Sleep deprivation

9. Yelling at kids

10. Looking in another direction

11. Changing radio station/CD

12. Using GPS navigation system

13. Looking for an address

PART 2 — STUDENTS ANNOTATE AND DISCUSS THE ARTICLE
(20 minutes)

STEP 1 **Give reading instructions** Pass out the article "Distractions Cause Most Car Crashes."

Strategy 2: **READ WITH A QUESTION IN MIND**

This article talks about how most car accidents are caused by the drivers being distracted. Remember, any distraction can increase your reaction time. As you read, I want you to look for the distractions we just listed. Then do three things: First, when you see one, put the number from our list by it.

Strategy 11: **CONVERSATION QUESTIONS**

Second, underline three statements or pieces of information that you thought were important or surprising. Third, next to each underline, jot down a related question that would be interesting to discuss.

STEP 2 **Pairs discuss** As kids finish up, call time. *Turn to your partner and compare what you found in the article. How did our class predictions compare with what this article discussed about dangerous distractions?* Allow pairs to discuss for a couple of minutes and then open up the question to the whole class for a quick discussion.

Strategy 10: **SAVE THE LAST WORD FOR ME**

Turn back to your partner again and take a look at the passages you underlined because you found them important or surprising. Take turns with your partner reading your passages aloud and using "save the last word." Rather than reading aloud and immediately explaining, have your partner first guess why you picked that passage. Then you can add any ideas they might not have mentioned or continue the discussion by asking your question. Be sure to switch after each passage.

Finally, display the projectable "big questions" listed on page 215. *Based on what you've read and discussed just now, how would you answer these questions? Take a couple of minutes with your partner to discuss them.*

STEP 3 **Whole class shares** As conversation winds down, call time. Ask for some volunteers to read their most interesting/surprising underlining aloud and explain. End by discussing the big questions and asking students if anything needs to be done about driving distractions, either through laws or personal responsibility.

EXTENSION JIGSAW *(30 minutes)*

STEP 1 **Introduce additional articles**

More and more organizations are starting to do studies on how distracted people become when they are talking on the phone or texting while trying to drive. Today I have two articles that describe these studies.

The first article is from Car and Driver *magazine. This piece describes an experiment they conducted as they tried to determine how a driver's reaction time lengthens when he is reading or writing a text.*

The second article describes a cell phone/texting study done by the Virginia Tech Transportation Institute. They studied distractions by installing cameras that recorded driver behavior and traffic conditions as well as other instrumentation that recognized and recorded dangerous driving events.

Strategy 23: **JIGSAW**

STEP 2 **Pairs assign readings** Pass out a set of articles to each pair and have them negotiate who reads what article. Since the Virginia Tech article is shorter, have extra copies of the *Car and Driver* article available for those kids who finish early.

STEP 3 **Give instructions for reading** Once negotiating is done, give these instructions:

As you read your article, be on the lookout for information that is surprising, connects with something in a previous article, or raises a question. Then I want you to do three things.

Strategy 4: **TEXT CODING**

When you see something that fits, underline it and mark a code by it:

! *exclamation point for surprising*

⊂⊃ *chain links for connection*

? *question mark for question*

Then, in the margin, jot down your thoughts or conversation questions. Remember that your goal is to bring interesting information, thoughts, and questions to the discussion you will soon be having with your partner.

STEP 4 **Partners discuss annotation and connections between all four texts** As they finish reading and coding, call time.

Turn to your partner and compare what you found in these articles. Read what you've underlined aloud to each other and discuss your thoughts, questions, and connections. Then figure out how all of the charts connect to one another.

STEP 5 **Share with the whole class** End with a short large-group discussion, sharing ideas about the articles and how the charts are interconnected. End by discussing these questions (project if possible):

- How do weight and speed increase your chances of getting into an accident if distracted?

- What advice would you give to someone texting or talking on their cell phone while driving? What facts would you use to convince them that this is creating dangerous conditions for themselves and others?

- Is controlling distracted driving purely the responsibility of the driver, or should laws be passed that prohibit electronic device use while driving?

Tips and Variations

■ **STAGE A REAL CRASH** Our colleague Ben Warner, who teaches science at Federal Hocking High School in Stewart, Ohio, shares another extension of the crash lesson. "A great way to get your students to see the relationship between mass and force is to have them build cars and then crash them. This is a variation on the 'egg drop' that ties in some safety engineering and design components. I use a physics cart as a base for their car and have kids build a body out of cardboard (or any other material they want). They incorporate safety features such as crumple zones, air bags, seat belts, and once even an ejector seat (that didn't work so well). The idea is for the team's egg to survive the impact of the car going down an eight-foot ramp into a large brick. The trick is that the car must be realistic in that the features must deploy on impact, not before (you wouldn't drive around packed in foam or wrapped in bubble wrap). In the end, the mass of the car and the impact velocity are used to determine the instantaneous force of impact that the egg hopefully survived."

Missouri Department of

Revenue

Driver Guide
Safe Driving Tips for Everyday Driving

Stopping Distance

http://dor.mo.gov/forms/Driver_Guide_Chapter8.pdf

Your *stopping distance* equals your *reaction distance* plus your *braking distance*. If you are driving fast, are very tired, or if your vehicle has bad brakes, you will need more space to stop your vehicle.

The *following distance* equals your *reaction distance* plus your vehicle's *braking distance* at different speeds. The reaction distance is the distance you travel after you see a danger and before you apply your brakes. In the chart shown below, the reaction distance is for 1.5 seconds. You have to be alert to react within one and one-half seconds.

The *braking distance* is the distance you travel after you apply your brakes and before your vehicle comes to a stop. In the chart shown below, the braking distance is for a vehicle with good brakes and tires, in good weather, and on a good road.

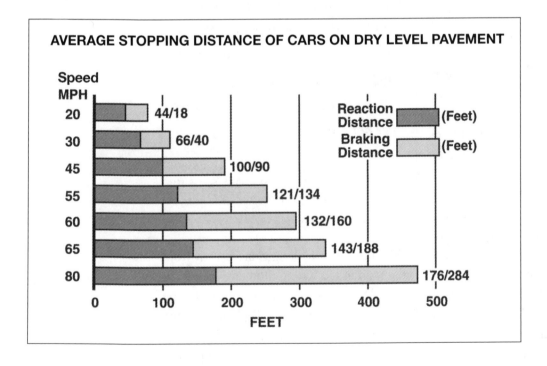

AVERAGE STOPPING DISTANCE OF CARS ON DRY LEVEL PAVEMENT

Speed MPH	Distance
20	44/18
30	66/40
45	100/90
55	121/134
60	132/160
65	143/188
80	176/284

Reaction Distance (Feet)
Braking Distance (Feet)

FEET

TEXT SET LESSONS / CRASH

San Francisco Chronicle

Study: Distractions Cause Most Car Crashes

By KEN THOMAS, The Associated Press, April 21, 2006

Those sleep-deprived, multitasking drivers—clutching cell phones, fiddling with their radios or applying lipstick—apparently are involved in an awful lot of crashes. Distracted drivers were involved in nearly eight out of 10 collisions or near-crashes, says a study released Thursday by the government.

"We see people on the roadways talking on the phone, checking their stocks, checking scores, fussing with their MP3 players, reading e-mails, all while driving 40, 50, 60, 70 miles per hour and sometimes even faster," said Jacqueline Glassman, acting administrator of the government's highway safety agency.

Researchers at the National Highway Traffic Safety Administration and the Virginia Tech Transportation Institute found that the risk of a crash increases almost threefold when a driver is dialing a cell phone.

Researchers said the report showed the first links between crash risks and a driver's activities, from eating and talking to receiving e-mail. "All of these activities are much more dangerous than we thought before," said Dr. Charlie Klauer, a senior research associate at the institute. Data from police reports had estimated that driver inattention was a factor in about 25 percent of crashes.

For more than a year, researchers studied the behavior of the drivers of 100 vehicles in metropolitan Washington, D.C. They tracked 241 drivers, who were involved in 82 crashes of various degrees of seriousness—15 were reported to police—and 761 near-crashes. The air bag deployed in three instances. The project analyzed nearly 2 million miles driven and more than 43,300 hours of data.

Drowsy driving increased the driver's risk of a crash or near-crash by four times to six times, the study said. But the study's authors said drowsy driving is frequently underreported in police investigations.

> "We see people on the roadways talking on the phone, checking their stocks, checking scores, fussing with their MP3 players, reading e-mails, all while driving 40, 50, 60, 70 miles per hour and sometimes even faster."
>
> —JACQUELINE GLASSMAN, ACTING ADMINISTRATOR OF THE GOVERNMENT'S HIGHWAY SAFETY AGENCY

When drivers took long glances away from the road at the wrong moment, they were twice as likely to get into a crash, the report said. Assessing cell phone use, the researchers said the number of crashes or near-crashes linked to dialing the phones was nearly identical to those tied to talking or listening on the phone.

CAR AND DRIVER

TEXTING WHILE DRIVING

How Dangerous Is It?

BY MICHAEL AUSTIN, June 2009

Texting is on the rise, up from 9.8 billion messages a month in December '05 to 110.4 billion in December '08. Undoubtedly, more than a few of those messages are being sent by people driving cars. Is texting while driving a dangerous idea? We decided to conduct a test. Previous academic studies—much more scientific than ours—conducted in vehicle simulators have shown that texting while driving impairs the driver's abilities. But as far as we know, no study has been conducted in a real vehicle that is being driven.

To keep things simple, we would focus solely on the driver's reaction times to a light mounted on the windshield at eye level, meant to simulate a lead car's brake lights. Wary of the potential damage to man and machine, all of the driving would be done in a straight line. We rented the taxiway of the Oscoda-Wurtsmith Airport in Oscoda, Michigan. Given the prevalence of the Black-Berry, the iPhone, and other text-friendly mobile phones, the test subjects would have devices with full "qwerty" keypads and would be using text-messaging phones familiar to them. Intern Jordan Brown, 22, armed with an iPhone, would represent the younger crowd. The older demographic would be covered by head honcho Eddie Alterman, 37, using a Samsung Alias.

Our Honda Pilot (four-wheel-drive SUV) served as the test vehicle. When the red light on the windshield lit up, the driver was to hit the brakes. The author, riding shotgun, would use a hand-held switch to trigger the red light and monitor the driver's results. Each trial would have the driver respond five times to the light, and the slowest reaction

AVERAGES AT 35 MPH	Reaction Time (sec)		Extra Distance Traveled (ft)	
	Brown	Alterman	Brown	Alterman
BASELINE	0.45	0.57	–	–
READING	0.57	1.44	6	45
TEXTING	0.52	1.36	4	41

AVERAGES AT 75 MPH	Reaction Time (sec)		Extra Distance Traveled (ft)	
	Brown	Alterman	Brown	Alterman
BASELINE	0.39	0.56	–	–
READING	0.50	0.91	11	36
TEXTING	0.48	1.24	9	70

time (the amount of time between the activation of the light and the driver hitting the brakes) was dropped.

First, we tested both drivers' reaction times at 35 mph and 70 mph to get baseline readings. Then we repeated the driving procedure while they read a text message aloud (a series of *Caddyshack* quotes). This was followed by a trial with the drivers typing the same message they had just received. Both of our lab rats were instructed to use their phones exactly as they would on a public road.

The results, though not surprising, were eye-opening. Intern Brown's baseline reaction time at 35 mph of 0.45 second worsened to 0.57 while reading a text, and improved to 0.52 while writing a text. At 70 mph, his baseline reaction was 0.39 second, while the reading (0.50) and texting (0.48), numbers

continues on next page

TEXTING WHILE DRIVING

continued from previous page

were similar. But the averages don't tell the whole story. Looking at Brown's slowest reaction time at 35 mph, he traveled an extra 21 feet (more than a car length) before hitting the brakes while reading and went 16 feet longer while texting. At 70 mph, a vehicle travels 103 feet every second, and Brown's worst reaction time while reading at that speed put him about 30 feet (31 while typing) farther down the road.

The key element to driving safely is keeping your eyes and your mind on the road. Text messaging distracts any driver from that primary task.

Alterman fared much, much worse. While reading a text and driving at 35 mph, his average baseline reaction time of 0.57 second nearly tripled, to 1.44 seconds. While texting, his response time was 1.36 seconds. These figures correspond to an extra 45 and 41 feet, respectively, before hitting the brakes. The results at 70 mph were similar: Alterman's response time while reading a text was 0.35 second longer than his base performance of 0.56 second, and writing a text added 0.68 second to his reaction time.

As with the younger driver, Alterman's slowest reaction times were a grim scenario. He went more than four seconds before looking up while reading a text message at 35 mph and over three and a half seconds while texting at 70 mph. Even in the best of his bad reaction times while reading or texting, Alterman traveled an extra 90 feet past his baseline performance; in the worst case, he went 319 feet farther down the road. Moreover, his two-hands-on-the-phone technique resulted in some serious lane drifting.

The prognosis doesn't improve when you look at the limitations of our test. We were using a straight road without any traffic, road signals, or pedestrians, and we were only looking at reaction times. Even though our young driver fared better than the balding Alterman, Brown's method of holding the phone up above the dashboard and typing with one hand would make it difficult to do anything except hit the brakes. And if anything in the periphery required a response, well, both drivers would probably be unable to react.

Both socially and legally, drunk driving is completely unacceptable. Texting, on the other hand, is still in its formative period with respect to laws and opinion. A few jurisdictions have passed ordinances against texting while driving. But even if sweeping legislation were passed to outlaw any typing behind the wheel, it would still be difficult to enforce the law.

In our test, neither subject had any idea that using his phone would slow down his reaction time so much. Like most folks, they think they're pretty good drivers. Our results prove otherwise, at both city and highway speeds. The key element to driving safely is keeping your eyes and your mind on the road. Text messaging distracts any driver from that primary task. So the next time you're tempted to text, tweet, e-mail, or otherwise type while driving, either ignore the urge or pull over. We don't want you rear-ending us.

Virginia Tech TRANSPORTATION INSTITUTE

| Home | News | About VTTI | Research | Public Access |

New Data from Virginia Tech Transportation Institute Provides Insight into Cell Phone Use and Driving Distraction

http://www.vtti.vt.edu/PDF/7-22-09-VTTI-Press_Release_Cell_phones_and_Driver_Distraction.pdf

BLACKSBURG, VA., JULY 27, 2009—Several large-scale, naturalistic driving studies (using sophisticated cameras and instrumentation in participants' personal vehicles) conducted by the Virginia Tech Transportation Institute (VTTI) provide a clear picture of driver distraction and cell phone use under real-world driving conditions. Combined, these studies continuously observed drivers for more than 6 million miles of driving.

VTTI's studies of light-vehicle drivers and truck drivers engaged in manual manipulation of phones such as dialing and texting of the cell phone show these behaviors lead to a substantial increase in the risk of being involved in a safety-critical event (e.g., crash or near crash). Text messaging on a cell phone was associated with the highest risk of all cell phone–related tasks.

Cell Phone Task	Risk of Crash or Near Crash Event
Light Vehicles/Cars	
Dialing cell phone	2.8 times as high as nondistracted driving
Talking/listening to cell phone	1.3 times as high as nondistracted driving
Reaching for object (i.e., electronic device and other)	1.4 times as high as nondistracted driving
Heavy Vehicles/Trucks	
Dialing cell phone	5.9 times as high as nondistracted driving
Talking/listening to cell phone	1.0 times as high as nondistracted driving
Use/reach for electronic device	6.7 times as high as nondistracted driving
Text messaging	23.2 times as high as nondistracted driving

VTTI's recommendations (based on findings from research studies)

Driving is a visual task and non-driving activities that draw the driver's eyes away from the roadway, such as texting and dialing, should always be avoided.

Texting should be banned in moving vehicles for all drivers. As shown in the table, this cell phone task has the potential to create a true crash epidemic if texting-type tasks continue to grow in popularity and the generation of frequent text message senders reach driving age in large numbers.

"Headset" cell phone use is not substantially safer than "hand-held" use because the primary risk associated with both tasks is answering, dialing, and other tasks that require your eyes to be off the road.

All cell phone use should be banned for newly licensed teen drivers. Our research has shown that teens tend to engage in cell phone tasks much more frequently, and in much more risky situations, than adults. Thus, our studies indicate that teens are four times more likely to get into a related crash or near crash event than their adult counterparts.

Text Set 8 | # Privacy

Grouping
Sequence:

Groups of 4 that sometimes work together, and other times split into 2 pairs; whole class

We are living in a time when personal privacy is disappearing. Some of our privacy is being stolen by ubiquitous surveillance cameras, prying agencies, and corporate intelligence gathering. But other elements of our personal lives we are blithely giving away ourselves. On social networking sites, we routinely offer the whole world access to information that once was kept among our actual, not virtual, "friends." On the other hand, maybe our loss of privacy provides some rewards. Police departments successfully use camera surveillance to solve crimes that might otherwise become cold cases. And Facebook offers busy people a way to sustain friendships that could so easily fall by the wayside.

In this lesson, students explore contemporary examples of potential privacy invasion. Big questions ripe for discussion:

On the Web

- How much privacy are we willing to give up in order to feel safe?

- How carefully will the government or a private corporation safeguard our information?

- What happens when this information about us is shared or used in ways that were not originally intended?

- Aren't citizens guaranteed the "right to privacy" under the U.S. Constitution?

TEXTS IN ORDER OF USE (teacher chooses one text for entire class to read)

"Eye Scan Technology Comes to Schools" (easier)

"Assembly Panel Backs Moratorium on Using ID Chips for School Kids" (easier)

"Growing Presence in the Courtroom: Cellphone Data as Witness" (easier)

"Microchips Everywhere: A Future Vision"

"FBI Prepares Vast Biometrics Database"

CURRICULUM CONNECTIONS

Social Studies: U.S. Constitution; Founding Fathers, the Supreme Court and judiciary; the right to privacy; how technology changes laws and society.

Science/Technology: Ethical use of technology, advantages/disadvantages of biometric databases, genetics.

Literature: 1984, Brave New World, The Hunger Games, The Giver, Feed, Unwind.

English Language Arts: Read a wide variety of nonfiction texts; use comprehension strategies to determine most important information; develop visual displays of one's thinking; join with peers to argue both sides of a complex issue.

STRATEGIES USED

Turn and Talk, Arguing Both Sides, Read with a Question in Mind, Text Coding, Two-Column Notes, Gallery Walk

MATERIALS NEEDED

Constitution information for projection, downloadable from the website; copied articles: choose one article and make enough copies for every student; chart paper; markers.

Steps and Teaching Language

Strategy 1: **TURN AND TALK**

| PART 1 | **INTRODUCE AND DISCUSS THE TOPIC** *(15 minutes)* |

STEP 1 **Form groups and brainstorm** Place kids in groups of four and then determine how they will split into pairs for the first two turn-and-talks. Pairs then brainstorm using this prompt: *What does the phrase "right to privacy" mean? Brainstorm in your pairs for one minute.* As conversation winds down, call time and invite pairs to share ideas with the whole class for two or three minutes.

STEP 2 **Explain the U.S. Constitution's privacy provisions**

Did you know that the phrase "right to privacy" exists nowhere in the Constitution? However, over the years, the Supreme Court has established that privacy is a basic human right protected by several different constitutional amendments. The court has pointed to the following amendments to show its reasoning. Project this information on the first, third, fourth, and ninth amendments.

On the Web

- **The First Amendment** provides that Congress make no law respecting an establishment of religion or prohibiting its free exercise. It protects freedom of speech, the press, assembly, and the right to petition the government for a redress of grievances.

- **The Third Amendment** prohibits the government from quartering troops in private homes, a major grievance during the American Revolution.

- **The Fourth Amendment** protects citizens from unreasonable search and seizure. The government may not conduct any searches without a warrant, and such warrants must be issued by a judge and based on probable cause.
- **The Ninth Amendment** states that the list of rights enumerated in the Constitution is not exhaustive, and that the people retain all rights not enumerated.

STEP 3   **Pairs discuss amendments**

Strategy 1: **TURN AND TALK**

In pairs, discuss what each of these amendments means and how each one might prevent government intrusion into our private affairs. Also, what questions do you have about any of these amendments? After a couple of minutes, call the class back; discuss the amendments' meanings and answer questions.

STEP 4   **Discuss the difference between limits on government versus the private sector**

These amendments were meant to limit the powers of the government. They say nothing about the conduct of private institutions or corporations. How many of you have typed in personal information in order to use the features of a website? Raise your hand. How many of you have a Facebook page? (Show of raised hands.)

What do you think companies do with the information you give them? Turn to your whole group of four this time and discuss for a minute. Take answers. *Though we know that companies sell our personal information to other organizations, we don't know for certain how these other organizations might use it.*

PART 2   **SEEING BOTH SIDES** *(25 minutes)*

Strategy 17: **ARGUING BOTH SIDES**

STEP 1   **Determine which article to use**   Beforehand, decide which article to use. (Note that the last two articles are a bit longer and will require more reading time.) If you would like to use multiple articles in a jigsaw format (more complicated), read the Tips and Variations section, which explains this option.

STEP 2   **Preview the article**

Today we're going to read an article about how personal information is collected and used, and think about whether our rights to privacy might be compromised. Let me give you a preview. (Use only the summary for the article you selected.)

"Eye Scan Technology Comes to Schools:" Have your parents ever visited your school during the normal school day? If so, they probably had to present an official photo ID and sign in. However, the district in this article has taken visitor identification a step further—regular school visitors must submit

to eye scan identification, a technique that until now you've seen only in some science fiction films.

"Assembly Backs Moratorium on Using ID Chips for School Kids": This article describes a school district that is trying to decide whether to incorporate chips into their student IDs. These chips would contain personal information that could be scanned for attendance or identification purposes. But what would happen if an ID got stolen or lost?

"Growing Presence in the Courtroom: Cellphone Data as Witness": Did you know that most cell phones constantly track the location of their owner? Have you ever texted something that might be incriminating? Did you know your cell phone could help convict you of a crime?

"Microchips Everywhere": The author presents a vision of the future where every product we buy, from our underwear to our toothpaste, would contain a permanent chip that could track, save, and sell our consumer preferences to the highest bidder.

"FBI Prepares Vast Biometrics Database": This article explains an ongoing, but little discussed government project. Its goal is to collect biological information about possible criminals or terrorists. Fingerprints, yes, but also included are iris patterns, face shape data, palm prints, and more.

STEP 3 ## Distribute the article and explain coding

Strategy 2: **READ WITH A QUESTION IN MIND**

This article is controversial because it raises the question: Is this a violation of my right to privacy?

As you read the article, I want you to think about the advantages and disadvantages of this technology as it relates to these big questions. (Project the list from page 226.)

+   Underline the advantages and mark them in the margin with a plus sign.

−   Underline the disadvantages and mark them with a minus sign.

Now take some time to read the article and mark your annotations.

Strategy 4: **TEXT CODING**   STEP 4 ## Students read, using text coding   Circulate, confer, and coach as needed.

STEP 5 ## Groups discuss and chart their findings

Strategy 6: **TWO-COLUMN NOTES**

OK pairs, move together so that you form a group of four (predetermined in Part 1, Step 1). Now, keep your article out while I give you this piece of chart paper and some markers. At the top of the paper, write the title of the article. Underneath the title, create two columns: For and Against. In each column, list three or four of your most powerful arguments for or against the use of this particular technology.

Under your arguments, write the word Conclusion. With your group, decide whether this technology is important enough to use, even though it threatens our privacy. Explain your determination beside the conclusion label. Refer students back to the projected set of big questions.

Be sure to use information from your annotation to support your arguments, but also feel free to use additional logical arguments that you think of together.

Go ahead. I'll come around and visit each group in case you have any questions.

STEP 6 **Support kids as they work** As you circulate, look for groups that may be struggling. If you need to nudge their thinking, remind them to think about those four big questions (listed in the strategy introduction), which you should leave posted or projected as kids discuss.

PART 3 **SEEING BOTH SIDES CONCLUSION** *(15 minutes)*

Strategy 19: **GALLERY WALK**

STEP 1 **Gallery walk** When groups have finished, post their charts around the room and conduct a gallery walk. Let groups circulate through the posters, comparing the arguments and conclusions that were reached by the different groups. For greater accountability, and to feed Step 2, have students take notes on each poster they read.

STEP 2 **Share with the whole class** Discuss with the class: *What similarities and differences did you notice when comparing the posters?* End by bringing the conversation back to the constitutional amendments and discuss:

Do these amendments provide enough protection for our privacy?

What laws might need to be passed by Congress so that nongovernmental organizations protect our privacy as well?

VARIATION 1, DAY 1

USING THE FULL TEXT SET IN PART 2 *(40 minutes)*

MATERIALS NEEDED

Amendment information and big questions, downloaded for projection; enough copies of all five articles so that each group can read a different article and each group member has a copy; chart paper; markers.

Using only one of the five articles makes this lesson quicker and easier to execute. However, if you would like to use the full text set in jigsaw fashion, plan on one and a half to two class periods and follow the directions below.

Grouping Sequence:
Groups of 4 that sometimes work together, and other times split into pairs, whole class

STEP 1 **Form groups** Discuss the U.S. Constitution's privacy provisions (see Steps 1 and 2 on page 227).

STEP 2 **Preview the articles**

Today we're going to read some different articles about how personal information is collected and used, and think about whether our rights to privacy might be compromised. Let me give you a preview. (Use the same preview blurbs listed in Part 2.)

STEP 3 **Distribute a different article to each group and explain coding** You may consider reading levels and students' interests as you do this; the first three articles are shorter and easier.

All of these articles are controversial because they raise the question: Is this a violation of my right to privacy?

Continue using instruction details from the original lesson through the rest of Part 2.

STEP 4 **Students read, using text coding**

STEP 5 **Groups discuss and chart their findings**

STEP 6 **Support kids as they work** As groups finish their charts, post them around the room to use the following day.

SEEING BOTH SIDES CONCLUSION *(40 minutes)*

Strategy 19: **GALLERY WALK**

STEP 1 **Gallery walk** The following day, have groups reconvene and conduct a gallery walk. *As your group circulates through the posters, look closely at the arguments for and against each particular technology as well as the conclusion the group drew. Discuss these with your group and jot down questions you have as well as ideas or conclusions you disagree with.*

Organize the groups so that each one begins at a different poster. Give groups four to five minutes to read and discuss the information at each poster station. Remind groups to take notes on their ideas and questions.

STEP 2 **Groups defend their conclusions** Have the gallery walk end with each group returning to its own poster.

Now that you've looked at all the posters, I want each group to discuss the conclusions you disagreed with. Why did you disagree? What questions can you pose to the groups who made those conclusions?

Give groups a couple of minutes for discussion. Then invite each group to explain and defend its conclusion as it takes questions and comments from the other groups.

STEP 3 **Share with the whole class** End by bringing the discussion back to the constitutional amendments and discuss:

Do these amendments provide enough protection for our privacy?

What laws might need to be passed by Congress so that nongovernmental organizations protect our privacy as well?

ARGUING BOTH SIDES *(50 minutes)*

MATERIALS NEEDED

One copy of chosen article for each student; projectable list of big questions.

The preceding lesson and variation use elements of argument but do not actually require students to individually advocate a position or refute an opponent's position. Variation 2 offers this experience. Variation 2 requires that you introduce the discussion of privacy and the U.S. Constitution (Steps 1 and 2 on page 227) on the previous day so that you have a whole period to argue!

For a complete review of the argument model, see Strategy 17.

STEP 1 **Preview and distribute the chosen article** Use the same article preview descriptions from Part 2, Step 2.

STEP 2 **Explain the coding** Use the same note-taking directions from Part 2, Step 3.

STEP 3 **Establish partners** Groups of four are divided into "face partners" (someone sitting across from you) and "shoulder partners" (someone sitting beside you) as described on pages 104–106. You must establish with the kids which is which before you continue to the next step.

Strategy 17: **ARGUING BOTH SIDES**

STEP 4 **Determine argument positions**

Keep your article out and get out a sheet of loose-leaf paper. I'm going to assign each of you a number, either one or two. When you get it, write the number at the top of your sheet of paper.

Assign the numbers so that all face partners are number ones and all shoulder partners are number twos.

Number ones, you are going to work with your face partner preparing an argument in favor of *the technology described in the article. Number twos, you are going to work with your face partner in preparing an argument* opposing *the use of the technology described in the article.*

STEP 5 **Give argument preparation instructions**

Strategy 6: **TWO-COLUMN NOTES**

Be sure to use information from your annotation to support your side, but also feel free to use additional logical arguments that you think of with your partner. Fold your paper so that you have two columns. List your arguments in the left-hand column. Across from each argument, in the right-hand column, write your support details.

Strategy 1: **TURN AND TALK**

Turn to your face partner and begin working. I'll come around and visit each pair in case you have any questions. If you are looking for a place to start, take a look at those four big questions I have posted [page 226].

Grouping Sequence: Two sets of pairs, face partners and shoulder partners; whole class

STEP 6 ## Conclude argument preparation with face partner

You have one more minute to wrap up your arguments. Thank your face partner and if you need to, turn around so that you can make eye contact with your shoulder partner.

STEP 7 ## Meet with argument (shoulder) partner

Now we are going to begin to argue. Number ones—those in favor of the technology—you are going to argue first. You have one minute to present your best arguments in favor of your technology. Shoulder partners can only listen and take notes on your partner's weak arguments. Go!

Ones, your time is up. Twos, it's time for you to explain why you oppose this technology. Ones can only listen and take notes on your partner's weak arguments. You have one minute. Go!

STEP 8 ## Refute the arguments

This is your chance to really argue. Review the notes you jotted. What were your partner's weak arguments? How do you disagree with him or her? Now it's time to point these weaknesses out and try to persuade your partner that they're wrong and you're right. You have three minutes. Go!

STEP 9 ## Drop advocacy, examine arguments rationally, and draw a conclusion with shoulder partner

You are no longer advocating a certain position. Together with your shoulder partner, I want you to create a new solution that incorporates the best points and ideas from both sides.

STEP 10 ## Share with the whole class

I am going to call on each pair in turn to explain the solution you came up with. As you listen to each pair report out, notice how similar or different the solutions presented are when compared to yours.

After all pairs have reported out, wrap up the discussion by asking kids for final comments on what they noticed about the similarities and differences of the solutions offered. End by bringing the discussion back to how these technological inroads impact the privacy guarantees given to us in the U.S. Constitution (information introduced the previous day).

Tips and Variations   ■   **SUBSTITUTE JIGSAW STRATEGY FOR ARGUMENT** If you'd rather not tackle the argument strategies outlined in these lessons, you can use jigsawing instead; the privacy collection also offers ample opportunity for this strategy. Decide which articles you want to use and then create the corresponding group size (two to five). Start with the discussion of the Constitution. Then pass out the prepared text sets to the groups. Let them negotiate who reads what, annotate according to your specifications, discuss in the group, and then end with whole class sharing. For a complete breakdown of jigsaw steps, see Strategy 23 on page 137.

Eye Scan Technology Comes to Schools
A New Jersey School District Is Piloting the Program

January 25, 2006–ABCNews.com

Parents who want to pick up their kids at school in one New Jersey district now can submit to iris scans, as the technology that helps keep our nation's airports and hotels safe begins to make its way further into American lives.

> When picking up a child, the adult provides a driver's license and then submits to an eye scan. If the iris image camera recognizes his or her eyes, the door clicks open.

The Freehold Borough School District launched this high-tech, high-wattage security system on Monday with funding from the Department of Justice as part of a study on the system's effectiveness.

As many as four adults can be designated to pick up each child in the district, but in order to be authorized to come into school, they will be asked to register with the district's iris recognition security and visitor management system. At this point, the New Jersey program is not mandatory.

When picking up a child, the adult provides a driver's license and then submits to an eye scan. If the iris image camera recognizes his or her eyes, the door clicks open. If someone tries to slip in behind an authorized person, the system triggers a siren and red flashing lights in the front office. The entire process takes just seconds.

This kind of technology is already at work in airports around the country like Orlando International Airport, where the program, known as Clear, has been in operation since July. It has 12,000 subscribers who pay $79.95 for the convenience of submitting to iris scans rather than going through lengthy security checks.

An iris scan is said to be more accurate than a fingerprint because it records 240 unique details—far more than the seven to 24 details that are analyzed in fingerprints. The odds of being misidentified by an iris scan are about one in 1.2 million and just one in 1.44 trillion if you scan both eyes. It's a kind of biometrics, the technique of identifying people based on parts of their body.

Phil Meara, Freehold's superintendent, said that although it was expensive, the program would help schools across the country move into a new frontier in child protection.

"This is all part of a larger emphasis, here in New Jersey, on school safety," he said. "We chose this school because we were looking for a typical slightly urban school to launch the system."

Meara applied for a $369,000 grant on behalf of the school district and had the eye scanners installed in two grammar schools and one middle school. So far, 300 of the nearly 1,500 individuals available to pick up a student from school have registered for the eye scan system.

San Francisco Chronicle

Assembly panel backs moratorium on using ID chips for school kids

June 22, 2006/Greg Lucas, Sacramento Bureau

SACRAMENTO—Citing privacy fears, a Bay Area state legislator is trying to ban the use of tiny chips embedded on identification badges as a way to keep track of schoolchildren until better ways are found to keep information on the chips secure.

The radio frequency devices are tiny chips with an antenna attached. When the chip passes a special reader, it transmits the information on it. The technology is commonly used by businesses to keep track of inventories, but it could be used on government identification cards, such as driver's licenses.

The bill, approved Wednesday by the Assembly Education Committee, stems in part from a controversy at Brittan Elementary School in Sutter County that angered some parents last year by being the first school in the country to experiment with the use of what's known as radio frequency identification devices to speed attendance taking.

Testing of the monitoring devices on the school's seventh- and eighth-grade students generated national attention as well as Internet and classroom debate over whether it improved campus security at the expense

> ## "We could not just let our child be tagged like cans or cattle."
>
> BRITTAN ELEMENTARY SCHOOL PARENT

of a student's privacy. The school board ultimately stopped the experiment following complaints.

"It's the educational equivalent of an ankle bracelet," countered Sen. Joe Simitian, D-Palo Alto, the author of SB1078, which would place a three-year moratorium on tracking students or recording attendance using the technology.

Paul Boylan, a Davis lawyer representing InCom, the company that developed the attendance-taking system and tested it at Brittan Elementary School, told the committee the technology was "astonishingly private." Use of it could help identify potential dropouts by showing their excessive absences.

Boylan noted that at Brittan Elementary School the chips used "unique identifiers"—a series of numbers representing each pupil—so that if someone tried to scan the chip with other than the correct reader all that would be revealed would be a "jumble of numbers."

Brittan Elementary School parent Michele Tatro spoke in favor of the bill at Wednesday's hearing. "We could not just let our child be tagged like cans or cattle," Tatro said.

But, as several parents told the school district last year, others see the tracking devices as a way to protect students. "I'm the mother of three boys. It would help keep our children safer," said Kelly McHugh.

Growing Presence in the Courtroom: Cellphone Data as Witness

July 6, 2009
By Anne Barnard

Mikhail Mallayev, who was convicted in March of murdering an orthodontist whose wife wanted him killed during a bitter custody battle, stayed off his cellphone the morning of the shooting in Queens. But afterward, he chatted away, unaware that his phone was acting like a tracking device and would disprove his alibi—that he was not in New York the day of the killing.

The pivotal role that cellphone records played in this murder trial highlights the surge in law enforcement's use of increasingly sophisticated cellular tracking techniques to keep tabs on suspects before they are arrested and build criminal cases against them by mapping their past movements.

But cellphone tracking is raising concerns about civil liberties in a debate that pits public safety against privacy rights. Existing laws do not provide clear or uniform guidelines: Federal wiretap laws, outpaced by technological advances, do not explicitly cover the use of cellphone data to pinpoint a person's location, and local court rulings vary widely across the country.

For more than a decade, investigators have been able to match an antenna tower with a cellphone signal to track a phone's location to within a radius of about 200 yards in urban areas and up to 20 miles in rural areas. Now many more cellphones are equipped with global-positioning technology that makes it possible to pinpoint a user's position with much greater precision, down to a few dozen yards.

> *Criminals are "unknowingly Twittering with law enforcement" whenever they use their cellphones.*

Civil libertarians do not oppose using cellphone surveillance to solve crimes or save people in emergencies, but they worry that the legal gray area is enabling it to happen without much scrutiny or discussion. "The cost of carrying a cellphone should not include the loss of one's personal privacy," said Catherine Crump, a lawyer for the American Civil Liberties Union.

"Law enforcement has a responsibility to keep pace with the latest advances in technology in order to improve its efficiency in combating crime," said Richard A. Brown, the Queens district attorney, whose office successfully prosecuted Mr. Mallayev, adding that criminals are "unknowingly Twittering with law enforcement" whenever they use their cellphones.

Civil libertarians say users whose phones have GPS-based services are unwittingly creating records that could give the government easy access to their movements.

Microchips Everywhere

A Future Vision

By **Todd Lewan, AP National Writer**
Jan. 29, 2008

Here's a vision of the not-so-distant future: Microchips with antennas will be embedded in virtually everything you buy, wear, drive and read, allowing retailers and law enforcement to track consumer items—and, by extension, consumers—wherever they go, from a distance. A seamless, global network of electronic "sniffers" will scan radio tags in myriad public settings, identifying people and their tastes instantly so that customized ads, "live spam," may be beamed at them. In "Smart Homes," sensors built into walls, floors and appliances will inventory possessions, record eating habits, monitor medicine cabinets—all the while, silently reporting data to marketers eager for a peek into the occupants' private lives.

Already, microchips are turning up in some computer printers, car keys and tires, on shampoo bottles and department store clothing tags. Companies say the RFID tags improve supply-chain efficiency, cut theft, and guarantee that brand-name products are authentic, not counterfeit. At a store, RFID doorways could scan your purchases automatically as you leave, eliminating tedious checkouts.

At home, convenience is a selling point: RFID-enabled refrigerators could warn about expired milk, generate weekly shopping lists, even send sig-

> It will be "difficult to know who is gathering what data, who has access to it, what is being done with it, and who should be held responsible for it."

nals to your interactive TV, so that you see "personalized" commercials for foods you have a history of buying. Sniffers in your microwave might read a chip-equipped TV dinner and cook it without instruction.

The problem, critics say, is that microchipped products might very well do a whole lot more. With tags in so many objects, relaying information to databases that can be linked to credit and bank cards, almost no aspect of life may soon be safe from the prying eyes of corporations and governments, says Mark Rasch, former head of the computer-crime unit of the U.S. Justice Department.

He imagines a time when anyone from police to identity thieves to stalkers might scan locked car trunks, garages or home offices from a distance. "The data is going to be used in unintended ways by third parties—not just the government, but private investigators, marketers, lawyers building a case against you . . ."

Even some industry proponents recognize risks. Elliott Maxwell, a research fellow at Pennsylvania State University who serves as a policy adviser to EPC global, the industry's standard-setting group, says data broadcast by microchips can easily be intercepted, and misused, by high-tech thieves. As RFID goes mainstream and the range of readers increases, it will be "difficult to know who is gathering what data, who has access to it, what is being done with it, and who should be held responsible for it," Maxwell wrote in *RFID Journal*, an industry publication.

The recent growth of the RFID industry has been staggering: From 1955 to 2005, cumulative sales of radio tags totaled 2.4 billion; last year alone, 2.24 billion

continues on next page

TEXT SET LESSONS / PRIVACY

Microchips Everywhere

continued from previous page

tags were sold worldwide, and analysts project that by 2017 cumulative sales will top 1 trillion.

Privacy concerns, some RFID supporters say, are overblown. Mark Roberti, editor of *RFID Journal*, says the notion that businesses would conspire to create high-resolution portraits of people is "simply silly." Corporations know Americans are sensitive about their privacy, he says, and are careful not to alienate consumers by violating it. Besides, "all companies keep their customer data close to the vest. There's absolutely no value in sharing it. Zero."

But industry documents suggest a different line of thinking, privacy experts say.

A 2005 patent application by American Express describes how RFID-embedded objects carried by shoppers could emit "identification signals" when queried by electronic "consumer trackers." The system could identify people, record their movements, and send them video ads that might offer "incentives." RFID readers could be placed in public venues, including "a common area of a school, shopping center, bus station or other place of public accommodation," according to the application.

In 2006, IBM received patent approval for an invention it called, "Identification and tracking of persons using RFID-tagged items." One stated purpose: To collect information about people

> *The documents "raise the hair on the back of your neck. The industry has long promised it would never use this technology to track people. But these patent records clearly suggest otherwise."*

that could be "used to monitor the movement of the person through the store or other areas."

But as the patent makes clear, IBM's invention could work in other public places, "such as shopping malls, airports, train stations, bus stations, elevators, trains, airplanes, restrooms, sports arenas, libraries, theaters, museums, etc." (RFID could even help "follow a particular crime suspect through public areas.")

The documents "raise the hair on the back of your neck," says Liz McIntyre, co-author of *Spychips*, a book that is critical of the industry. "The industry has long promised it would never use this technology to track people. But these patent records clearly suggest otherwise."

Corporations take issue with that, saying that patent filings shouldn't be used to predict a company's actions.

So, how long will it be before you find an RFID tag in your underwear? The industry isn't saying, but some analysts speculate that within a decade tag costs may dip below a penny, the threshold at which nearly everything could be chipped.

In the United States, RFID is not federally regulated. And while bar codes identify product categories, radio tags carry unique serial numbers that—when purchased with a credit card, frequent shopper card or contactless card—can be linked to specific shoppers. And, unlike bar codes, RFID tags can be read through almost anything except metal and water, without the holder's knowledge.

The Washington Post

FBI prepares vast biometrics database

$1 billion project to include images of irises and faces

By **Ellen Nakashima, staff researcher; Richard Drezen contributed to this report**
Dec. 22, 2007

CLARKSBURG, W. Va—The FBI is embarking on a $1 billion effort to build the world's largest computer database of peoples' physical characteristics, a project that would give the government unprecedented abilities to identify individuals in the United States and abroad.

Digital images of faces, fingerprints and palm patterns are already flowing into FBI systems in a climate-controlled, secure basement here. Next month, the FBI intends to award a 10-year contract that would significantly expand the amount and kinds of biometric information it receives. And in the coming years, law enforcement authorities around the world will be able to rely on iris patterns, face-shape data, scars and perhaps even the unique ways people walk and talk, to solve crimes and identify criminals and terrorists. The FBI will also retain, upon request by employers, the fingerprints of employees who have undergone criminal background checks so the employers can be notified if employees have brushes with the law.

The increasing use of biometrics for identification is raising questions about the ability of Americans to avoid unwanted scrutiny. It is drawing criticism from those who worry that people's bodies will become de facto national ID cards. Critics say that such government initiatives should not proceed without proof that the technology really can pick a criminal out of a crowd.

The Department of Homeland Security has been using iris scans at some airports to verify the identity of travelers who have passed background checks and who want to move through lines quickly. The department is also looking to apply iris- and face-recognition techniques to other programs. The DHS already has a database of millions of sets of fingerprints, which includes records collected from U.S. and foreign travelers stopped at borders for criminal violations, from U.S. citizens adopting children overseas, and from visa applicants abroad. There could be multiple records of one person's prints.

If successful, the system planned by the FBI, called Next Generation Identification, will collect a wide variety of biometric information in one place for identification and forensic purposes. In an underground facility the size of two football fields, a request reaches an FBI server every second from somewhere in the United States or Canada, comparing a set of digital fingerprints against the FBI's database of 55 million sets of electronic fingerprints. A possible match is made—or ruled out—as many as 100,000 times a day.

Soon, the server at the FBI's Criminal Justice Information Services headquarters will also compare palm prints and, eventually, iris images and face-shape data such as the shape of an earlobe. If all goes as planned, a police officer making a traffic stop or a border agent at an airport could run a 10-fingerprint check on a suspect and within seconds know if the person is on a database of the most wanted criminals and terrorists. An analyst could take palm prints lifted from a crime scene and run them against the expanded database. Intelligence agents could exchange biometric information worldwide.

At the West Virginia University Center for Identification Technology Research (CITeR), 45 minutes north of the FBI's biometric facility in Clarksburg, researchers are working on capturing images of people's irises at distances of up to 15 feet, and of faces from as far away as 200 yards. Soon, those researchers will do biometric research for the FBI. Covert iris- and face-image capture is several years away, but it is of great interest to government agencies.

To safeguard privacy, audit trails are kept on everyone who has access to a record in the fingerprint database, said Kimberly Del Greco, the FBI's biometric services section chief. People may request copies of their records, and the FBI audits all agencies that have access to the database every three years, she said.

Privacy advocates worry about the ability of people to correct false information. "Unlike say, a credit card number, biometric data is forever," said Paul Saffo, a Silicon Valley technology forecaster. He said he feared that the FBI, whose computer technology record has been marred by expensive failures, could not guarantee the data's security. "If someone steals and spoofs your iris image, you can't just get a new eyeball," Saffo said.

TEXT SET LESSONS / PRIVACY

Pandemic

Grouping Sequence:

Pairs; groups of 4 for discussion, tableaux, and extension jigsaw; whole class

Though the word *pandemic* is most associated with the Black Death of the fourteenth century and the Spanish influenza of 1918, the first recorded pandemic occurred in 430 BC, during the Peloponnesian war. It killed thirty thousand Greeks. Today we see the phrase *potential pandemic* every time a new flu strain appears. It seems like every year the world is threatened by some kind of exotic flu. Sometimes these turn out to be false alarms, while other times, thousands die. Some of this danger actually may arise from the way we keep animals, as described in the factory farming text set (pages 180–194).

The readings in this lesson are divided into two categories. While the first two help students understand how viruses work, the last four extend the topic by examining a historical or literary context, the process for creating vaccinations, or, in the case of "Path of a Pandemic," how our current food production methods encourage more deadly mutations. Within these readings, the following big questions arise:

On the Web

- How dangerous is the flu?
- How do viruses take advantage of various opportunities to mutate and spread?
- How do people often react in the face of a pandemic?
- What steps can we take to reduce the chance of a pandemic?
- How might current food production practices contribute to the rise of new and antibiotic/antiviral resistant diseases?

TEXTS IN ORDER OF USE

Main Lesson:

"What's in a Name?" (diagrams and charts with text; easier)

"Swine Flu: Virus' Invasion Sets Off Battle Inside the Body"

Extension:

"The Masque of the Red Death"

"The Path of a Pandemic"

"The Great Pandemic 1918–1919"

"Expediting Production of a Vaccine" (diagram)

CURRICULUM CONNECTIONS

Biology: Cell structure, viruses, infections, epidemics, pandemics.

Health: Common diseases and the immune system, disease prevention.

Social Studies: How disease shapes society and history.

Literature: Edgar Allan Poe, as well as the numerous fiction and nonfiction books that touch or focus on the topic of pandemic: *Fever 1793; The Astonishing Life of Octavian Nothing, Traitor to the Nation; When Plague Strikes; Wickett's Remedy; The Demon in the Freezer; The Hot Zone; The Stand; The Plague Tales.*

English Language Arts: Drawing on fiction and nonfiction text to understand a topic or era; choosing the right note-taking strategy for the text genre under study; representing one's thinking visually and dramatically; joining in structured small-group discussions to deepen understanding.

STRATEGIES USED

Pair Reading, Text Annotation, Conversation Questions, Tableaux, Text Coding, Sketching Through the Text, Jigsaw, Save the Last Word for Me

MATERIALS NEEDED

For the main lesson, copies of the first two articles for each student; index cards. For the extension, one set of all four articles for each group (copy the articles single-sided so students can write on the back; also, it is least confusing if you number the choices one through four or copy each article on a different color paper); projectable set of big questions.

Steps and Teaching Language

Strategy 9: **PAIR READING**

| PART 1 | **PAIR READING OF DIAGRAM** *(15 minutes)* |

STEP 1 **Introduce the topic** Have students sit with a partner (their choice or teacher determined). *Has anybody ever gotten the flu?* Ask for a show of hands. *When you get the flu, what are the symptoms? How is it different from a cold?* Call on some volunteers. *Believe it or not, most of the symptoms you just named are caused by your own body in reaction to the flu virus's invasion. Today we're going to take a closer look at how the flu virus works.*

STEP 2 **Students read the diagram silently** Pass out a copy of "What's in a Name?" to each student. *This diagram is complicated and filled with information. I want you to take a couple of minutes to just read through it silently.*

STEP 3 **Pairs reread and discuss the diagram** After time is up, say: *Now I want you to look over these diagrams and charts a little bit more closely with your partner. Start with the diagram that begins in the upper right with the number 1 under the heading "The Flu Enters the Body."*

Partners, you are going to take turns reading the numbered steps of this diagram aloud. One person reads the text beside number 1, then stops and lets his or her partner explain what is happening in the diagram. Then add anything your partner didn't mention and move on to the next number. Now the other partner does the reading aloud. Continue taking turns as you discuss the rest of this diagram.

Once you've finished moving through the numbers on that first diagram, take turns picking something else off the page to read and discuss. You do not need to go in any particular order. As you discuss the information, be sure to talk about what is surprising and seems important to remember.

STEP 4 **Monitor groups** It is more important that pairs complete their discussion of that initial diagram than discuss everything on the page. Also, make sure that students are following the pair reading instructions you outlined.

STEP 5 **Share with the whole class**

OK, pairs, what was something you noticed on this handout that was interesting or surprising? Going back to that first diagram about how the flu works when it enters the body, did anyone have any questions? I know that drawing is complicated. Spend a few minutes sharing and clearing up any confusion.

| PART 2 | **ANNOTATE AND DISCUSS** *(15 minutes)* |

STEP 1 **Introduce the text and explain reading directions** Direct pairs to form groups of four. Pass out the text "Swine Flu: Virus' Invasion Sets Off Battle Inside the Body."

This article goes into more detail about how your body reacts to a flu invasion. As you read, please annotate in three ways. Mark passages:

★ *that seem important*

? *that raise a question*

⚭ *that connect with what we have already learned*

As always, beside your annotations, jot down some notes on your thoughts or a conversation question that will spark some interesting discussion.

STEP 2 **Monitor reading** Work the room, helping kids to find all three kinds of responses within the text. If you notice students finishing early, prompt them to first go back and add to their annotations or return to the pair reading diagram and see if they can find any other connections between the diagram and the article.

STEP 3 **Groups discuss** *Turn to your group of four. Share and discuss your annotations. Read aloud what you've underlined before discussing a part. Remember to pose your conversation questions as well.* Allow about five minutes for discussion.

Strategy 3: **TEXT ANNOTATION**

Strategy 11: **CONVERSATION QUESTIONS**

PART 3

TABLEAUX *(20 minutes)*

STEP 1 **Explain the tableaux assignment** Students remain in their groups of four. Pass out an index card to each group.

Working together, pick out one important piece of information you learned about how viruses invade and write that information as an action-filled caption on the index card I gave to your group. As you word your caption, think about how the scene might be described if it were a balloon caption in a superhero comic book.

Give groups a few minutes to come up with their captions. As always, monitor the groups in order to answer questions and keep them on task. Following is a list of potential captions students might create. If a group seems really stuck, nudge them toward one of these.

Possible Tableaux Captions

1. A single sneeze spreads billions of viruses.

2. A new virus strain can sneak past the immune system's gatekeepers.

3. The virus shows its host cell its virus blueprints.

4. The virus hijacks a healthy cell and turns it into a virus factory.

5. A cell explodes and virus copies attack other healthy cells.

6. Cytokines sound an alarm that alerts T-cells to destroy the infected cells.

7. The alarm system creates flu symptoms like fever and aches.

Strategy 21: **TABLEAUX**

Now create a corresponding action-packed tableau that illustrates your caption. Stand up, practice, and keep revising your scene to make it more informative and visually interesting. Since there is a lot of action in a virus invasion, it's OK if you want to add some movement as well; you do not have to be absolutely still this time! Your job is to help your viewers better understand how viruses work. All of your members need to be part of the scene; your caption will be read by someone in another group.

STEP 2 **Monitor groups** Give students five minutes or so to practice. As you observe, cajole groups to get out of their chairs and practice. If a group says they are done, make them show you their tableau. Don't be afraid to make suggestions that will enhance the drama, visual effect, or meaning.

STEP 3 **Groups perform tableaux** Once time is up, have groups elect someone in another nearby group to dramatically read their caption when it is their turn. Have each group perform. Remind the rest of the class that silent attention is needed during each performance and a large round of applause is needed afterwards. After the performances have concluded, group members should write all of their names on their caption card and turn it in to you.

STEP 4 **Review content; share with the whole class** Once performances are concluded, ask students this question: *What important information was portrayed about viruses in these tableaux?* Send students back to the diagram and the article for a quick review and then ask for responses.

EXTENSION

JIGSAW *(45 minutes)*

STEP 1 **Introduce the activity** Form groups of four and talk students through the text choices.

"The Masque of the Red Death" is a shortened version of the Edgar Allan Poe classic. In the story Prince Prospero tries to save his friends from a pandemic by locking away everyone in his castle and then throwing a big party.

"The Path of a Pandemic" explains how H1N1 evolved—and how the current way we produce food may produce future and more dangerous pandemics.

"The Great Pandemic 1918–1919" describes how the flu virus spread around the globe, creating death and terrible consequences for tens of thousands.

"Expediting Production of a Vaccine" is a diagram that explains how two different kinds of flu vaccines are produced, but only one of these methods is approved for use in the United States.

STEP 2 **Groups negotiate reading assignments** Pass out a complete text set to each group and have students decide who will read each piece. Then give the directions.

STEP 3 **Give instructions for reading**

Now that you've chosen your articles, I want you to stop, think, and react along the way.

Underline at least three passages that you think would be surprising or interesting to other members of your group.

Strategy 4: **TEXT CODING**

Mark information that connects back to the diagram and article we read as a class with chain links ⬭⬭*, and jot a quick note explaining the connection.*

Strategy 5: **SKETCHING THROUGH THE TEXT**

Then, after you're finished, on the back side of the article, please draw a picture or diagram that captures the important information in your article. And, in the case of those who have the vaccine production text, you have to think about how to visually represent the information in a new way versus just copying the pictures in the article.

Allow at least ten or twelve minutes for this three-way note-taking.

Strategy 23: **JIGSAW**

STEP 4 **Expert pairs meet** As students finish reading and annotating, call time. *Everybody stand up and stretch. Pick up your article and pen. Now, we're going to regroup by article. All the ones* [or blues, etc., if texts are color coded] *gather in this corner, twos in that corner, threes over here, fours over there. Go!* Give everyone a minute to move. *Now that you are with all the others who read the same article, I want you to break into pairs and compare what you annotated. Decide which two or three pieces of information are most important, discuss any connections, and be sure to check out each other's drawings. When you return to your original group, you will be the expert on this article, so make sure you are prepared.*

Give students about five minutes for this pairs discussion and then tell them to return to their *original groups.*

STEP 5 **Groups discuss readings**

Strategy 10: **SAVE THE LAST WORD FOR ME**

Now that you are back in your original groups, you need to first share your information. Start with your drawing and use Save the Last Word for Me. Hold it up and have the other members explain what is in your picture and what it means. Once they're done, add any further explanation and then read one or two of your most important passages aloud, once again using Save the Last Word. Take a few minutes for each member to show their drawings and read a couple passages.

Monitor carefully and end discussion as soon as groups appear to be finished.

STEP 6 **Groups prepare answers to discussion prompts**

Now that everyone is done sharing, I want your groups to take the discussion a step further and come up with some answers to these questions. Once your group decides on an answer, everyone should jot it down. (Post these on the board or project.)

- How dangerous is the flu?

- How do viruses take advantage of various opportunities to mutate and spread?

- How do people often react in the face of a pandemic?

- What steps can we take to reduce the chance of a pandemic?

- How might current food production practices contribute to the rise of new and antibiotic/antiviral resistant diseases?

STEP 7 **Share with the whole class** Once groups have finished, end with some large-group sharing in response to the big questions posed.

What's in a name?

2009 H1N1 and the seasonal flu are more similar than many people might realize.
Graphics and research by Chelsea Williams and Brandon Schatsiek

THE ABCs OF INFLUENZA

To understand the differences between 2009 H1N1 and the seasonal flu, it is first important to understand the different types of flu virus – A, B and C. Influenza A is the most common.

TYPE	HOSTS	SYMPTOMS	SUBTYPES	EPIDEMIC OR PANDEMIC?
Influenza A	Humans or animals (primarily wild birds)	Cough, sore throat, runny or stuffy nose, fever, headache, fatigue, muscle ache	Two based on proteins on the surface of the virus: hemagglutinin (H) and neuraminidase (N)	Can cause both epidemics and pandemics
Influenza B	Humans	Less severe than Influenza A	None	Causes epidemics; has not yet caused pandemic
Influenza C	Humans	Causes mild illness	None	Does not cause either

REPLICATION REPLICATION REPLICATION

2009 H1N1 and the seasonal flu enter the body, attack and spread in the same way. Both break down the cell membrane of a healthy cell and replicate their RNA to make new viruses that spread throughout the body.

Despite their similarities, H1N1 differs from the seasonal flu in that populations that are normally at risk for severe illness or death from the seasonal flu, such as young children and the elderly, have not been most affected by H1N1. Also, it seems to thrive in the summer, outside of the normal flu season.

UNSEASONAL FLU DEATHS

The number of deaths of people who had 2009 H1N1 increased over the summer months, when most strains of flu are said to die off.

U.S. DEATHS ATTRIBUTED TO H1N1
By month from April 2009

Month	Deaths
April	1
May	14
June	113
July	240
August	315

	2009 H1N1*	SEASONAL**
Cases, worldwide	254,206	3 to 5 million
Cases, U.S.	9,079	200,000
Deaths, worldwide	2,837	25,000 to 50,000
Deaths, U.S.	593	36,000

*From April to August 2009
**Annual average

HOW H1N1 NUMBERS ARE COLLECTED

The Centers for Disease Control and Prevention and the World Health Organization originally tested every probable case of 2009 H1N1. However, because there were so many cases around the world, "reporting this information becomes questionable," said Kristen Nordlund, a CDC spokeswoman. The groups have since recorded only serious cases and hospitalizations due to H1N1. On Sept. 17, Missouri had its second confirmed death from H1N1, but the most recent state-by-state numbers are through the end of August.

Sources: WORLD HEALTH ORGANIZATION; CENTERS FOR DISEASE CONTROL AND PREVENTION; THEISPOT.NET; MICHAEL COOPERSTOCK, MU HEALTH CARE; BETHANY STONE, MU DIVISION OF BIOLOGICAL SCIENCES

① THE FLU ENTERS THE BODY

Virus is inhaled and attaches to the cells in the nose, throat and lungs

Virus

② Protein spikes on the surface of the virus bind to the cell

Protein spike

③ The virus is engulfed by the cell

Cell membrane

NUCLEUS

④ The virus releases its RNA (nucleic acid that carries pieces of information)

⑤ In the nucleus, viral RNA copies are made

⑥ Viral messenger RNA causes the cell to make viral proteins

Viral proteins

⑦ RNA and viral proteins combine to make more viruses

⑧ Newly formed viruses leave the cell and spread throughout the respiratory system

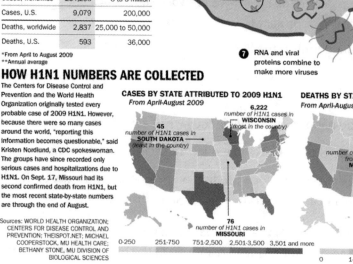

CASES BY STATE ATTRIBUTED TO 2009 H1N1
From April-August 2009

6,222
number of H1N1 cases in
WISCONSIN
(most in the country)

45
number of H1N1 cases in
SOUTH DAKOTA
(least in the country)

76
number of H1N1 cases in
MISSOURI

0-250   251-750   751-2,500   2,501-3,500   3,501 and more

DEATHS BY STATE ATTRIBUTED TO 2009 H1N1
From April-August 2009

266
number of people who died from H1N1 in
NEW YORK
(highest in the country)

1
number of people who died from H1N1 in
MISSOURI

17
number of people who died from H1N1 in
ILLINOIS

0   1-14   15-22   23-53   More than 53

Chicago Tribune

Swine flu: Virus' invasion sets off battle inside the body

May 1, 2009
By Robert Mitchum and
Trine Tsouderos

Like a sleeper agent, the flu virus causes its damage from within, turning an organism's cells against itself. A single virus can hijack a healthy cell and transform it into a virus factory, making thousands of copies in a couple of hours. The cell then bursts, allowing the copies to infect other healthy cells and start the process anew. The body fights back by launching a self-sacrificing counterattack: molecules designed to kill the hijacked cells before the virus does.

Not all flu particles are infectious, but doctors said it takes only a small number to spread infection, whether via a cough on a crowded subway train or an escalator handrail recently touched by a sick person. A single sneeze can contain billions of viruses.

Yet for an infection to take root, the virus particles need to get past the immune system's gatekeepers: antibodies. Previous flu exposures and vaccinations build a security system that can recognize and attack viruses. But the swine flu circulating now is a virus humans have not seen before. And although some scientists theorize that previous exposure to strains from the same family, called H1N1, may offer limited protection, for the most part the swine flu virus can sneak untouched through the antibody grid. From there, the virus is free to pursue its goal: multiplying as swiftly as possible.

"A virus is like a blueprint and a cell is like a factory," said Dr. Kenneth Alexander, chief of pediatric infectious diseases at Comer Children's Hospital at the University of Chicago. "The virus carries in its own blueprints and says to the cell: Make this."

The presence of the virus, as well as the husks of cells left by the replication process, alerts the immune system that something is wrong. The body sends out an alarm in the form of molecules called cytokines and recruits attackers called T-cells to kill infected cells before they release their toxic cargo. These defenses come with a cost. Most of the symptoms we attribute to a flu virus are actually the result of the body's defensive maneuvers. For example, fever occurs when cytokines tell the brain to

> *"A virus is like a blueprint and a cell is like a factory. The virus carries in its own blueprints and says to the cell: Make this."*
>
> —Dr. Kenneth Alexander, chief of pediatric infectious diseases,
> Comer Children's Hospital, University of Chicago

raise the body's temperature, which helps the immune system fight its enemies.

Especially alarming to public health officials are flu strains that kill young adults, as was seen in 1918 and is being reported from Mexico. In these cases, a person's healthy immune system may overreact, causing a "cytokine storm" that can cause excessive inflammation in the lungs, leading to death. As scientists unravel the genetic makeup of swine flu strains collected in Mexico, the U.S. and New Zealand, they are relieved to find differences between the 1918 strain and the current strain that suggest a lower potential for severe illness.

The Masque of the Red Death (Abridged)

By Edgar Allan Poe

THE "RED DEATH" had long devastated the country. No pestilence had ever been so fatal, or so hideous. Blood was its avatar and its seal—the redness and the horror of blood. There were sharp pains, and sudden dizziness, and then profuse bleeding at the pores, with dissolution. The scarlet stains upon the body and especially upon the face of the victim, were the pest ban which shut him out from the aid and from the sympathy of his fellow-men. And the whole seizure, progress and termination of the disease, were the incidents of half an hour.

But the Prince Prospero was happy and dauntless. When his dominions were half depopulated, he summoned to his presence a thousand hale and light-hearted friends and with these retired to the deep seclusion of one of his castellated abbeys. A strong and lofty wall girdled it in. The abbey was amply provisioned. With such precautions the courtiers might bid defiance to contagion. The external world could take care of itself.

It was toward the close of the fifth or sixth month of his seclusion, and while the pestilence raged most furiously abroad, that the Prince Prospero entertained his thousand friends at a masked ball of the most unusual magnificence. And the revel went whirlingly on, until at length there commenced the sounding of midnight. Before the last echoes of the last chime had utterly sunk into silence, there were many individuals in the crowd who had found leisure to become aware of the presence of a masked figure which had arrested the attention of no single individual before. The figure was tall and gaunt, and shrouded from head to foot in the habiliments of the grave. The mask which concealed the visage was made so nearly to resemble the countenance of a stiffened corpse. The mummer had gone so far as to assume the type of the Red Death.

Prince Prospero, maddening with rage, bore aloft a drawn dagger, and approached the figure. There was a sharp cry—and the dagger dropped gleaming upon the sable carpet, upon which, instantly afterwards, fell prostrate in death the Prince Prospero. The revelers at once threw themselves into seizing the mummer, whose tall figure stood erect and motionless, but, gasped in horror at finding the grave-cerements and corpse-like mask which they handled with so violent a rudeness, untenanted by any tangible form.

And now was acknowledged the presence of the Red Death. He had come like a thief in the night. And one by one dropped the revelers in the blood-bedewed halls of their revel, and died each in the despairing posture of his fall. And Darkness and Decay and the Red Death held illimitable dominion over all.

THE PATH OF A PANDEMIC

How one virus spread from pigs and birds to humans around the globe. And why microbes like the H1N1 flu have become a growing threat.

Laurie Garrett, May 18, 2009

Around Thanksgiving 2005 a teenage boy helped his brother-in-law butcher 31 pigs at a local Wisconsin slaughterhouse, and a week later the 17-year-old pinned down another pig while it was gutted. In the lead-up to the holidays the boy's family bought a chicken and kept the animal in their home, out of the harsh Sheboygan autumn. On Dec. 7, the teenager came down with the flu, suffering an illness that lasted three days. It was an H1N1 swine influenza. Largely ignored at the time, the Wisconsin virus was a step along the evolutionary tree, leading to a virus that four years later would stun the world.

Flash-forward to April 2009, and young Édgar Enrique Hernández in faraway La Gloria, Mexico, suffers a bout of flu, found to be caused by a similar mosaic of swine/bird/human flu, also H1N1.

Back in 2005, Centers for Disease Control scientists discovered that the H1N1 virus had pieces of its RNA genetic material that matched a human flu seen earlier, two swine types that had been circulating in Asia and Wisconsin for several years and an unknown avian-flu virus. Last year researchers from Iowa State University in Ames warned that pigs located in industrial-scale farms were being subjected to influenza infections from farm poultry, wild birds and their human handlers. As a result of the constantly changing genetic makeup of individual influenza viruses in pigs, the U.S. swine industry is continually scrambling to respond to the influenza viruses circulating within individual production systems.

Investigation of the 1918 influenza pandemic, which is now estimated to have killed up to 100 million people worldwide in 18 months, revealed that the viral culprit was a type H1N1 human flu that had infected pigs, and then circulated back to humans. Today pigs are still an ideal mixing vessel for the creation of new avian/mammalian influenza viruses capable of causing novel diseases with the potential for producing pandemics in the human population. It is apparent that, in the U.S. swine industry, transmission of influenza viruses between swine and humans is fairly common.

It is a strange world wherein billions of animals are concentrated into tiny spaces, breeding stock is flown to production sites all over the world and poorly paid migrant workers are exposed to infected animals. And it's going to get much worse, as the world's once poor populations of India and China enter the middle class. In 1983 the world consumed 152 million tons of meat a year. The United Nations Food and Agriculture Organization estimates that by 2020 world consumption could top 386 million tons of pork, chicken, beef and farmed fish.

This is the ecology that, in the cases of pigs and chickens, is breeding influenza. It is an ecology that promotes viral evolution. And if we don't do something about it, this ecology will one day spawn a severe pandemic that will dwarf that of 1918.

| Home | Life in 1918 | The Pandemic | Your State | Documents |

The Great Pandemic 1918–1919

Throughout history, influenza viruses have mutated and caused pandemics or global epidemics

http://1918.pandemicflu.gov/the_pandemic/01.htm

INFLUENZA STRIKES

In early March of 1918, officials in Haskell County in Kansas sent a worrisome report to the Public Health Service. Eighteen cases of influenza of a severe type had been reported there. By May, reports of severe influenza trickled in from Europe. Young soldiers, men in the prime of life, were becoming ill in large numbers. Most of these men recovered quickly but some developed a secondary pneumonia of "a most virulent and deadly type."

> As the bodies accumulated, funeral parlors ran out of caskets and bodies went uncollected in morgues.

Within two months, influenza had spread from the military to the civilian population in Europe. From there, the disease spread outward—to Asia, Africa, South America, and back again to North America. In Boston, dockworkers at Commonwealth Pier reported sick in massive numbers during the last week in August. Suffering from fevers as high as 105 degrees, these workers had severe muscle and joint pains. For most of these men, recovery quickly followed. But 5% to 10% of these patients developed severe and massive pneumonia. Death often followed.

Public health experts had little time to register their shock at the severity of this outbreak. Within days, the disease had spread outward to the city of Boston itself. By mid-September, the epidemic had spread even further with states as far away as California, North Dakota, Florida and Texas reporting severe epidemics.

The pandemic of 1918–1919 occurred in three waves. The first wave had occurred when mild influenza erupted in the late spring and summer of 1918. The second wave occurred with an outbreak of severe influenza in the fall of 1918 and the final wave occurred in the spring of 1919.

Entire families became ill. In Philadelphia, a city especially hard hit, so many children were orphaned that the Bureau of Child Hygiene found itself overwhelmed and unable to care for them. As the bodies accumulated, funeral parlors ran out of caskets and bodies went uncollected in morgues.

As the disease spread, schools and businesses emptied. Telegraph and telephone services collapsed as operators took to their beds. Garbage went uncollected as garbage men reported sick. The mail piled up as postal carriers failed to come to work.

Public health officials sought to stem the rising panic by censoring newspapers and issuing simple directives. Posters and cartoons were also printed, warning people of the dangers of influenza.

In November, two months after the pandemic had erupted, the Public Health Service began reporting that influenza cases were declining.

By the time the pandemic had ended, in the summer of 1919, nearly 675,000 Americans were dead from influenza. Hundreds of thousands more were orphaned and widowed.

Expediting production of a vaccine

Drugmakers around the world have received or are awaiting strains of the H1N1 swine flu virus to begin making a vaccine. The urgency of the situation provides an opportunity for companies to further develop a relatively new cell-based method of creating vaccines, which can potentially reduce the amount of time it takes to bring the product to market.

Egg-based

Production time: 20-28 weeks

1 About a week after chicken eggs are fertilized, the virus is injected into the fluid surrounding the embryo of the eggs

2 The virus multiplies within the fluid

3 After several weeks, the fluid is removed from the eggs and is spun in centrifuges to separate and concentrate the virus

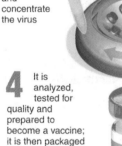

4 It is analyzed, tested for quality and prepared to become a vaccine; it is then packaged and distributed

Advantages
- A well-established method for vaccine production
- Relatively inexpensive

Disadvantages
- Requires large amounts of eggs that are not produced on demand (a single vaccine dose requires 1-2 eggs)
- Extensive planning and preparation can limit the effectiveness on quickly-developing viruses

Source: Baxter, New England Journal of Medicine, GlaxoSmithKline
Graphic: Max Rust and Phil Geib, Tribune Newspapers

Cell-based

Production time: 12-15 weeks

1 The virus is injected into kidney cell cultures from the African green monkey

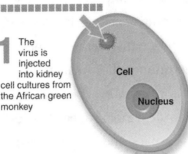

2 The virus infects the cells, which multiply with the virus inside them, producing additional samples of the virus

3 The initial cells are harvested and the virus particles are separated into pools

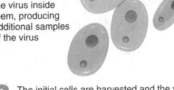

4 The pools are injected into large fermenters containing more cells and the process is repeated on a much larger scale

5 The virus is removed and prepared to become a vaccine; it is then packaged and distributed

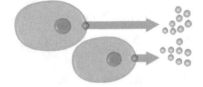

Advantages
- Faster method, which could result in creating vaccines in time to prevent the spread of the virus
- Avoids potential impurities that can occur in the egg-based method

Disadvantages
- High initial costs to set up the process
- Still unestablished; no cell-based vaccine has been approved by U.S. regulators for commercial use

TEXT SET LESSONS / PANDEMIC

Encounters

Grouping Sequence:

Pairs, groups of 4, whole class

An eternally important topic, both in school and society: what happens when one group of people decides to take over somebody else's homeland? In our country, native-settler encounters tell a long story of conquest, resistance, accommodation, displacement, exploitation, and sometimes, warfare. In the American West, the mantra was "manifest destiny"—the idea that God wished for Europeans to push back the frontier, and the native peoples with it, to expand and occupy the continent from Atlantic to Pacific. This same human struggle has been reenacted around the world and throughout the ages.

This lesson uses a combination of images and print to get students to think about the westward expansion and settlement of the United States, including these big questions:

- What role did the U.S. Army play in western expansion and Native American removal?
- How did visual images and newspaper accounts shape public opinion?
- How were Native Americans impacted by ever-encroaching settlements?

Our use of pictures here goes well beyond creating manageable reading opportunities for struggling readers. Contemporary life bombards us with images from the time we get up until the time we go to sleep. Most of your students, if asked, would describe themselves as visual learners. But are they really highly skilled viewers, or just image-skimmers? This lesson teaches students to stop and look thoughtfully at an image, noticing the details and thinking about how those details shape the viewer's opinion.

TEXTS IN ORDER OF USE

Main Lesson:

Indians Attack Settlers (image; easier)

Newspaper Accounts of Native American Hostility (easier)

American Progress (image; easier)

Extensions:

Distant View of Niagara Falls 1830 (image; easier), Extension 1

Niagara Falls 1930 (image; easier), Extension 1

"The Long Walk—Hwéeldi" (copy back to back with Navajo Stories), Extensions 2 and 3

"Navajo Stories of the Long Walk Period" (easier), Extensions 2 and 3

"The Navajo Code Talkers," Extension 4

CURRICULUM CONNECTIONS

Social Studies: American history; westward expansion, Manifest Destiny; the effects of "progress" on indigenous people; how public opinion is swayed by media; assimilation of cultures.

Mathematics: Codes and symbols.

Literature: Blood and Thunder, Bury My Heart at Wounded Knee, The Absolutely True Diary of a Part-Time Indian, Dances with Wolves, Montana 1948.

Language Arts: Getting information from visual images; looking at topics from different points of view; using a text annotation strategy that suits the genre at hand; collaborating with classmates to represent ideas in physical and dramatic form.

STRATEGIES USED

Reading a Visual Image, Turn and Talk, Point of View Annotation, Save the Last Word for Me, Text Annotation, Tableaux, Alternative Perspective Writing

MATERIALS NEEDED

For the main lesson: Projectable images of *Indians Attack Settlers* and *American Progress* (full images as well as framed/masked images that show only one quadrant at a time); copy of "Newspaper Accounts of Native Hostility" for each student. (Image note: *Indians Attack Settlers* can be found on the book's website. *American Progress* can easily be found via Google Images—we found fifteen different images on the first page—but we recommend searching the Autry Museum's website: www.theautry.org/search-the-autry.)

For Extension 1: Projectable images of *Indians Attack Settlers, Distant View of Niagara Falls,* and the *Niagara Falls 1930* photo. (Image note: The *Niagara Falls 1930* photo can also be found on the book's website. *Distant View of Niagara Falls* can easily be found via Google Images, but we recommend searching the Art Institute of Chicago's website: www.artic.edu/aic/collections.)

For Extension 2: Copy of "Long Walk—Hwéeldi" and "Navajo Stories of the Long Walk" for each student (copied back to back), index cards, projectable list of big questions (page 252).

For Extension 3: Copy of "Long Walk—Hwéeldi" and "Navajo Stories of the Long Walk" for each student (from Extension 2).

For Extension 4: Copy of "Navajo Code Talkers" for each student; projectable list of big questions.

Steps and Teaching Language

Strategy 7: **READING A VISUAL IMAGE**

Strategy 1: **TURN AND TALK**

Strategy 16: **POINT OF VIEW ANNOTATION**

PART 1 **READING A MEDIA IMAGE** *(10 minutes)*

STEP 1 **Group students and prepare materials** Seat students in groups of four and then have the groups break into pairs for the initial activity (teacher can assign the groups or have students choose). *OK, please get out a sheet of loose-leaf paper and fold it in half vertically, then again in half horizontally, so that you have four sections (as we say in Chicago, first fold hot dog style, then hamburger). Unfold your paper.*

STEP 2 **Project the first full image for study** Project the *Indians Attack Settlers* image. *Study this image for a minute. Think about what you notice and the story it tells.*

STEP 3 **Students take notes on each quadrant**

Now we're going to look at each section of the picture separately. Show each quadrant of the image, following the framing instructions given in Strategy 7, page 58. (You might also refer to the earlier image examples for the child labor text set, page 195.) *As you study each section, jot down notes in the corresponding square on your paper.*

STEP 4 **Partners compare notes**

Now, take a look at the entire picture again. Remove the mask and show the full image. *With your partner, compare what each of you noticed in each of the sections and talk about how the details tell a story. And, if you were going to give this story a title, what would you call it?*

STEP 5 **Share with the whole class** Call time after a couple of minutes and ask volunteers to share details that they noticed as well as possible titles for the picture. Ask students what they think this picture was used for. You can tell them that it was a common illustration used to accompany newspaper articles reporting on Indian attacks.

PART 2 **POINT OF VIEW ANNOTATION** *(20 minutes)*

STEP 1 **Explain roles and allow groups to negotiate** Tell the pairs to recombine with their established groups of four (see Part 1, Step 1). Then pass out "Newspaper Accounts of Native American Hostility." *These short articles, written between 1855 and 1863, are about encounters between the U.S. Army and Native Americans. Before reading, I want you to meet quickly with your group and decide which of these four roles each of you will take: army officer, settler, Native American, government official.*

STEP 2 **Give instructions for reading**

Now that you've chosen your roles, I want you to read the three short articles. But, as you read, I want you to take on your role and imagine how that person would respond to the article. What would they think is important, problematic, or outrageous? Underline these parts and jot notes about your reaction based on your role.

STEP 3 **Allow time for reading and annotating** Help kids to stay in their roles as they annotate the text.

STEP 4 **Initiate discussion**

Strategy 10: **SAVE THE LAST WORD FOR ME**

Now you can pull together with your group and discuss the articles. Focus on comparing how you reacted to the information depending on your role. However, rather than just explaining, please use Save the Last Word for Me. When it's your turn, remind the group what role you are and just read the passage aloud. Then let the rest of the group explain why you picked it and how your role reacted. Add your thoughts and opinions last. Be sure to take turns at reading passages. Do not let the same person read more than one passage at a time.

STEP 5 **Share with the whole class** As discussion winds down, call time and ask for some volunteers to share what their groups discussed—and then, how their various roles influenced how they viewed the news articles.

STEP 6 **Make connections** Return to the previous image, *Indians Attack Settlers,* and ask groups to brainstorm connections between the news articles and the image. Also, have students discuss the reaction their role would have upon viewing this image. Remind students that this image might have actually accompanied any of these articles.

| PART 3 | **READING AN IMAGE—*AMERICAN PROGRESS*** *(10 minutes)* |

STEP 1 **Groups of four break into designated pairs and prepare materials**

Now return to your earlier pairs. Can you find each other? Good. We're going to take a look at another image, using the quadrant format once again. Turn your folded sheets over to the back side.

Strategy 7: **READING A VISUAL IMAGE**

STEP 2 **Project the second full image for study** Project the *American Progress* image. *Study this image for a minute. Think about what you notice and the story it tells.* (You can comment on or ignore the female icon's imminent wardrobe malfunction, as you wish.)

STEP 3 **Students take notes on each quadrant** As in Part 1, show the image in sections, revealing one quadrant at a time.

As with the previous image, we're going to look at each section of the picture separately. As you study each section, jot down notes in the corresponding square.

Strategy 1: **TURN AND TALK**

STEP 4 **Partners compare notes**

Take another look at the entire picture. With your partner, compare what each of you noticed in each of the sections and talk about how the details tell a story.

STEP 5 **Share with the whole class** Call time after a couple of minutes and ask volunteers to share details that they noticed as well as possible titles for the picture. Ask students what they think this picture was used for; then offer this information and prompt:

> John Gast painted this in 1872 on commission. The image was intended for a series of western travel guides. Knowing that, what kind of feelings did the publisher hope to inspire in potential readers by using this picture? And, if you were going to give this painting a title, what would you call it? Let students brainstorm for a minute.

Let's hear some titles that you thought up for this picture. Take some suggestions and discuss how the name fits with specific details of the image. Many kids may expect the image to be called "Manifest Destiny," but *American Progress* fits the picture well, too.

Note that the volume being held is a schoolbook, not a bible. That's a point worth discussing for a minute or two.

EXTENSION 1

READING AN IMAGE (20 minutes)

STEP 1 **Project the entire image for study** Seat students in pairs (teacher determined or student chosen). Project the *Distant View of Niagara Falls*. Study this image for a minute. Think about what you notice and the story it tells.

Strategy 7: **READING A VISUAL IMAGE**

STEP 2 **Partners compare what they noticed**

Strategy 1: **TURN AND TALK**

Turn to your partner and share what you noticed. What is the story? What feelings does the painting elicit from the viewer? What would you title this painting?

STEP 3 **Compare images** Project the *Indians Attack Settlers* image again. This is the image we started our study with. I want you to look carefully at both images and think about what each is trying to say about Native Americans. After a minute, return to *Distant View of Niagara Falls*. Have students brainstorm with their partner and share some responses.

Give painting background information

Most of you noticed that both pieces take an unrealistic, extreme view. While the first picture depicts Native Americans as savage, primitive, cold-blooded killers, Thomas Cole, painter of the second picture, evokes nostalgia, an era when times were better and Native Americans were the stewards of nature. This second picture depicts the famous Niagara Falls located in upstate New York. Though painted in 1830, the majority of Native Americans were removed from or left upstate New York after the Revolutionary War. The scene depicted in this painting is the artist's imaginative creation. Ironically, though still rugged, Niagara Falls in the 1830s was becoming increasingly commercialized, a popular tourist attraction. And thirty years later industrialization had taken root.

STEP 5 **Project the second Niagara Falls image, a photograph**

What do you notice in this later photograph, taken in 1930? Give students a minute to study the image and then return to Cole's painting for comparison.

STEP 6 **Discuss bias that is present in images**

Though we often perceive a painting or photograph as historically or contextually accurate, how does an artist or photographer really create an image that reflects his or her opinion, thoughts, or imagination? Why is it that art and photographs are seldom objective? Discuss this with your partners and then be ready to share with the class.

EXTENSION 2

TEXT ANNOTATION AND TABLEAUX *(30 minutes)*

STEP 1 **Give instructions for reading** Have students form groups of four (teacher directed or student chosen). Pass out the texts "The Long Walk—Hwéeldi" and "Navajo Stories of the Long Walk Period."

Strategy 3: **TEXT ANNOTATION**

These pieces explain in more specific terms how westward expansion affected the Navajo Indians. While the article called "Long Walk" gives some background, "Navajo Stories" tells a story of personal loss that one family has passed down through generations. Start by reading "Long Walk" and turn the sheet over to read "Navajo Stories." As you read, underline important information and jot down just enough notes so that you can remember what you were thinking when we discuss them.

STEP 2 **Students discuss articles in groups** As they finish up, call time and have students meet quickly in their groups for discussion. Direct them to turn first to the "Navajo Stories" piece. *What did you find surprising, shocking, or disturbing as you read this account? If you were Navajo, what would your attitude toward the military be?*

Strategy 21: **TABLEAUX**

STEP 3 **Give instructions for the tableaux assignment** Once groups have finished discussion, say: *It's time for you to get up and portray your thoughts in a different way than just reporting out. With your group of four, I want you to pick two scenes from the "Navajo Stories" piece and create a tableau to illustrate each one. Remember that a tableau is a frozen scene, like a statue. Each statue will also need a thoughtful, interesting caption. Write each of your captions on one side of the index card I give to each group.* Pass out index cards while students begin planning their scenes.

STEP 4 **Monitor groups** Make sure groups get out of their seats and hone their statues. Give groups only five to seven minutes for preparation.

STEP 5 **Students perform tableaux** Call on each group to come up and perform their tableaux. Since all four members will be part of the statue, have each group give their captions to another group to read as they perform. Remind students to give each group their full attention during performance and a big round of applause afterwards.

STEP 6 **Groups review texts studied, discuss big questions, and share with whole class** Project these big questions:

- What role did the U.S. Army play in western expansion and Native American removal?

- How did visual images and newspaper accounts shape public opinion?

- How were Native Americans impacted by ever-encroaching settlements?

EXTENSION 3

ALTERNATIVE PERSPECTIVE WRITING *(20 minutes)*

STEP 1 **Organize materials and give writing directions** After the tableaux, have students get out a sheet of loose-leaf paper; then give this prompt:

Strategy 15: **ALTERNATIVE PERSPECTIVE WRITING**

The Long Walk 1864—you are there . . .

You have surrendered to the American cavalry and walked 300 miles to a relocation facility. Along the way, friends and loved ones died: victims of disease, starvation, exhaustion, enemies. Fort Sumner conditions are no better. Crops fail and starvation is rampant. After four long years, you are finally able to return to your native land. Determined to see Navajo dignity and self-reliance reemerge, write a letter to future generations that acknowledges these atrocities yet encourages hope and strength.

You'll have about seven minutes to work on this.

STEP 2 **Monitor writing** Call time when most students have half to three quarters of a page. Rather than ending the writing suddenly, tell students when they have a minute left. And when you call time, they should finish their last sentence as well as sign off with a personalized closing (yours truly, sincerely, etc.).

STEP 3 **Group members share writing with each other** Students move back into their groups of four and each take a turn reading their letters aloud. If time permits, have each group select one letter (or a portion of a letter) for a member to read aloud to the class.

STEP 4 **Plan for the next extension piece** Students will use their Long Walk alternative perspective piece for the next extension. If you plan to do Extension 4 on a future day, be sure to collect their Long Walk pieces so that you can return them for that final step.

EXTENSION 4

ANNOTATION AND ALTERNATIVE PERSPECTIVE WRITING (40 minutes)

STEP 1 **Retrieve materials and organize groups** In this stage, kids meet in the same pairs and groups of four as used in the tableaux and alternative perspective writing extensions. Return the Long Walk alternative perspective pieces if you collected them earlier or have students retrieve pieces if they kept them. *Keep your pieces out because we will be using them later for another piece of writing.*

STEP 2 **Introduce the topic** Ask students what they know about secret codes. Listen to responses. *Believe it or not, having an unbreakable code is crucial to winning a war. Codes are used to relay information and strategy. If an enemy is able to break a country's code, the enemy can get the upper hand, know an opponent's battle tactics in advance, and win the war. During World War II, the Navajo language was used to create an unbreakable code.*

Strategy 3: **TEXT ANNOTATION**

STEP 3 **Give instructions for reading** Pass out the article "Navajo Code Talkers." *As you read this article, annotate by underlining important information and jotting notes in the margin.*

STEP 4 **Monitor reading** Circulate and check for sufficient and detailed annotation. Nudge quick finishers to reread for additional information and understanding.

STEP 5 **Give instructions for writing**

Strategy 15: **ALTERNATIVE PERSPECTIVE WRITING**

Keep this article out but also get out the Long Walk letters that you wrote earlier. Reread your letter. Give students a couple of minutes to read. When they are finished, continue instructions. *Now turn the letter over so you have a blank sheet to work with. Imagine that you are one of the Navajo code talkers.* Use this prompt:

Navajo Code Talkers—You are there . . .

Imagine that you are one of the men who helped devise and implement U.S. military encryption based on the Navajo language. Found in a trunk belonging to your elders is a letter describing the atrocities the Navajo suffered under the U.S. Army, an army you are now a part of. Though sad, this letter also encourages future generations to retain a culture that is hopeful, strong, and dignified. In response to this letter, write a letter back to your ancestors, addressing their concerns and conveying your accomplishments and your success in keeping the Navajo culture alive.

STEP 6 **Monitor writing** Call time when kids have written half to three quarters of a page. Rather than just ending the writing suddenly, tell students when they have a minute left. When you call time, they should finish their last sentence as well as sign off with a personalized closing.

STEP 7 **Groups share writing with each other** Once done, students should move into their groups of four and each take a turn reading their letters aloud. If time permits, have each group select one letter (or a portion of a letter) for a member to read aloud to the class.

Tips and Variations

■ **ALTERNATIVE IMAGES** There are lots of interesting photos of Niagara Falls from around 1830 on. If interested, try these websites:

www.niagarafrontier.com/

www.nflibrary.ca/

The second one is the website of the Niagara Falls Public Library, Canada. Find the heading "Historic Niagara" and then click on the Art or Images database link.

On the Web

Indians Attack Settlers, vintage illustration that often
accompanied newspaper reports of Indian attacks

Newspaper Accounts of Native American Hostility

Difficulties with the Utah and Apache Indians

NEW YORK DAILY NEWS, May 1, 1855

On April 19th, two companies of United States Troops under Colonel Faunkeroy, met 90 Utah and Apache Indians, well armed and mounted, in Chowatch Pass. A conflict ensued between them. Five Utahs were killed and two dragoons were wounded. The next day they came upon the Apaches, who retreated in two bodies. Of these, six were killed and some prisoners taken.

On the 22nd, Kit Carson, Lieutenant Magruder, and Captain Williams and his Company were leaving Punche Pass. They met a party of Utahs, whom they followed, killing one and wounding another.

HOSTILITY OF THE CAMANCHES

NEW YORK TIMES, March 22, 1859

We have been favored with a private letter of a Santa Fe correspondent, of the date of February 21:

On the 2nd, I went in company of Lieutenant Beale and Kit Carson out into the Camanche country. The chiefs sent for Lieutenant Beale to come out and see them, as they wanted to make arrangements in reference to emigrants passing through their country as they call it. The chiefs tell Lieutenant Beal the emigrants, together with the United States mails, may pass through unmolested, but if any person undertakes to settle, or build a house, they will surely kill them. So here is a nut for Uncle Sam to crack. The Camanches are a powerful tribe and are well armed with rifles and pistols; and I am told they have made it their boast that they will fight the American army man to man.

VICTORY OF KIT CARSON OVER THE INDIANS

NEW YORK TIMES, September 4, 1863

From Albuquerque (New Mexico) newspapers of August, we learn that on the 28th of July, Colonel Kit Carson, with part of the First New Mexican regiment, had a fight with the Navajoe Indians beyond Fort Canby. The Indians were defeated, with the loss of 13 killed and over 20 wounded, and many prisoners.

John Gast, *American Progress*

Thomas Cole, *Distant View of Niagara Falls 1830*

Niagara Falls 1930

The Long Walk—Hwéeldi

Hubbell Trading Post National Historic Site

For centuries before the coming of European settlers, the Navajo (Diné—The People) were accustomed to roaming freely over the vast distances of the great Southwest. This is the land that their Holy People had created for them, "Dinétah," the land within their Four Sacred Mountains. Life was hard, but good.

> In 1863, Carleton ordered Colonel Christopher "Kit" Carson to follow the "scorched earth" policy to destroy Navajo subsistence, break up family units, and round up the Navajo population.

When the United States took possession of the southwestern territories in 1846 after the war with Mexico, the Euro-American inhabitants were promised protection from tribes perceived as warlike. Military posts were established within Navajo country, but the Diné fiercely resisted the intrusion into their sacred land. The oral history of the Diné is to protect this land that the Holy people had created for them. In the early 1860s, American expansion continued west into Dinétah. General James H. Carleton believed gold existed within Navajo country and he wanted to *"establish a military post in the very heart of the gold country. The people will flock into the country (once the Navajo are removed), and will soon farm and have stock enough for the mines."*

In 1863, Carleton ordered Colonel Christopher "Kit" Carson to follow the "scorched earth" policy to destroy Navajo subsistence, break up family units, and round up the Navajo population. The People fled, hiding in canyons and mountains. Carson's troops burned their crops, killed livestock, and massacred men, women, and children. Faced with starvation and so much loss, many Navajo surrendered during the winter of 1863–1864. After surrendering, more than 8,000 Navajos were forced to march in "The Long Walk," over 300 miles to a flat, 40-square-mile windswept reservation in east-central New Mexico, located on the east bank of the Pecos River, known as Fort Sumner or Bosque Redondo.

From the start, the reservation experiment was doomed; Navajos had lived for generations in dispersed family groups and possessed no pattern of communal living on the scale imposed by the military. Pests, drought, and hail destroyed their crops. Irrigation water from the Pecos River contained so much salt that the land lost its productivity. Wood was scarce. Thousands of Diné died from diseases, starvation, and exposure.

In May of 1868, a federal peace commission headed by General William Sherman arrived at Fort Sumner to investigate complaints and to hear the Diné claims. Three days later the two sides agreed to the Treaty of 1868. The Diné were to return to their homeland at last, closing this bleak episode in their history. But the memories of the suffering of Hwéeldi remain a dark cloud over the Diné even to this day.

TEXT SET LESSONS / ENCOUNTERS

Navajo Stories of the Long Walk Period

Howard W. Gorman

Mr. Gorman, who lives in Ganado, Navajo Nation, Arizona, has been a member of the Navajo Tribal Council for the past 36 years—since 1937—and was its vice chairman from 1938 to 1942. He was 73 years of age at the time of publication of this book. He was born into the Todichiinii (Bitter Water) clan, and his account of the Long Walk and the Fort Sumner experiences was passed down to him by various ancestors.

The Long Walk to Fort Sumner—what was the cause of it? It began because of the behavior of a few Diné. A handful, here and there, riding horseback, killed white people and others that were traveling overland, and took their belongings. Today they would be referred to as gangsters. So the soldiers, commanded by Kit Carson, were ordered out.

The Navajos started on their journey in 1864. They headed for Fort Wingate first, and from there they started on their Long Walk. Women and children traveled on foot. That's why we call it the Long Walk. It was inhuman because Navajos, if they got tired and couldn't continue to walk farther, were just shot down. Some wagons went along, but they were carrying army supplies. So the Navajos had to keep walking all the time, day after day. They kept that up for about 18 or 19 days from Fort Wingate to Fort Sumner.

On the journey the Navajos went through all kinds of hardships, like tiredness and injuries. And, when those things happened, the people would hear gun shots in the rear. But they couldn't do anything about it. They just felt sorry for the ones being shot. Sometimes they would plead with the soldiers to let them go back and do something, but they refused. This is how the story was told by my ancestors. It was said that those ancestors were on the Long Walk with their daughter, who was pregnant and about to give birth. Somewhere beyond Butterfly Mountain, the daughter got tired and weak and couldn't keep up with the others or go any farther because of her condition. So my ancestors asked the Army to hold up for a while and let the woman give birth. But the soldiers wouldn't do it. They forced my people to move on, saying that they were getting behind the others. The soldiers told the parents that they had to leave their daughter behind. "Your daughter is not going to survive, anyway; sooner or later she is going to die," they said in their own language.

"Go ahead," the daughter said to her parents, "things might come out all right with me." But the poor thing was mistaken, my grandparents used to say. Not long after they had moved on, they heard a gunshot from where they had been a short time ago. "Maybe we should go back and do something, or at least cover the body with dirt," one of them said. By that time one of the soldiers came riding up from the direction of the sound. He must have shot her to death. That's the way the story goes.

The Navajo Code Talkers

U.S. National Archives and Records Administration

Maintaining secrecy, particularly during wartime, is vital to the national security of every country. On the battlefield, maintaining military secrecy and breaking enemy codes was necessary to gain the advantage and shorten the war. The ability to send and receive codes without the risk of the enemy deciphering the transmission was the most desirable end result of military secrecy. This ability, however, often required hours of encrypting and decrypting the code to ensure the highest security of the message. During World War II, the U.S. Marine Corps, in an effort to find quicker and more secure ways to send and receive code, enlisted Navajos as "code talkers."

> With proper training, Johnston was sure that Navajos who fit the age and education requirements for military service could be taught to transmit messages in their native language.

Philip Johnston was the initiator of the Marine Corps' program to enlist and train the Navajos as messengers. Although Johnston was not a Navajo, he grew up on a Navajo reservation as the son of a missionary and became familiar with the people and their language. Johnston's report stressed the complexity of the Navajo language and the fact that it remained mostly "'unwritten' because an alphabet or other symbols of purely native origin" did not exist. Furthermore, the languages of Native American tribes varied so significantly that one group of Native Americans could not understand another's language. With proper training, Johnston was sure that Navajos who fit the age and education requirements for military service could be taught to transmit messages in their native language.

On February 28, 1942, four Navajos assisted Johnston in demonstrating his idea. Prior to the demonstration, General Vogel had installed a telephone connection between two offices and wrote out six messages that were typical of those sent during combat. One of those messages read "Enemy expected to make tank and dive bomber attack at dawn." The Navajo managed to transmit the message almost verbatim: "Enemy tank dive bomber expected to attack this morning." The remaining messages were translated with similar proficiency, which duly impressed General Vogel. A week later on, March 6, 1942, Vogel wrote a letter to the U.S. Marine Corps commandant recommending the initial recruitment of two hundred Navajos for the Amphibious Corps, Pacific Fleet.

The initial recruitment of code talkers was approved, with the stipulation that the Navajo meet the normally required qualifications for enlistment, undergo the same seven-week training as any other recruit, and meet strict linguistic qualifications in English and Navajo. On May 5, 1942, the first 29 Navajos arrived at the Recruit Depot in San Diego, California, for basic training, where they trained in the standard procedures

continues on next page

The Navajo Code Talkers

continued from previous page

of the military and in weapons use. Afterward, they moved to Fleet Marine Force Training Center at Camp Elliott, where they received special courses in the transmission of messages and instruction in radio operation.

It was at Camp Elliott that the initial recruits, along with communications personnel, designed the first Navajo code. This code consisted of 211 words, most of which were Navajo terms that had been imbued with new, distinctly military meanings in order to compensate for the lack of military terminology in the Navajo vocabulary. For example, "fighter plane" was called "da-ha-tih-hi," which means "humming bird" in Navajo, and "dive bomber" was called "gini," which means "chicken hawk." In addition, the code talkers also designed a system that signified the twenty-six letters of the English alphabet.

> The primary strengths of the code talkers were the amount of secrecy that they ensured and the versatility with which they could be used.

The Navajo soon demonstrated their ability to memorize the code and to send messages under adverse conditions similar to military action, successfully transmitting the code from planes, tanks, or fast-moving positions. The program was deemed so successful that an additional two hundred Navajos were recommended for recruitment as messengers on July 20, 1942.

Overall assessments from Iwo Jima and other battles showed that there was an interest to continue the development of Navajos as code talkers. The primary strengths of the code talkers were the amount of secrecy that they ensured and the versatility with which they could be used. When compared to other messengers, the Navajos provided a valuable line of communication by radio that was both secure and error-free. Capt. Ralph J. Sturkey, in his Iwo Jima Battle Report, called the Navajo code the "the simplest, fastest, and most reliable means" available to transmit secret orders by radio and telephone circuits exposed to enemy wire-tapping.

It is estimated that between 375 to 420 Navajos served as code talkers. The Navajo code talker program was highly classified throughout the war and remained so until 1968. Returning home on buses without parades or fanfare and sworn to secrecy about the existence of the code, the Navajo code talkers are only recently making their way into popular culture and mainstream American history. The "Honoring the Code Talkers Act," introduced by Senator Jeff Bingaman from New Mexico in April 2000, and signed into law December 21, 2000, called for the recognition of the Navajo code talkers. During a ceremony at the U.S. Capitol on July 26, 2001, the first 29 soldiers received the Congressional Gold Medal. The Congressional Silver Medal was presented to the remaining Navajos who later qualified to be code talkers.

TEXT SET LESSONS / ENCOUNTERS

Works Cited

Allington, Richard. 2011. *What Really Matters for Struggling Readers* (Third Edition). New York: Allyn and Bacon.

"Ask an Algorithm." 2010. *Wired*. August, 86.

Beers, Kylene. 2006. *When Kids Can't Read, What Teachers Can Do*. Portsmouth, NH. Heinemann.

Common Core State Standards. 2010. The National Governor's Association and the Council of State School Officers.

Daniels, Harvey, ed. 2011. *Comprehension Going Forward: Where We Are, What's Next*. Portsmouth, NH: Heinemann.

Daniels, Harvey, and Marilyn Bizar. 2004. *Methods That Matter. Teaching the Best Practice Way*. Portland ME: Stenhouse.

Daniels, Harvey, and Nancy Steineke. 2006. *Mini-lessons for Literature Circles*. Portsmouth, NH: Heinemann

Daniels, Harvey, and Steven Zemelman. 2004. *Subjects Matter: Every Teacher's Guide to Content-Area Reading*. Portsmouth, NH: Heinemann.

Daniels, Harvey, Steven Zemelman, and Nancy Steineke. 2005. *Content-Area Writing: Every Teacher's Guide*. Portsmouth, NH: Heinemann.

Harvard College Library. 2011. "Interrogating Texts: 6 Reading Habits to Develop in Your First Year at Harvard." http://hcl.harvard.edu/research/guides/lamont_handouts/interrogatingtexts.html.

Harvey, Stephanie, and Harvey Daniels. 2009. *Comprehension and Collaboration: Inquiry Circles in Action*. Portsmouth, NH: Heinemann.

Harvey, Stephanie, and Anne Goudvis. 2004, 2008. *The Comprehension Toolkit* (Intermediate and Primary). Portsmouth, NH: Heinemann.

Ivey, Gay, and Joan Broaddus. 2007. "A Formative Experiment Investigating Literacy Engagement Among Adolescent Latina/o Students Just Beginning to Read, Write, and Speak English." *Reading Research Quarterly* 42, no. 4 (October): 512–545.

Johnson, David W., and Roger T. Johnson. 1995. *Creative Controversy: Intellectual Challenge in the Classroom.* Edina, MN: Interaction Book Company.

Pearson, P. David, Gina Cervetti, and Jennifer Tilson. 2008. "Reading for Understanding and Successful Literacy Development." In *Powerful Learning: What We Know About Teaching for Understanding*, edited by Linda Darling-Hammond, 71–112. San Francisco: Jossey-Bass.

Pearson, P. David, and Margaret Gallagher. 1983. "The Instruction of Reading Comprehension." In *What Research Says to the Teacher*, 2nd edition, edited by S. J. Samuels and A. E. Farstrup, 145–199. Newark, DE: International Reading Association.

Steineke, Nancy. 2003. *Reading and Writing Together.* Portsmouth, NH: Heinemann.

Steineke, Nancy. 2009. *Assessment Live! 10 Real-Time Ways for Kids to Show What They Know—and Meet the Standards.* Portsmouth, NH: Heinemann.

Tovani, Cris. 2007. *I Read It But I Don't Get It.* Portland, ME: Stenhouse.

Vopat, James. 2009. *Writing Circles: Kids Revolutionize Writing Workshop.* Portsmouth, NH: Heinemann.

Wilhelm, Jeffrey D., Tanya N. Baker, and Julie Dube. 2001. *Strategic Reading: Guiding Students to Lifelong Literacy, 6–12.* Portsmouth, NH: Heinemann.

Zemelman, Steven, Harvey Daniels, and Arthur Hyde. 2005. *Best Practice: Today's Standards for Teaching and Learning*, 3rd edition (4th edition in press). Portsmouth, NH: Heinemann.

The **bestselling books**

that changed how tens of thousands
of language arts, math, science,
and social studies teachers
use reading and writing in their classrooms

Subjects Matter

Every Teacher's Guide to
Content-Area Reading

Harvey "Smokey" Daniels
and **Steven Zemelman**

978-0-325-00595-9 / 2004 / 288pp / $28.50

Content-Area Writing

Every Teacher's Guide

Harvey "Smokey" Daniels
Steven Zemelman
and **Nancy Steineke**

978-0-325-00972-8 / 2007 / 288pp / $28.50